"WHEN I SAY THIS ... ," "DO YOU MEAN THAT?"

Enhancing On-the-Job Communication Skills
Using the Rules and the Tools
of
The Improv Comedy Player

❧

By Cherie Kerr

Foreword by Julia Sweeney

ExecuProv Press
Printed in the United States of America
First Edition
ISBN#: 0-9648882-3-8

For: Barb, Cathy, Carol Ann, Carol C., Deanna, Gretchen, Jane, Janet, Jody, Judy, Nancy, Sheila, Ruth and Teri.

With them, communication doesn't get any better...

To: MM – If only this, then …

ACKNOWLEDGMENTS

Love to sons Sean, David, Keith and Drake. Love as well to God's special envoy to my soul, Shannon. Cameron, may you grow up unafraid and awe-inspired.

Deepest thanks to those who encourage and assist me in my work—my relentless pursuit to bring the improv message to the business world—Shirley Prestia, John Michalski, Michael Gellman, Dick Frattali, Gary Austin and Brian Spillane. Profound thanks to Tom Maxwell, who continues to cheer me on, Cathy Shambley for believing from the start, and Tracy Newman for her ongoing kindnesses.

Much affection to Gus Lee, a triumph unto himself and a model of humility.

Julia: May God continue to be as generous to you as you have been to all of us.

Appreciation to Deborah Way for the thoughtful edit, Sherrie Good for her generous help, Audrey Bohan and Alex Kappas for carefully guiding me down worthwhile paths, Mama Patsy and Cille for filling in. Aunt Mary and Uncle Louie; I adore you both.

Gratitude to hundreds of ExecuProv students, especially those who continue to make me proud. Among them: Tom Orbe, Ben Rasberry, H.K. Desai, Gary T., Laverne David, Ed Poll, Marhnelle Hibbard, Bill Ellermeyer, Morelle Ellison, Lowell Anderson and Bob Crites.

In addition to "the Girls," I am indebted to other friends: Rowena Stoughton, Greg Williams, Sim Middleton, Merry Neitlich, Victoria Betancourt, and Brenda Blackburn.

Eternal gratitude to Judy. We are fused at the soul.

Thanks for passing down your drive and your courage, Mom. Dad, your jazz is my salvation. Play on!

Heather, meet you at the Mecca.

Masha Irvine, Peter Seidenberg, Randy Schneider and Phil Hartman: wish you could have stayed a little longer.

TABLE OF CONTENTS

PART ONE: THE RULES

PART TWO: THE TOOLS

PART THREE: THE SHOW

FOREWORD

by Julia Sweeney

As an improv player it's important that everything we do on stage works and works well. This doesn't happen by accident. We learn rules and have tools that make this possible. It takes time to learn these principles and it takes time and diligence to make them habit. But once we learn them and once we use them, we please every audience. We also find great joy in working with the others on stage.

Knowing about Cherie's work — her effort in using these techniques to assist business professionals through her ExecuProv training — it made perfect sense to me that she would write a book that clearly defined what we improv players know. Her concept that every piece of communication is a "scene" is absolutely correct. There really is no difference where a scene takes place — the workplace or the stage — it's all the same. With that in mind then, sharing improv comedy secrets with the business community makes perfect sense.

The book you're about to read will definitely give you an inside edge when it comes to making all your communications work, and to giving you the positive upper hand in getting more out of your on-the-job relationships.

I've known Cherie for a number of years and have always been fascinated at how well she has taken the business professional through improv training making people better presenters and communicators. I, too, share her belief that everyone should study improv comedy — that everyone should use it to get far more out of relationships. Especially at work!

You'll like this book because it's full of useful and helpful information. You'll also like it because it's written in a fun and interesting way — with humorous sketches. They'll make you laugh, but they'll also hit home.

If you take her lessons to heart and do all the assignments in this book, there's no question that you'll get far more out of your workplace communications, and in the end, no doubt be even more successful than you already are!

Don't forget that old adage about the world being a stage ...

Julia Sweeney, who like Kerr was also a former member of the Los Angeles Groundlings, is a TV and film actress. She is a "Saturday Night Live" veteran and creator of that most memorable character, "Pat". She is also the creator of "God Said, Ha!", the highly acclaimed monologue/film.

PART ONE

THE RULES

Chapter 1

Behind The Scenes
Introduction

Don't you sometimes wish you could script every meeting you had to attend? If even just for one day? You could walk in, pass out copies of the scripts to everyone in the room, and then yell "Action!" Things would certainly go your way. The reality is, we never know how a given scene will unfold. We can't control the other guys. Sometimes we can't even seem to control ourselves. We often choke, stutter, freeze up, say something stupid, or—this is my favorite — say something we're not even aware of saying. I once asked, "Would anyone like coffee?" right after the host of the meeting said, "Coffee, anyone?"

The truth is, communication can be a very tricky business. All too often, our business encounters end in frustration and confusion. Many of our one-on-one exchanges leave us feeling unresolved, incomplete—like wide receivers hanging out alone on the ten-yard line. We're often tackled mentally by distractions or disjointed thoughts. We offer up inappropriate responses, replies that have little to do with the conversation on the other end. Or we think out loud, on the other guy's time.

But still, like manic football players, we keep running up and down that verbal field trying to gain some ground.

Often we're intercepted by someone's retort from the other side; sometimes we fumble all by ourselves; sometimes our efforts are thwarted, and we alone push ourselves backwards. Sometimes we go forward inch by inch, only to find that the clock has run out.

Sometimes our conversations move only laterally. Sometimes our comments are off-sides, but we ignore the flags. Sometimes we make giant strides; yet just as often we fall hard and painfully, skidding along on our proverbial verbal ass. That's why, in the game of communication, sometimes we score, but just as often, we don't.

But enough about football. This book is about improv comedy techniques — how to use them to improve on-the-job communication skills. And the first thing to know about improv is that the actors, the players, thrive on nail-biting challenges. They love the unexpected and respond to it by flexing their mental muscles with strength and agility. As these communication daredevils will tell you, the mere thought of the verbal unknown electrifies them.

Well, here's something to ponder: What improv actors do on stage, you, the business professional, do on the job. All day, every day. You create and engage in one scene after another, and, within those various scenes, you function improvisationally. Like the improv player, you operate without a script. Unlike the improv player, however, you haven't been trained to do so.

Many of you have seen improv comedy players in action. You've watched as the audience called out suggestions, and you've witnessed the brilliant results as the improv actors assimilated those ideas and, without any planning, translated them into meaningful and often hilarious results. In improv, the actors receive the information and, just like that(!), create an entire scene out of it.

As business professionals, then, we need to understand that before we can be truly effective on — or rather, *in* — any field, we first need to master our communication skills. The basics. The question is: How do we do this?

Well, I've spent 30 years studying, performing and directing improvisational comedy theater, and nearly the same amount of time working with the business community, and one day the answer finally struck me — and it hit me hard, like a Heimlich maneuver. I reasoned that since the best training camp for good communication skills is an accredited improvisational comedy school, a business professional who received training in the techniques of improv would be able to communicate effectively every time, everywhere. Aha!

In fact, as a business professional myself, one who has had to score on very competitive turf in order to stay in the game, I can certainly attest to the advantage that improv training has given me. Wow! What an edge. In fact, Catholic to the very core, I used to feel almost guilty about using this training on the job, because those around me were so unsuspecting. In awe. It always worked. Others thought I was perceptive and charming. I knew I was simply receptive and well-trained.

After much reflection — and some midnight soul-searching — I decided I was in enough of a missionary position, so to speak, to spread the word to others. The business professionals I've taught tell me I'm clever; I tell myself I'm lucky — lucky to have improv training in my professional background.

Here is something else to ponder: Wouldn't it be nice to always be prepared for the unexpected? To be able to gracefully handle an agenda that you didn't anticipate? Similar to your reaction to a surprise birthday party: "Hey, this is great ... how nice of you ... you shouldn't have, but since you did, let's party!" Unfortunately, few of us can adopt this same easygoing attitude when we suddenly discover at a meeting that something new is about to happen. On the contrary, it makes us crabby. Or it can be startling, like someone suddenly dropping a bowling ball from the ceiling onto the table. In fact, terror is a common reaction for many of us. And in any of these states of mind, it's hard for us to be effective communicators.

If you haven't been fortunate enough to witness an improv performance, let me tell you that the process can be astonishing to watch.

Experienced improv players are so skillful at assimilating audience input and then using it in a meaningful way that cynical first-time viewers are apt to suspect that audience "plants" were used. But for the improv player, there are no plants. The information is fresh and without pre-planning, the actor uses it to converse and interrelate with the other members of the improv team. (As you'll see later, teamwork is an important part of good communication.)

So how do improv players do what they do so convincingly? So spontaneously? So confidently? How do they always seem to say the right thing? Well, the answer is, they train for it. The training is demanding, it's fun, and it's perhaps the finest preparation there is for any human being who needs to talk as part of making his or her living. (As a matter of fact, I think the art of improv acting is the highest form of verbal communication available on this planet!) And in this book you're about to learn how improv training applies to you as a business professional: how to bolster, refine, and enhance all of your communications using the same techniques that the improv actor employs.

Now, don't get discouraged, thinking that you're suddenly going to be asked to be an improv player. In fact, the majority of improv players aren't "naturals" — they have to work at it.

They must first learn the fundamentals of presenting themselves well in front of others. Then they delve into the study of what makes a scene a scene, and how to behave effectively in various scenes. Fun as it is, it's also a serious science. But take heart. Anyone who can talk can learn the techniques. And you're not expected to be funny — just improvisational.

The bottom line is: Improv comedy training teaches you all there is to know about successful communication. Just like improv actors, you'll learn how to take information and then implement, integrate, infuse, and coordinate the various components to ensure that any scene, every scene, will always work. You'll use what we term "the rules and the tools" of improv to produce communication that has substance, clarity, meaning, and resolution. (And maybe you won't always get what you want from a given scene, but your chances will be greatly improved!)

Consider this book, then, as your improv scene-study/great communication training manual. Contained within it are all the theories and tricks used, scene in and scene out, by experienced improv actors. I'll say that once again. These are the rules and the tools that improv players utilize in all their work on stage. And you're going to learn their secrets.

Maybe you're saying to yourself that the training sounds like a cool idea for the other guy but not for you. Well, you're wrong. As I said before, if you can talk, you can learn the basics of improv. As a consequence, you'll communicate more fully and successfully — in business situations and in your personal life, too.

The reality is that our remarks and our interpretations of information are extremely important and powerful. In the workplace, especially, we are mandated to interact with others. We are required to communicate — be it ideas, thoughts, feelings, or needs. In fact, we trade words all day long, despite our frequent preferences to the contrary (for example, there have been days when I'd rather be with a coloring book than a client!).

The problem is that we're often rather sloppy communicators. We enter into conversation as nonchalantly as we do a walk-in closet. Opening our mouth is like opening a door, but far too often, we don't let the other guy in. We're just too much into ourselves, our needs, our wants. But the competitive world we live in requires that we communicate effectively — if we want to succeed, that is.

"When I Say This ... ," "Do You Mean That?" will expose you to a number of alternative methods for upgrading your communication skills. Don't worry. It's not another one of those heavy, pop psychology type of books. Nor is it a quick fix. In a nutshell, this book will teach you how to process and respond to information differently. That's all. It's not new; it's not revolutionary. It's just different. And while it may require a little behavior mod on your part — and some mental discipline, too — you won't be reinventing yourself. Think of it instead as a sort of revamping. Retooling, so to speak.

The information in the following chapters will give you an array of appropriate communication choices and the opportunity for increased spontaneity, greater clarity, deeper insights into others, and methods for bolstering your self-confidence. Along the way, you'll learn how to achieve a greater awareness and understanding of the ways in which you convey information to others — and the ways in which others present it to you.

I'll be introducing real conversations, many of which will undoubtedly sound very familiar to you. (You'll laugh!) And at the end of each chapter, you'll see the conversations again — revised in accordance with the improv strategies you'll be learning. In addition, I'll be suggesting some fun homework assignments as we go along.

In effect, you'll be taking my basic ExecuProv II/People Skills course — the same one I've been teaching for years. According to the feedback from my students, it's a joyful way to learn, one that makes it easy to grasp improv concepts and implement them into your day-to-day business "scenes." It's just a matter of understanding the rules and the tools of improv scene-study.

Ultimately, the message and overall purpose of this book is about maximizing communication in scenes that do go well, and taking the "n't" out of scenes that don't. With that in mind, be sure to get into the habit of looking at all of your communications in terms of "scenes"; each communication constitutes a separate scene. After all, the elements and mechanics of a scene are the heart of this book and the reason for this training.

So then, just as I do with my improv students at the start of their training, I advise you to: Let go, let your mind go blank, and just let it happen as you read on ... as you explore your potential to be the most effective communicator you can be.

Chapter 2

Setting the Scene
Covering the Basics

TAKE ONE: "Zonkzoogie Boogie"

(Int. business office. Early afternoon. As the lights come up, a three-piece-suited-gentleman sits behind his desk. A second man, also dressed in business attire, is just beginning to seat himself. He has a briefcase on his lap. He pops it open and, leaning around it, begins to speak to the man across the desk — his would-be client. It's Mr. Outthur's fifth one-on-one for the day)

MR. OUTTHER

(Fumbling and looking hurriedly inside his briefcase)
Thanks so much for agreeing to see me this afternoon.

MR. WOODBEE

(Half rising out of his chair, slightly extending his right hand for a shake) I only have a few min —

MR. OUTTHER

(**Never sees extended hand. Still searching for something in his briefcase. Peers around top of it briefly**) You're going to love our new Zonkzoogies. They can out-produce your current line of Plefwoogies two to one.

MR. WOODBEE

(**Pulls brochure out of desk drawer**) I've already looked at the catalogue (**Gestures toward it**) and I have a few quest —

MR. OUTTHER

(**Still digging, scrambling. Flashes one sample of Zonkzoogie**) Did I mention that these can out-produce what you're putting out now two to one, and —

MR. WOODBEE

(**Pointing to picture in catalogue**) These?

MR. OUTTHER

(**Glancing toward him quickly. Still digging**) Those?

MR. WOODBEE

(**Pointing at brochure picture again**) I'm asking about *these* ... this.

MR. OUTTHER

(**Digging deeper**) Huh? This.

MR. WOODBEE

(Irritated. Almost poking a hole in brochure picture)
I don't think you understand. When I say this ...

MR. OUTTHER

**(Cuts him off. Finally produces some obscure sample.
Holds it up and points to it)** Do you mean that?

-Lights-

Chapter 2

Setting The Scene
Covering the Basics

Can you see why I suggested that you get into the habit of thinking about every piece of communication you engage in as a scene? The exchange between Mr. Outther and Mr. Woodbee is a scene that occurs all too frequently in many offices. Mr. Outther and Mr. Woodbee could be you and me.

Metaphorically, this particular scene speaks volumes. One guy trying to get the other to understand his needs; the other with his head up his briefcase.

Sometimes we're simply not in the same scene with another person, even though we're both in the same room. Sometimes there are two separate scenes going on simultaneously. Oftentimes there's no scene at all. Or, there is, but it looks like something out of "Twin Peaks." Remember, though, where there is dialogue, there's also a scene — or there should be. And ideally, we want to make all our scenes work to our communication advantage.

Let's return to the world of improv. In that medium, the actors have one goal: to create scenes that work. And work is the operative word. What the audience sees on stage doesn't just evolve accidentally. Each performer in every scene is following specific guidelines and rules to make certain that the scene succeeds.

Even though improv actors don't know what will happen as the scene unfolds and have little control over where it ends up, they do by adhering to those same rules and guidelines — exercise considerable control — over the *direction* the scene will take. The rules will always steer the actors down the path together, in a tight, unified fashion. And the actors are well aware that violation of the guidelines is a risk *not* worth taking. None of them wants to end up like Mr. Outther or Mr. Woodbee.

In addition to producing communication that is tight, sequential, and meaningful, the improv code also guarantees that an individual scene will always have an end result; it will have closure. Without adhering to the basics, though, improv players would do what most of us as business professionals do in our scenes: hit and miss. They'd flail around, their conversations holding together about as well as defective Lincoln Logs.

Now, along with rules, improv players also rely on various tools. In contrast to the rules, which *must* be followed, the use of tools is optional. Some are appropriate in one scene, others in another (think kitchen utensils and you'll get the idea). These tools are employed to enliven, bring clarity, foster interest, and perhaps introduce new ideas into a scene; sometimes they actually save it.

In addition to the rules and tools, improv actors have a certain checklist of "must haves" that they must satisfy in order for a scene to qualify as a scene. As the scene moves along to its eventual, unpredictable outcome, the actors check the list off as they go (almost like putting groceries in a basket).

Throughout their scenes, in fact, improv actors are threading one piece of information into the next — using the rules, tools, and must-haves — to produce communication that resembles a finely woven tapestry. How different from the business world, where so many of our conversations end up looking like asymmetrical doilies!

As I reveal the improv player's secrets to you, I ask that you consider how each precept could apply in scenes at your workplace. You don't have to memorize the precepts yet; you don't even have to sit up straight in your chair. I only request that you run their ideas around on your mental Big Wheel to see if any of them resonate, or drive home a needed point.

Many of the improv tricks are simply good common sense. And whether you're a CEO, salesperson, administrative assistant, attorney, doctor, whatever, remember that the fundamentals of improv apply to you just as much as they do to the professional improv player. There's only one difference: They're doing it on stage; you're probably doing it in an office, in front of an "audience" of clients and colleagues.

As I explore, one by one, in the following chapters the rules and tools of improv comedy, I'll also be including scenes like the one between Mr. Outther and Mr. Woodbee. Each scene will highlight a particular principle, to provide a more complete understanding of how the precepts work in real life. You'll see that they play a vital role in a scene's progress and ultimate success. At each chapter's end, you'll see those same scenes revamped to illustrate how the communication might have been exchanged more effectively.

Before moving on, let me first give a quick overview of the improv principles to come. (And you can mentally insert the term "business professionals" whenever I say "improv actors" or "players.")

First and foremost, improv players must establish and maintain "Trust." That's at the core of everything.

In addition, players must agree to be and remain "Committed" to the scene and its process, whether or not they agree with its context.

Building on the initial principle of trust, improv actors must "Give and Take" — not always leading, not always following, but taking turns being dominant and submissive. Improv players strive for balance in this regard, because without it, the equilibrium of the piece is disturbed. Harmony is an inalienable right for every citizen of the improv world.

In addition, the actors ensure cooperation among themselves by adhering to the principle of "Division of Responsibility." All actors are equally accountable for making a scene work. If there are three people in a scene, each assumes 33 ⅓ percent of the burden for success.

Another important rule is "Attending To," which simply means looking at the person who is talking. In real life, that's plain old good manners.

"Refusal and Denial" are the mortal sins of improv. To "refuse" is to ignore what someone is saying; to "deny" is to change or undercut another's words or ideas. Much more on this later on — including penance!

The "Yes, and ... " principle is to improv what the core is to an apple. Without it, there's nothing to hang onto, and everything eventually splits apart. "Go With" is another way of wording this precept.

"Adding Information" is just that — the players add on to the prior thing said or idea held.

"Listening" is big in the improv player's book (and should be in yours, too). I'm not just talking about the literal spoken word, either. In fact, the "subtext" — what is unsaid — is often even more important. Few of us listen carefully to the spoken words, let alone pay attention to the nuances; but it's in the hidden stuff that we — and the improv players — find real meaning and the treasures.

To qualify as a legitimate scene, a piece must have a "Beginning, Middle and End." Those three elements are like Manny, Moe and Jack. Without all three, no Pep Boys. Without a beginning, middle and end, no scene.

"Creating Into Certainty" is an absolute necessity because it forces improv actors to deal in specifics rather than generalities. How much time do you waste in ambiguity? As I'll demonstrate for you, more than you probably think.

"Answering the Question" means that the actors are required to clearly and explicitly play out a scene the way the audience set it up. Contrast this with the typical business set-up, where we often run around questions like breezes on a wind chime.

The principle of "Economy of Dialogue" dictates that the improv players will say only what is necessary and essential. The more concise and succinct, the better. Less is more — and more meaningful. Oh, yeah.

Now, for the three most important guidelines of all — the rules that scream at the improv player constantly, like garish neon on a desert diner, the rules that are held in his or her consciousness every minute on stage. This trilogy is to improv what the Holy Trinity is to Catholicism. You can't have one without the other two. And this indivisible combo *must* be honored and respected at all times, under all circumstances.

The trio of guidelines consists of: "Serve and Support," "React and Respond" and "Be Here Now." They are absolutely essential to every improv situation. And after reading this book, they should be as handy to you as your everyday silverware. Used properly, they confer communication omnipotence! In fact, once you become familiar with each of them, you'll feel strange trying to communicate without them (sort of like leaving the turkey off the Thanksgiving table — Oops, something's missing!). And even if you were to forget every other lesson in this book, by using the Big Three I can just about guarantee that you'll improve your communication at least 100 percent. I can't stress their importance enough.

Of course, everything I've mentioned so far is important, and that's why I've devoted a chapter to each principle. The chapters will define the mechanics of the individual rules and demonstrate how they apply to you in the business environment.

With additional scripted scenes, you'll be able to see for yourself what happens when the rules are violated, and how powerfully they operate when followed. Soon you'll be evaluating your own real-life scenes, rewriting certain passages and lines. You'll begin to know when a scene is working and when it's faltering. And if you find yourself stuck in the dynamics of a scene that isn't working, you'll learn how to recover quickly. Overall, you'll begin to understand the complete evolution of a scene — including how it's born, how it develops positively, and how simple it is to bring to resolution.

From this point forward, then, I'm asking you to think of every communication you engage in as, first and foremost, a scene.

One final point about the rules of improv: Improv actors are never allowed to bail from a scene. To just quit. To walk off the stage. Instead, they're instructed to resolve every single situation. It's like solving a Rubik's Cube, but with words. Scenes have to fit together logically and end with a sense of completion.

For the improv player, this means sticking it out — a lesson we could all stand to learn. I, for one, was once married to a man who never completed a scene that involved controversy. We'd get into it. He'd make a short speech (usually something sanctimonious or self-serving). I'd get ready to reply, thinking we were going to communicate and he'd simply leave the room. Make an exit. I'd be furious. We eventually found an ending, of course. A final one. Too bad he hadn't learned improv!

So, although what you're about to learn are systems and procedures as they relate to communication skills for work, the very same principles can — and should be — applied to your personal relationships, as well. You'll be amazed at the results. (If I had my way, every intermediate-school student would take improv comedy training as routinely as PE; it would also be included in every corporate training program across the country.)

Now that I've set the scene, so to speak, let's move forward. Soon, very soon, you'll begin to appreciate how these principles can easily and positively be put to work for you, day after day, scene after scene.

Ready? Here we go! But first, let's run that earlier scene again — with changes!

TAKE TWO: "Zonkzoogie Boogie"

> **(Int. business office. Early afternoon. As the lights come up, one three-piece-suited gentleman is seated behind his desk. A second man, dressed in business attire as well, is just beginning to seat himself. He has a briefcase on his lap. He pops it open and, leaning around it, begins to speak to the man across the desk — his would-be client. It's Mr. Outther's fifth one-on-one for the day)**
>
> MR. OUTTHER
>
> **(Pulling some papers and samples from the briefcase, which he had carefully organized before the meeting, and quietly closing it, setting it on the floor)** Thanks so much for agreeing to see me this afternoon.

MR. WOODBEE

(Half rising out of his chair, slightly extending his right hand for a shake) I only have a few minutes.

MR. OUTTHER

(Stands. Shakes hands genuinely) I understand, so I'll get right to the point. I wanted to let you know today that I'm sure you'll love our new Zonkzoogies. **(Smiling broadly, with confidence)** They can out-produce your current line of Plefwoogies two to one.

MR. WOODBEE

(Pulls brochure from desk drawer) I've already looked at the catalog. **(Gestures toward it)** I have a few questions.

MR. OUTTHER

Sure. What are they?

MR. WOODBEE

(Pointing to the picture in the catalog) These?

MR. OUTTHER

(Looking intently at the picture) Those?

MR. WOODBEE

(Pointing to the picture again) Yes. I'm asking about this.

MR. OUTTHER

(**Looking closer. He points**) Ah, this!

MR. WOODBEE

(**Feeling comfortable; smiling**) Yes. Good. I'm glad you understand that when I say this ...

MR. OUTTHER

(**Already pulling a sample of it from his briefcase and pointing back and forth from it to the picture**) You mean *that!*

Chapter 3

On The Scene
Be Here Now

TAKE ONE: "Delicate Procedure"

(Int. office cubicle. Two guys standing at the doorway chatting, drinking coffee, styro cups in hand. They're waiting for Ms. Crastnait)

MR. KNOTNOW

(Looking at paper produced by the other guy) I don't want to deal with the Ramrod report. Let's talk about what we'll say to her if she hates the new procedure idea.

MR. ETHEARIAL

(Pulling the paper out from under his nose and waving it around as he speaks) Just now, I was thinking about the nontangibles of that procedure. The unknowns, the what-ifs, the what-might-be's ... the effect it could have on the mid-management staff in November.

MR. KNOTNOW

(Almost dizzy from following the bouncing paper) But it's July.

MR. ETHEARIAL

(**Looking skyward**) It *was* June.

MR. KNOTNOW

(**Grabbing the paper and shoving it in the back of his file folder**) Glad that's over. (**Suddenly deep in thought**) June was hell.

MR. ETHEARIAL

Remember two Junes ago ... ? (**Squinting**) Let's make up a new name for the month, you know, call it something else. And the June after that we could change Flag Day ...

MR. KNOTNOW

Let's talk about the effects of that procedure twenty years from now.

MR. ETHEARIAL

Let's talk about the rebellion over the non-vacation procedure of May '77. What a ballbuster.

MS. CRASTNAIT

(**Looks harried, papers flying as she enters the cubicle. Drops some**) I'll get 'em later.

MR. KNOTNOW

(**Looks at Ethearial**) Well?

MR. ETHEARIAL

(**Squinting, deep in thought**) Well. Well. I'll never forget the time my mother said, "Don't go near there, Harold; you'll fall in ... "

MS. CRASTNAIT

(**Annoyed**) I hate the new procedure, gentlemen.

(**The two men look helplessly at each other**)

MR. KNOTNOW

Let's talk old procedure.

MR. ETHEARIAL

What about calling it something other than a procedure?

MS. CRASTNAIT

(**Shooing them out of her small space**) Later!

Chapter 3

On The Scene
Be Here Now

As you can tell from Take One, the three characters involved were anywhere but in the here and now. If they had been, their communication would have had some unity, not to mention a more reasonable ending — some resolution about the so-called "procedure." How many of you are involved in scenes like that every day? I know I'm raising *my* hand!

Take One is a good illustration of the most critical rule in improv: the law called "Be Here Now." In brief, this means that when you're engaged in a scene, you cannot be in the past, nor can you be projecting forward into the future. Without exception you must always *be*; in other words, you must remain in the present moment. As the scene unfolds, you unfold with it. It's like riding a wave. You want to stay in the midst of the momentum.

On the surface, this fundamental improv rule may appear easy; but in the scope of our everyday business activities, it really isn't. Too many times in business meetings, telephone conversations, and other interactions, our minds go whirling around, spinning unpredictably like aluminum tops. It's hard to "Be Here Now" every second, every minute. (Robin Williams is really stellar in this regard, as are other improv veterans, but I don't know too many business types who can pull it off.)

There are so many ways we get distracted. Perhaps we get fixated on a thought, leaving us behind the "moment"; or our minds take off to God knows where—maybe to what's for dinner. Our minds flit from topic to topic so rapidly that our fragmented thoughts are like race cars zigzagging around brightly colored cones.

As you might have guessed, while we're engaged in all that mental hot-rodding, we're probably missing out on some important details in the moment. For example, somebody might be saying something that we really need to be attending to. In fact, any time someone is speaking to us, we should be listening. I once had a client named Paul; every time we'd meet, he was always in another world. But he continued to fake me out. Each time he would sit across the table from me and look me straight in the eye. I would say something — ask a question, for instance. He kept a penetrating, alert fix on me — eyeball to eyeball — and I felt very connected, even special to see him so attentive. Then after I posed my important question, he would say, "Huh? What? I gotta remember to give Jill the Delamer file." My surprised look would all but say, "What the hell is the Delamer file?" He later confessed he had Attention Deficit Disorder.

Another danger of checking out is that when we do, it's impossible for us to assimilate new information or focus on the part we're playing in the scene. Too, we quickly lose track of why we're in the scene in the first place. Like Paul. We space out. And if we're mentally coming and going in the scene, it's difficult to participate — to communicate.

For improv actors, staying totally current in a scene is an absolute prerequisite to its progression. Once again, however, improv players enjoy a significant advantage over the business professional in this regard: Having had so many hours of practice in class and rehearsal on stage, being "in the moment" becomes as natural to them as breathing.

Lacking this type of training, the average business professional easily strays from the "Be Here Now" mode, as in the following example. Suppose you're in a meeting, and someone is talking. Something they say triggers an idea that you want to express. Several lines of dialogue later, you jump in to say your line. Unfortunately, it may have very little to do with the line of dialogue that preceded it. But you don't care, you're hellbent on articulating the thought you're stuck on. You're no longer in the "now"; you're unable to assimilate new information and move forward in the scene. You're mired in the conversational past.

The same thing happens when you anticipate, when you think ahead beyond where a conversation is presently. For example, someone might say something that triggers a connecting thought in your own mind that you know needs to be brought up at a later point in the meeting. As your mind travels ahead to that thought, you miss the moment; you're already "over there," in the future.

What typically occurs in a meeting where everyone is on his or her own mental pogo stick is a version of what improv players call "Locked into Activity." That is, all involved grab onto their individual ideas and go off in their own directions. As they stay fixated on their own pet ideas, as they belabor and mentally rehearse their creations, it becomes impossible for them to remain in the here and now. Each person is in his or her own scene, his or her own private moment. They're not really listening to anybody else. As a result, the people in the scene can't connect with one another, and there's little, if any, communication between them.

You saw this previously with Knotnow, Ethearial, and Crastnait — all of whom were somewhere other than the present moment of their conversation. If they had *been there now*, you'd have witnessed ideas and thoughts that followed in sequence from one another. (If you re-read the scene, you'll notice that each was anywhere *other* than where the other two were at any given verbal juncture.)

If the parties in a conversation attempt to force preconceived topics and ideas into the scene regardless of appropriateness to the actual moment, the integrity of the scene's flow is severely disturbed. In the sample scene, you can see the result: very quickly, you have three different scenes occurring at the same time. Even worse, you actually have three separate, concurrent monologues taking place. As the participants express their own points of view, elaborate on these points, or jump ahead to new ones, the conversation breaks down. Communication-wise, the players get further and further apart. You can't commune with others when you're alone.

The basic problem here is the need for control, with each person going forward to do his or her own thing so that no one's in the collective moment. What starts this runaway train? The need to analyze, filter, monitor, dissect, rationalize, reason — the list goes on and on.

On the other hand, if we strive to stay in the moment in all of our business dealings, we've practically guaranteed that the communication won't go astray. Wherever the conversationalists go, they'll go there together.

Now that you've seen the pitfalls of violating the "Be Here Now" principle, you're ready to learn how to train yourself to avoid them. Again, let's take our cue from the improv player's notebook.

Improv actors go into scenes with their eyes and ears wide open. They listen to all of the specifications called out by the audience, assimilate the information, and swing into action. At no time do they decide how the scene should develop, how it should end, or what they will say in the interim. They just "go with" whatever seems to develop naturally, by staying in the moment, from moment to moment, confident that an ending will present itself at a strategic time.

In a typical improv setting, one improv player speaks, and another makes a direct response to the last piece of dialogue spoken. By operating within the bounds of one response-to-another, the piece is threaded together; the actors are like a verbal assembly line. In fact, many improv actors will tell you that doing improv isn't nearly as demanding as it would seem, because they don't feel any pressure to make the piece work. Rather, their only mandate is to remain in the present.

Improv actors are unlikely to fret about where a scene will go, or even whether it will go anywhere at all. It's like skiing. When you look down and see the entire hill, it can be a frightening sight. But when you traverse, taking one piece of the mountain at a time, never thinking about getting to the bottom of the hill, just remaining with what's right there in front of you, it's a lot easier to stay confident and calm.

So, just like the beginning skier trains, the improv actor continues the drill one step at a time: being right there, right then, over and over again. Each scene provides another workout. After a while, the "Be Here Now" process becomes second nature.

If you want to see this principle in action, watch Robin Williams being interviewed sometime on TV. As you'll see, he's always very present. He never hesitates; he never lags behind; he never jumps ahead. Sure, he sometimes goes off into the yonder, but those trips of his are always relative to the present. He just keeps threading things together, from one moment to the next. And yes, he does it rapidly.

What are some other ways to train relevant to the "Be Here Now" principle? Well, in addition to listening, which we'll talk about in a later chapter, improv actors learn to concentrate, to focus. They also train themselves to be good observers. They develop the ability to stay anchored and centered, locked into place, solidly aligning themselves with the prevailing energy. Self-discipline in all these areas assists the improv player with staying in the present.

Repetition is yet another way to gain consistency in terms of the ability to settle down and not be distracted. The more a person works out, the stronger his or her mental muscles will become.

I'm big on rehearsal. Someone said to Fred Astaire, "Gee, Fred, you're such a great dancer." His response was: "No, I'm not; I'm a great rehearser." He made that statement after performing a two-minute dance number for which he'd spent eight hours in rehearsal.

Granted, you may not have eight straight hours just to practice the "Be Here Now" game, but you *can* practice on the job on a daily basis. I advise my students to pick a specific time each day to work on one or more of the improv principles. Eventually, the principles will become an ingrained part of your communication behavior.

There are many reasons that we engage in communication: to inform, to persuade, to connect. No matter what the reason, staying in the moment will enhance the effectiveness of every communication you engage in, whether business or professional.

Remember the chaos you saw in the "communication" between Knotnow, Ethearial and Crastnait? If that's not for you, then you'll want to practice the "Be Here Now" principle. It'll bring order to all your communications.

The following is a list of homework assignments to aid you in this task:

1. Select a time each day when you will devote yourself to doing nothing other than staying with each moment as it occurs. It may be a phone call, it could be a conversation with a co-worker, it could be drafting a letter or a sales pitch. Notice how many times your mind skips ahead or lags behind, and how easy it is to get off track from the present. This will take tremendous mental discipline at first. Later, you will find yourself with the superb ability to shut out all else and be "with" whatever is happening, right there, right then.

2. Select examples of times when it is really easy and comfortable to "Be Here Now." For many, it may be watching a movie or a sporting event. My personal favorite is counting money. You tend to stay right with "it" as you go along. Now compare that to things you do when you are definitely not in the "here"—like washing the car, getting dressed, vacuuming. Many of the tasks you do all day are done mindlessly. We tend to be doing one thing while our minds are somewhere else. The lesson here is to start becoming aware of how it feels to be and *stay* in the moment.

3. Choose everyday activities — listening to a song, working at your desk, chopping salad ingredients — and do them with total and complete focus on what you are *currently* doing. You will be surprised at how difficult it will be at first not to slip away mentally. Keep this in mind: For every day that you exercise your "Be Here Now" muscle, you will increase your ability to become and stay immersed in anything as it is transpiring. This will build on itself until, finally, it becomes habitual and the way in which you mentally function. Improv players exercise in this way for several hours each day until it becomes rote.

4. Take a few minutes each day to read something. Anything. As you read, make sure you pay close attention to *what* you are

reading. Take it sentence by sentence, then word by word. Reading is an activity where people tend to space, jump ahead or get stuck behind. This is a great homework assignment to step up your reading comp skills.

5.   Make a deliberate effort to choose another time of day to sit down at your desk for at least 15 minutes doing one task at a time. Stop between tasks, regroup, then go on to the next task. For instance: Let's say you are going to look up a phone number on your Rolodex. Look it up. Now, dial the phone. Now prepare yourself to be ready for the voice on the other end. When you hear that voice, take the conversation as it comes. Don't jump ahead. Stay with each sentence. Don't get mired in something that was just said, either. See if you can stay with each word as it is spoken. You see, most of us in a desk setting will often be doing two or three things simultaneously. We'll be looking up that phone number, writing a note about something we hope not to forget, while we're also looking through a stack of papers for yet another thing. My worst habit in this category is to look up a phone number, dial it, then start looking up the next phone number for the subsequent call. When the person I first called answers the phone, I have often had to ask them who I called. Talk about making a bad impression! At first, it may seem like you're moving in slow motion, but slowing down is the way to tackle this discipline. You can gradually increase your speed at taskdoing. Soon you will go at a reasonable pace; however, as you do each "thing," you will be with *that* "thing" and nowhere else.

6.   Practice having conversations when you don't react to anything but what is being said now. (More on this in Chapter 5). This too, takes effort, but eventually you will find it easy to go with the flow and pay attention to the immediate.

7.   Note the times when you're not very flexible or agile in chang-ing course, whether it's during an activity or a conversation. Keep telling yourself you want to stay current, stay present, be

willing to go with the flow — and soon you will. You may even want to keep a diary for a certain part of each day to track such moments. I guarantee you will find review of such notes extremely helpful. They'll be like instant replays. It seems we all learn a great deal more when looking back. One more tip along these lines: You want to learn to relinquish control in conversations, something we'll talk about in greater detail later.

8. Dance. Pay attention to each step as you perform it. To me, this is a really fun way to learn the technique of "Be Here Now."

9. Try the technique of detaching from yourself in any given task, and make it feel as though you are simply observing yourself. Let's say you're putting clothes away in the closet or dusting a table. Being in a state of mind where you watch yourself do the chores will cause you to stay immersed through each detail. It will automatically force you to "Be Here Now."

10. Get in the car and don't plan where you're going. Just enjoy everything along the way. When you finally arrive at some destination, experience that "place" as if you're looking for something new. Discover something different – something you've never noticed before.

11. Do an activity in slow motion. Let's say you decide to put laundry into the washer. Deliberately do so as slowly as you can, staying focused on each and every second of activity – each clothing item. This, too, increases your ability to travel in the here and now.

12. Lastly, sit in the middle of the floor and close your eyes. Now, just listen. Listen to every single sound, even your own breathing. See if you can do this for about five minutes each day. Again, it forces you to remain in the present.

One final note about "being here now": You will begin to see how much better your sense of focus becomes; how much easier it is to retain information; and, most importantly, how perceptive you become about others. All this only serves to make you a stronger communicator.

Now, let's redo the scene that preceded this chapter and see what happens when those three apply the "Be Here Now" principle.

TAKE TWO: "Delicate Procedure"

(Int. office cubicle. Two guys standing in the doorway chatting, drinking coffee, styro cups in hand.) They're waiting for Ms. Crastnait)

MR. KNOTNOW

(Looking at paper produced by the other guy) Ah, the Ramrod report. Hate dealing with that thing.

MR. ETHEARIAL

Hate it? Loathe it. **(Throws it over his shoulder)**

MR. KNOTNOW

Ari, the new procedure. What'll we say to her if she hates it?

MR. ETHEARIAL

We'll have to sell her on its benefits.

MR. KNOTNOW

Oh, yes, the benefits. Perks, extras, the bonus factor.

MR. ETHEARIAL

I'll skip the nontangibles, the what-ifs, what-might-bes.
Especially the effect it could have on the mid-management
staff in November. **(Laughs)** Hell, those things may never
happen.

MR. KNOTNOW

Yeah, or the effects of it twenty years from now. Who
cares? Heck, we're right smack in July.

MR. ETHEARIAL

Yep, smack dab in July! We were smack dab in June
not long ago.

MR. KNOTNOW

Yes, we were. Soon we'll be smack dab in August.
But hey, this is today.

MR. ETHEARIAL

Yes. Currently, we're right here ...

MR. KNOTNOW

... right now.

MS. CRASTNAIT

**(Looking harried, papers flying as she enters the
cubicle. Drops some)** I'll get 'em later.

MR. KNOTNOW

(Looks at Ethearial) We'll get them for you.

(Both men scramble to pick them up)

MS. CRASTNAIT

(Annoyed) I hate the new procedure, gentlemen.

(The two men look helplessly at each other)

MR. KNOTNOW

What is it you hate about it?

MR. ETHEARIAL

We're all ears.

MS. CRASTNAIT

You got two weeks?

(They nod in the affirmative)

MS. CRASTNAIT

Sit down!

(As the scene ends, the three are engaged in conversation about the procedure)

-Lights-

Chapter 4

Scene Savers
Serve and Support

TAKE ONE: "On Their Own"

(Int. business office. Three women sitting at a small conference table organizing what appear to be notes and reports. They are obviously about to begin a meeting)

MRS. PREOCK

(Looking in a compact mirror) I've been trying to fix my pompadour all morning. It just won't lay right.

MRS. MEEFURST

(Pulling poster boards from her portfolio case) I really need to get an approval on this ad so I can get it into production right away.

MRS. UPSORBED

(Trying to read her notes without her glasses) Well, I have two new agenda items that we forgot to talk about last meeting, ladies.

MRS. PREOCK

(**Jumping up and looking out the window**) Did I put money in that meter?

MRS. UPSORBED

(**Going back and forth with her pencil**) Let's talk about item two first, because it affects item one, which is the budget.

MRS. MEEFURST

I've got an ad that'll miss deadline unless you sign it off. (**Shoving it over to Mrs. Preock and covering up her mirror**)

MRS. PREOCK

Hmmm. (**Briefly looking at the ad copy in front of her**) Do either of you know what the responsibilities of a team mother are? (**Under her breath**) Did I feed the dog?

MRS. UPSORBED

Well, if we covered item one first, then we could move on to two, which would be a far more logical progression.

(**A pager beeps. They each reach for their own**)

MRS. MEEFURST

Oh! That's Bonehead. He's ready for our 3:30.

-Fade to Black-

Chapter 4

Scene Savers
Serve and Support

One of the biggest faux pas for would-be communicators is entering into conversations from a pre-set agenda — from *their* own point of view, with little regard for the other guy. Maybe some of these people are truly selfish, but I tend to think that most who do this are simply preoccupied.

Whatever the reason, these people have violated another rule of improv — the principle of "Serve and Support." Improv players, rather than concentrating on themselves, are trained to put their focus on the others in a scene. They think in terms of how they can best take care of everyone else. They're like safety nets, doorstoppers, paramedics; they're the great protectors, the ultimate helpers, like grips, flight attendants. As individuals, improv actors cater to each other like ever-ready busboys.

They are as reactive an ensemble as a corp of Red Cross. In fact, the term "first aid" has a whole different meaning for improv actors, who learn to listen to, and anticipate, the others on stage. When improv players speak, they provide information that tends to bolster and embellish the ideas already set forth by their fellow actors in the scene. Their attention is consistently focused away from themselves and onto the needs of others.

Here's how the "Serve and Support" theory operates during a scene. Let's say there are three actors in a piece. Each takes the stage with only one thing on his or her mind: how to take care of the other two. Even though nothing within the scene is planned, the actors know going in that it's their job to focus on the others and then provide them with the conversation that supports the ideas put forth. As they launch into the piece, the actors pay close attention to where their co-participants are coming from, both verbally and physically. In this way, they're able to absorb vital information much more quickly — a big advantage, since there's no such thing as downtime for the improv actor. (I don't know that downtime exists for business professionals, either. Some business days I feel like the Roadrunner.)

In the midst of a rapid turnaround of information, the performers also pick up on such essentials as the attitude and demeanor of their co-actors. They are laser-quick at tuning into the others' subtexts (what is unsaid). Because of this — and by adhering to the "Serve and Support" rule, in general — improv actors have a seemingly miraculous ability to become an integral part of a scene only moments after the scene has gotten underway. For those in improv, "Serve and Support" is a law; if they break it, everyone gets busted. In fact, this particular improv tenet gives an entirely new meaning to the term "buddy system."

As a business professional, your first assignment in improv training was to "Be Here Now." Your second assignment, then, is to "Serve and Support" by taking care of everyone else in a given conversation. (And actually, by doing so, you'll also be taking very good care of yourself.) Think about the dynamic that will result if everyone is focused on making the communication go smoothly for the others involved. Since no one will be making self-centered efforts to control the direction of the conversation, there'll be unbelievable harmony among the participants. Talk about rapport building!

Suppose, however, that you're the only one in the conversation who knows about the rule of "Serve and Support." Well, you can still make it work. You can still impact others through your own behavior. (As is true in so many things, what you put out is also what you get back.)

If others are unaware of the rule, your chances for tight communication do improve when there are fewer participants in the scene. Luckily, most business encounters are one-on-one. (Think about all those phone calls, for example.) When you're operating on the premise that your only job is to "Serve and Support" the other actor — your client, your co-worker, your boss — you just increase your chances not only of controlling the way that person responds to you, but also getting what you want.

If you have a caretaking approach, the other person usually responds positively, often without even understanding why. I've seen this on stage and in business situations, too. When you put the focus on the other person, you gain an edge. You quickly learn what's important to that individual, and you can then back up this knowledge with the correct responses. Paradoxically, by not trying to control the outcome of an encounter, you'll actually be retaining much greater control than you're accustomed to.

So when we begin, within the scenes of our daily lives, to take care of the communication needs of others — business prospects, colleagues, subordinates, existing clients, or whomever — things just have a way of falling into place. Unfortunately, though, many a scene goes awry because the players are so focused on their individual agendas that they don't even bother to listen to one another. Even if the participants in these "conversations" aren't talking simultaneously, they might as well be. Certainly, no one involved in the exchange is giving any thought to the needs and wants of the others. I see this happen in business situations all day, every day. Especially with salespeople.

All too often, salespeople will approach their prospective customers like pit bulls on a pant leg. They lunge right into their prey and won't let go until they've verbally expostulated on every possible reason why Customer X should buy Product Y.

You may not realize it, but whether we're salespeople or not, we're all selling something — a product, a service, a philosophy, an idea, or, if you're an actor, a part. So it's incumbent upon us to understand that while there are different ways to hook a prospect, the best way is by deferring to him or her — by putting our focus on that *other* person. That's how we learn about other people. And what we learn can be key. Learn first. Sell later.

To backtrack just a bit, we want to begin each of our scenes with the mindset of being, and staying, "in the moment." From that starting point, we can begin to "Serve and Support" by becoming very conscious of the others involved. Functioning in that mode tends to foster tight verbal exchanges — for both the improv actor and the business person. Remember, a scene is a scene.

Ask yourself how many times — let's say yesterday — you approached each situation or scene by focusing on the other guy(s) and taking the attention off yourself. Did you try to get inside their heads, or were you content to stay in your own? Did you concentrate on your own agenda and the ideas you wanted to discuss, or were you more concerned with listening to others? Did you allow yourself to be distracted with thoughts about your appearance (good hair day or bad)? Others' opinions of you? Whether or not you forgot to unplug the iron or close the driveway gate so the dog wouldn't get out? There are a million disjointed thoughts that can divert us from tuning in to the needs of others. We're so important to ourselves. That can be good but it can also be quite harmful to effective communication.

Here's an example: I used to attend a weekly meeting for one of my PR clients, a big Orange County developer. He thought he was the center of the universe. Truly a legend in his own mind. But not in the minds of the eight people who sat around his marble table. All of us were tired of his "I," "me," "mine" orientation. The day that took the cake was a Tuesday afternoon when, as usual, he was late. Forty-five minutes late. We tapped our pencils on the table, heads drooping, almost dozing. Finally, he graced us with his presence. When we began to show him the essentials of our new public relations campaign, he reluctantly approved them. Unlike other campaigns, this one was not his creation. His marketing director sat nearby; she was enthused. Until, that is, he began to bark orders at her, insisting she turn around the needed printed materials in 48 hours. She tried to remind him that she had already asked for two days off (she worked seven days a week, this gal) to take her small daughter on a trip to Sea World. "Well, change your plans," he ordered.

She gasped. We gasped with her. Then he rose, "I got what I needed. Gotta go. As it is, I'll only get in nine holes." As the door closed, almost on cue, each of us shot him an " ... if looks could kill" stare through the mahogany door. Talk about lack of Serve and Support **all** the way around! He didn't care about making that scene work. He had no regard whatsoever for us as a creative team — or for his assistant, who was also in support of him. Everything emanated from his point of view. His needs. His wants. We were just incidental fixtures in his self-decorated world. (Shortly after his award-winning departure, by the way, our creative team insisted on helping the marketing director complete her task. We worked as a team and got the job done on time. We opted to "Serve and Support" and everyone won.)

As I mentioned previously, improv actors don't have the luxury of being self-absorbed or self-centered. Not even for a moment. But that kind of focused attention takes diligence, discipline, practice, and a whole new way of processing information and relating to others.

Currently, I have ExecuProv students rehearsing every day in business meetings what they've learned in my classes. In the beginning, they might be able to work on only one thing at a time, because the precepts — when used in conjunction with one another — can become as complicated as, let's say, laughing, talking and eating all at once. It takes time for the improv basics to become conditioned, subconscious reflexes. But, remember how hard you had to concentrate when you first learned how to tie your shoes?

Over time, with enough repetition and practice, you'll actually be able to recondition your mind to function and respond in accordance with the principles of improv theory. And with the substantial groundwork you've laid for successfully establishing and maintaining rapport with others, you'll soon be running circles around your competition. Why? Because once you've established rapport, everything else will fall into place. More on that later!

For now, just run around in your head this idea of serving and supporting others. Try it out. Experiment. Next time you find yourself in a "scene," ask yourself what you can do to "Serve and Support" the others who are in it with you. Ask, "What can I do to assist, to help, to bolster, to fortify, to aid, to facilitate, to encourage, to validate, to advocate" — the list goes on and on. If you want the scene to work, make sure you're focused on others.

Forget about yourself.

If you get stuck on exactly what this means or how to do it, just dwell on the Golden Rule — the "Do unto others ... " thing. It'll rapidly snap your perspective right back into alignment — like a kiddie car on a Disney ride!

One last thing about "Serve and Support": Just because you're in a caretaker mode doesn't mean you can't have controversy or conflict in a scene. Although we'll address this in detail in a later chapter, I want you to understand that serving and supporting simply means being prepared to put your focus "over there," and to put others' needs before your own in order to foster more effective communication.

Another wonderful by-product of "Serve and Support" is that when you take the focus off yourself, you become less self-conscious. It really helps relieve pressure. And when your attention is "over there," you're not as apt to flub up — flubbing up is often the result of being too self-focused. It's a wonderful principle for the meek and the timid to stand behind!

Like so many improv rules, it has more than one benefit or purpose.

Here's some homework to aid you in the task of serving and supporting.

1. Take at least one business encounter a day and approach it from an attitude of total "Serve and Support." Forget **your** needs. Put your agenda on the back burner. Focus only on perceiving what the others need and want, and when you've perceived it, provide it. Soon you'll create a habit of doing this. The end result: Your clients will come back for more, you'll feel unusually powerful, and people in general will tell everyone what a great person you are.

2. If you don't do this already, volunteer for some organization in need and assist them once a week or once a month — whatever your schedule allows. No matter how important your station in the business world, this donation of your self will serve to

keep you humble, to remind you that we all "serve somebody" (in the words of Bob Dylan).

3. Unbeknownst to anyone in your office, pick someone you can focus on for a few weeks as a person you will make a conscious effort to support. Be helpful to them, listen to them, let them take center stage. Tune into their needs and wants, then serve them. This is great boot-camp training because you're mandated to do it every day. Make certain your selection includes someone with whom you come into contact several times daily. Again, no one has to know what you're up to!

4. See if you can get everyone in your department or office to agree to take a day when you change places with each other. I once did this when I had a bustling, 15-person advertising/PR firm. We drew names and then showed up for work that Friday taking over the person's desk. By day's end, we had a much greater understanding and compassion for that person's workload. And when we returned to our regular jobs, there was no effort in serving and supporting. We were eager to do just that. This became a regular monthly event.

5. Spend an afternoon going to the mall, any mall, and placing yourself at the door of any major store. Open that door for at least a half hour for all those passing by. It's another reminder of taking care of "them" and not you. I do this at Christmas time. It makes me feel good.

6. Make your own list of activities that drive this point home. Now, make sure you spend at least 30 minutes a day doing one or more of them. Some examples might be tidying up a co-worker's work space, playing catcher for your Little League youngster who wants to practice hitting the ball, or cleaning up the kitchen when it's not your turn. Any activity is valid so long as it puts you in a state where you're fully cognizant of serving and supporting.

With all that in mind, let's now take a second look at our

friends who were so obsessed with their own agendas.

TAKE TWO: "On Their Own"

**(Int. business office. Three women sitting at a small confer-
ence table organizing what appear to be notes and reports.
They're obviously about to begin a meeting)**

MRS. PREOCK

(Looking in a compact mirror) I've been trying to fix
my pompadour all morning. It just won't lay right.

MRS. MEEFURST

(Pulling poster boards from her portfolio case) Here,
try this. **(She whips out a tube of gel)** Now, ladies, I really
need to get an approval of this ad so I can get it into
production right away.

MRS. UPSORBED

(Trying to read without her glasses) Looks good to me.
(Holds it up to show the woman with the hair problem)
Entense, what's your opinion?

MRS. PREOCK

Sure. Looks good to me, too. I say it's a go.

MRS. UPSORBED

You know, ladies, I have two new agenda items that
we forgot to talk about last meeting.

MRS. MEEFURST

Yeah?

MRS. PREOCK

What are they?

MRS. UPSORBED

Item one is the budget. Item two is expenditures.

MRS. PREOCK

Ladies? Before we cover those, may I just interrupt to ask you both something?
(Both women nod in the affirmative)

MRS. PREOCK

Do either of you know what the responsibilities of a team mother are? Oh! I can't remember if I put money in the meter...or fed the dog.

MRS. MEEFURST

First of all, Entense, a team mother does everything the coach doesn't want to do. I'll go down and put money in the meter for you. I parked right behind you and have to check mine anyway.

MRS. UPSORBED

... And the hell with the dog. I once forgot to feed Rover for three days, and he got by on goldfish and —

(A pager beeps. They each reach for their own)

MRS. MEEFURST

Oh! That's Bonehead. He's ready for our 3:30. As soon as we're done, what'ya say let's get right back to those agenda items.

(Together, the three women bolt for the door)

-Fade to Black-

Chapter 5

Scene One/Act, Too
React and Respond

TAKE ONE: "Where's the Beef?"

(Two men sitting across from one another at a conference table working on a business proposal they are soon due to present. They've been there for hours)

MR. SLUGGARD

(Scribbling desperately on a piece of paper) Help! I can't think of a good enough adjective to describe how chewy our beef jerky is.

MR. SNAILEICH

(Feet on the desk, eyes skyward. The tempo of his voice akin to a trumpet playing taps) We better address the salt factor. There's 47 grams of sodium in every 1.5 bites. Oh, and don't forget the water retention deal with our jerky.

MR. SLUGGARD

(Biting the eraser off the pencil and trying to wedge it into the small cracks between his bottom incisors)I need help, man! We've only got two more hours to get this to word processing and... **(He blurts)** INSCRUTABLY CHEWY...SHARKTEETH CHEWY... MARSHMELLOW CHEWY...Hey, Bud, I'm dying here, throw something out....

MR. SNAILEICH

(Slowly pulls a small plastic container from his pocket protector pocket. It rattles slightly) You want a TicTac?

MR. SLUGGARD

(Chewing on the wooden part of the pencil. Spitting splinters so harshly they lodge between the moussed strands of the other man's coif) I want a lifesaver!!!

MR. SNAILEICH

Hmmm. A Lifesaver. **(His head tilts skyward. He squints as if peering into the noonday sun as he speaks)** Those are the candies with the holes in the center. Or, are they the holes with candies on the outside? They're not a subject of this proposal, are they? **(He slows)** Besides, look at how many more bugs are trapped inside that flourescent. Count 'em ... 14, 15, 16 ... .

MR. SLUGGARD

(**The wooden portion of the pencil is no more.
He's spitting lead balls now with every outburst**)
CADDILAC CHEWY .. .CAPGUN CHEWY ...
CATACLYSMIC CHEWY ... CHUNKY CHEWY ...
CLARINET CHEWY ... CHUCKSTEAK CHEWY ...
CHROMOCHOME CHEWY ... CHIPPENDALE
CHEWY ... I'm dyin' here, I'm sinkin' (**He's caught
up by his own undercurrent as he slides out of his
chair, helplessly bonking his chin on the tabletop as he
begins to slip out of sight. His final words are
muffled**) I'm failin', I'm reachin', I'm graspin', Holy
Moly, (**Only the top of his crewcut is visible**) I'm
gonna crash ... .

MR. SNAILEICH

(**Still peering skyward as though he's waiting for the
ceiling to part**) Oh, yeah, let's see ... an adjective for
beef ... .

MR. SLUGGARD

(**He's spent. Screams loudly from underneath
the table**) JeRRKKKK!

-Lights-

Chapter 5

Scene One/Act, Too
React and Respond

What we just witnessed is as commonplace a verbal get-together as "Hello, how are you?" As you can see, these two people are not having a conversation with one another. There is no "Fine, and you?" kind of thing in their ongoing remarks. True, Sluggard was trying to connect with Snaileich by saying things like "throw something out ... I need a Lifesaver ... I'm failin', I'm gonna crash ... " but Snaileich wouldn't bite. Wouldn't engage. He wouldn't give anything back. There was no repartee. And the idea of repartee is essential in any substantial conversation — in any substantial scene.

Snaileich seemed to be in his own little world with his own little thoughts simply focused on his own little needs, ideas and agenda. What a pinhead.

I know a lot of pinheads. In fact, I was in a meeting full of them not long ago, where one guy, named Harold, was trying desperately to get help from his colleagues with the configuration of a living room on an architectural design plan for a single-family home. Every time Harold spoke about his plight, the other architects kept talking about the other rooms in the house and what would work relative to their design elements. Harold would say things like, "I think I need another option for the fireplace, guys; it's too close to the central wall." The head pinhead at this meeting said in response to that: "Let's put a spa in the master bedroom itself rather than on the deck." Poor Harold. He may just as well have been talking to himself. He kept throwing out bits like those of Sluggard; bits that required help or assistance – needed ideas, suggestions – when all he got for his efforts was some form of resistance and a string of non-sequiturs. In fact, Harold got so frustrated, he started sketching in fireplaces along every portion of the back wall of the living room. (His words and his absurd drawings gained him nothing. As much as he tried to throw out dialogue that begged for sequential responses, he got, in the words of Mick Jagger, "no satisfaction.") Sluggard and Snaileich-style conversations happen to all of us every day. We are either the victims or the perpetrators. But these types of conversations shouldn't happen, ever. They just don't have to. Not if you follow the final rule in the sacred trilogy that I've been talking about: the rule of "React and Respond."

"React and Respond" is another fundamental tenet used by the improv player to make absolutely sure that all verbal exchanges on stage will thread together in a unified way.

What I'd like to make known at this point is just how the improv actor makes certain that each conversation is just that, a conversation (an oral exchange of sentiments, observations, opinions or ideas). In true conversation, comments are bounced back and then forth, back and then forth, and so on.

Now, during this conversation process, the improv player's comments are always based on appropriate responses. What defines an appropriate response is simple: You simply reply with a comment that is a direct response or reaction to the **last thing said or last idea held.** In other words, each of your comments responds to the idea of the comment that precedes it.

For example, if Snaileich had replied to Sluggard's initial piece of dialogue by displaying concern or an idea that would have assisted Sluggard (an adjective that described the new beef jerky), they would not only have had a meaningful conversation, but also may have come upon some viable solutions to the problem.

Similarly, if Harold had been given some interest relative to his fireplace concerns, he could have moved on to another interior feature.

Both men could have taken a tip from improv players, who behave in a manner that is always mindful of what was just said. Every response, every reply, is in direct accordance with what was just uttered, and everyone involved feels secure and safe because they know they are all going down the same verbal road. In step. It's magic to watch. And, there's a sense of comfort and appreciation in the audience, because while they watch, they come to trust that each scene (each conversation) will unfold and progress with meaning, clarity, and most of all, congruency.

So then, each improv actor is trained to "React and Respond." In other words, to address, exclusively, the last thing said or last idea held. In so doing, the actors tend to buttress improv's two other basic principles: "Be Here Now" and "Serve and Support." If you're reacting and responding, you're no doubt serving and supporting, giving the other actors what they need to produce a reasonable conversation. In addition, if you're reacting and responding, you're necessarily in the moment (you couldn't react and respond if you weren't "here now").

In the words of my dear friend, Michael Gellman, one of the most skilled directors and teachers at Chicago's Second City, "Improv is like playing tennis. It's like hitting a ball back and forth to and fro." He's quick to point out that you must be ready at all times to return the ball, no matter which way it comes to and at you.

Gellman is right. Improv dialogue is just like tennis. You never know what will be said or what will be done, but you must be ready to provide a reasonable return; you must be willing to "React and Respond" appropriately. And again, each verbal hit must be aimed with the intent of staying within reasonable bounds of the conversation at hand.

As I said, "React and Respond" is the last rule in that all important trilogy I've been hammering on. And it's really very simple. All you ever need to do as a business professional or an improv player is "React and Respond" to what is happening at every moment, right there, right then. When you play tennis well, you ready yourself for each release that comes at you. You never remain positioned for the last ball; instead, you focus on the one that's coming at you now. So when you think of "React and Respond," think tennis, think volleyball, think Ping-Pong or any other game that requires that back-and-forth rhythm. And, hey, how 'bout those pro basketball rebounds? Same concept!

In improv, responses and reactions are lightning quick. Your eyes and ears shift with them. You're caught up. And, all they've done, these improv players, is practice this rule till it's become as automatic as slipping on slippers. But once again, it's learned behavior. It's repetition and drill. Remember what I said earlier (it's the key to this new way of communicating): The rule of "React and Respond" is just another way of **processing** information. After awhile, you're not even conscious of doing it.

It sounds easy, doesn't it? Simply offer words and actions that fit with previous words and actions. But, we as business professionals rarely listen to each release of dialogue, let alone "React and Respond" to it. Instead, we jump ahead or lag behind, or more typically, introduce new information into the conversation that isn't at all a natural progression or natural response.

I'm asking that you pay attention to how many of your conversations are nonsensical, disjointed, disconnected, discontinuous and severed. How many of your conversations are partial; how many meander?

I think when you begin to assess the quality of your "scenes," you'll take serious note of how often you trip out of verbal bounds. Too, you'll come upon an awareness of why you actually feel lonely during some conversations.

Another thing: I have an issue with time. Wasted time. And when I think about how many meetings I've been in where people are talking in circles, or not really talking with each other, or throwing out bits and pieces of ideas and thoughts like cheap confetti, I get so irritated I want to chew viciously on my day planner. Why bother even talking? What's the point? Such communication is about as purposeful to the meeting as a deck chair to the Titanic.

One more note: When people opt not to "React and Respond" to one another every step of the way, it's almost impossible to connect in thought, feeling, purpose and goal. That's why people feel misunderstood, isolated, frustrated and lonely. That's why, very often, very little gets accomplished. I say time is just too precious. Why get together for a conversation if you're going to gain nothing?

In closing, I want to share my favorite story about "React and Respond." I know a woman, a highly sought-after interior designer, who, though she tricked you into thinking, at first glance, that she was as quiet and meek as Jackie O., was quite bold at all her business meetings. She was mid-fifties. Had no patience for small talk. She had things to do and places to go. She had the crust of a chicken pot pie and a mind that could outrun the space shuttle. Whenever the conversation went askew, she would begin answering her own questions or responding to her own comments. What I loved about her digressions is that she was always in sequence with her last response to herself. And, of course, she could always make people laugh.

She would say things like: "Great suit." If the suit in question didn't respond, or random chatter ensued, she would say something like, "Thanks, I got it on sale." "How much was it?" "Not as much as the hourly increase you're going to have to give me for my consulting services effective as of this meeting." "Oh, really, how much is that?" "$450 per hour." Abrupt silence would fill the room. The sound of numbers tends to do that. "Oh," she would innocently exclaim, "is it something I said?"

She would always talk to herself out loud, she says, in an attempt to keep her mind on course when everyone else was "tripping" (she was a product of the '60s), and to bring the conversation back into sharp focus. She was known for her back and forth sole conversations and for her witty eargrabbers. I'm proud to say I, too, was present the day she announced casually that her ass had slipped helplessly down to the back of her knees.

I'm not suggesting that you begin to engage in conversations with yourself so that eventually someone in a white coat comes to fetch you. I'm merely asking that you pay greater attention to the way in which your "scenes" transpire.

Which brings me to your homework assignments:

1. Take the opportunity at least once a day to monitor a conversation between others. Identify the purpose of the communication by listening to the first couple of things that are said. See who reacts and responds to those particulars, and who doesn't. See if you can jot down various bits of conversation that either uphold the "React and Respond" principle, or violate it. If you have the opportunity to do this exercise more than once a day, do so. It will definitely strengthen your tendency to "React and Respond" appropriately, rather than verbally steer off course. Soon you'll be a keen observer, catching the slightest digression.

2. Have a conversation either on the phone or in a meeting with one person. Focus on reacting and responding to everything the other person says or does. Ask yourself as you go along: are your responses in accordance with what the other person said, or are your responses coming from your own agenda? (It's that old "Serve and Support" concept.) Later, see if you can write down various things that were said, things that either supported the theory or didn't. With regard to this exercise and the one above: If it's not too intrusive, record these conversations. You will be amazed at what you hear when you play them back. If you're fortunate enough to get to study this way, write down preferred reactions and responses should you have the chance to redo the "scene." See if you can compare the two, then see what you've learned from the distinct differences.

3. As silly as it may seem, attend a tennis match, volleyball game or other sporting event where the ball is rapidly sent back and forth. Just the rhythm of it all should create a new awareness and feel for the true meaning of "React and Respond." Watch those playing the game; note how they are ever ready to meet the challenge of the ball's direction.

Now, let's rerun that scene between the two guys in the conference room. Let's see what happens when they "React and Respond" to immediate statements and remarks.

TAKE TWO: "Where's the Beef?"

(Two men sitting across from one another at a conference table working on a business proposal they are soon due to present. They've been there for hours)

SLUGGARD

(Scribbling desperately on a piece of paper) Help! I can't think of a good enough adjective to describe how chewy our beef jerky is.

SNAILEICH

(Feet on desk, eyes skyward. The tempo of his voice akin to a trumpet playing taps) Ohh, Chewy, Chewy ... hmmm ... how 'bout Gummy, or Gooey ... ?

SLUGGARD

(Biting the eraser off the pencil and trying to wedge it into the small cracks between his bottom incisors) Ah, that sounds like taffy. I need help, man. We've only got two more hours to get this to word processing and...**(he blurts)** INSCRUTIBLY CHEWY ... SHARKTEETH CHEWY ... MARSHMELLOW CHEWY ... hey, Bud, I'm dyin' here, throw something out.

SNAILEICH

(While tossing him a box of breath mints from his

pocket protector) How 'bout TAFFY-PULL CHEWY?
TOBACOO-CHEW CHEWY? CHOO CHOO
CHEWY? Oh, I know ... COW-CUD CHEWY?

SLUGGARD

**(Chewing on the wooden part of the pencil. Spitting
splinters so harshly they lodge between the moussed
strands of the other man's coif)** I want a lifesaver!!!

SNAILEICH

Hmm. A Lifesaver. **(His head tilts skyward. He
squints as if peering into the noonday sun as he speaks)**
Those are the candies with the holes in the center. Or,
are they the holes with the candies on the outside? Or,
are you referring to a better idea?

SLUGGARD

**(The wooden portion of the pencil is no more. He's
spitting lead balls now with every outburst)** Yes, I'm
referring to something that will save our necks ... Oh,
wait ... .**(He's spitting them out furiously. Snaileich
is deflecting them right back as they bounce off his
forehead)** CADILLAC CHEWY ... CAPGUN
CHEWY ... CATACLYSMIC CHEWY ... CHUNKY
CHEWY ... CLARINET CHEWY ... CHUCKSTEAK
CHEWY ... CHROMOCHOME CHEWY ... CHIP-
PENDALE CHEWY...Hey, I'm dyin' here. I'm sinkin,
**(He's caught up by his own undercurrent as he slides
out of his chair, bonking his chin on the tabletop as he
slips out of sight. His final words are muffled.)** I'm
failin'. I'm goin' down. I'm gonna crash.

SNAILEICH

Oh yeah, that might work … (**still peering skyward as though he's waiting for the ceiling to part**) CRASH-COURSE CHEWY … or CAR-CRASH CHEWY … or, CRASH CORRIGAN CHEWY … those could be adjectives for beef … .

SLUGGARD

(**He's spent. Screams loudly from underneath the table**) JERRRK!

SNAILEICH

(**Unfazed**) Yeah, but don't forget the "e": our product has a "e" on the end Slug, so it's Jerrr-keeeeee!

-Lights-

Chapter 6

Making A Scene
Beginning, Middle and End

TAKE ONE: "We Get Letters"

(Int. conference room. Three people are seated, futzing with prototype containers and boxes, writing notes. A fourth person enters. Sits himself down, reaches for scraps of notes. They fly from his day planner. He begins to speak)

MR. SPACEY

(Clears his throat) Well, it probably would be better to take M from U and put it in the F cases.

MS. SWEETNIZ

(Timidly) M from U?

MR. SPACEY

(Arrogantly) I think that's what I just said.

MR. TRYARD

(Looking about the room at his colleagues. Kindly)
I think we are all wondering why just M and U, sir?

MR. SPACEY

(Almost impatient but somewhat patronizing)
Fine, then, let's just move on to the F cases.

MR. BRAUNOS

(Trying to impress Spacey) Hey, why don't we just
cover the P and XY Problem, which would take care of
the whole packing dilemma, including the F cases?

MR. SPACEY

Well said, Braunos. I think that covers it. **(Looks
around)** Same time tomorrow?

MS. SWEETNIZ

But, but … we didn't handle M or U … and what's all
this with P and XY?

MR. TRYARD

(Trying to mediate) Perhaps we could just finish
M — and U -- then figure out P another time?

MR. BRAUNOS

I think we've accomplished a great deal at this meeting
and Mr. Spacey has addressed the issue.

MR. SPACEY

**(Spacey flashes Braunos a smile, then displays
a perplexed look because he doesn't know why he
smiled. Then with finality)** So, tomorrow then we'll
meet again and put out another fire here at Hair-On-End!

-Lights-

Chapter 6

Making A Scene
Beginning, Middle and End

The essentials that comprise a scene, the basics that constitute a scene, include a beginning, a middle and an end. Always. That holds true not only for improv players when they're engaged in their on-stage dialogue, but for us as business professionals each time we participate in our daily business verbal exchanges.

Now, as you can well see, the goings-on between the parties in our last vignette illustrate anything but a beginning, middle and end. Instead, we had random bits of conversation with no sequential flow, no logical segues. Ultimately, we were left with no idea as to what was really going on or what the point was. For example, we never really got clear on what the meeting was about, the purpose for getting together. Next, no one was dealing conclusively with any particular issue. And most certainly, there was no closure as the meeting was summed up. You can't have closure when you have so much ambiguity.

If you take an honest look, however — even though that scene was exaggerated — I'm sure you could picture yourself in one of those chairs. Or, at least similar circumstances.

I have sat through many a meeting that was not too far off from what we just witnessed. People assemble. They begin to talk. Some attendees don't know what the initial verbiage means. Then others begin to talk around fragmented ideas, but no one in particular seems to zoom in on the heart of the matter. Next thing we know, time is up and the issue never gets thoroughly dealt with. As a consequence, there is no resolution. As a rule: All this equals wasted time and confusion.

Your work, and the work of the improv player, is one and the same: We constantly improvise in all our scenes. Therefore, it is to our advantage to train as improv players do because their scenes always work. In order to do this, we must first begin to think of all our communication in terms of three parts: a beginning, a middle and an end. That is a minimum requirement if we want full and complete communication. It doesn't matter, incidentally, if the communication lasts a few minutes or a few hours; for strong communication, we need to think in those three chunks.

Every scene — before it's over — should reveal a who, what, where and when. Also, each scene has a "why", a purpose to deal with, whether that's a conflict, an issue, a problem, a circumstance, a situation or difficulty. Every scene — every piece of work — must have a reason for being presented or expressed. The "how" — the way the purpose is dealt with — usually gets us to our final destination in a scene; it gets us to an ending through some type of resolution.

I don't know about you, but, as I said earlier, one of the things that bugs me more than anything is wasting time. I guess because I've spent most of my life as a freelancer and consultant (time is money for everyone, but especially for freelancers and consultants), I have very little patience for lack of productivity. Too much minutae and I begin to display exaggerated signs of PMS. No matter what time of the month it is.

Thinking back, I'm sure you can remember — maybe as recently as last week – when you were in a scene that had no real beginning. Or, perhaps there was a beginning, but no middle. And an inconclusive ending. No resolve.

Consider those get togethers where someone jumps to the middle, stays there, never reaches an ending, and completely leaves out the beginning. Then, the meeting is over. Everyone gets up, leaves. There is no real result. A key idea can be left hanging in mid-air, like a trapeze artist without a bar.

So then, it's no surprise that many of our conversations and communications do not produce a scene in its entirety. When this is the case, we have misunderstandings, misconstrued information and, very often, negative feelings.

Now, improv, as I have suggested, if done right, is the most synergistic method of communication on the planet. The study of this area of improv work — how it works, why it works, and how to do it — begins with a complete understanding of the nature of a scene — what constitutes one. Remember: beginning, middle and an end.

Before I go further, let me explain that there is a difference between improv theater games (you see many of these on the comedy channel) and improv theater scenes. Games are snippets of improv dialogue, clever moments of repartee, whereas scenes are complete pieces of work. It's like comparing an orange slice to the entire orange. Scenes can be fully fleshed out from a handful of audience suggestions, while games are usually acted out with quick reference to a singular suggestion. If you were performing a theater game, you might, for instance, be asked to sing "Yankee Doodle Dandy" backwards, or talk endlessly about a subject based on a word that was spelled funny. In contrast, a scene is based upon specific particulars given by the audience. The person hollering out the assignment might say: "You're two bus drivers with no buses to drive and your shoes are too tight." Based on that input you can create and flesh out an entire scene. Again, the difference is that in a scene, you must provide the clarifying and substantive trilogy: a beginning, a middle and an end.

Scenes in improv can happen in a relatively short period of time. Sometimes no more than two minutes. Sometimes longer. To really dissect the meaning of what makes a scene a scene, think of a scene this way: It's a segment of something that, within its confines, is nevertheless a complete entity. Given more time and development, this entity could provide a link to another entity. Given more time and development, there could be more linking, with the various entities eventually threading together to provide an entire, full-length story. We see scenes in plays and films. Read them in novels. They're all around us.

If we were to examine various movies or novels, we could see that many provide a logical string of complete and satisfying moments. And each of these moments actually has the properties of a beginning, middle and an end. I have seen many improv scenes become the beginning of what later developed into a full-length play. It's complicated and demanding work, but those who perform in such scenes all started by learning the basics. As they extemporaneously write their scenes, they have a sense of the need for an evolution, so they stay conscious of what juncture they are at as they go along. They have great regard for the essentials: the beginning, middle and end.

As you know, many of our moments are neither complete nor satisfying. Nor are we very conscious of any structure in presenting or responding to information. In fact, very often when we engage in dialogue, our sentences are like clothes in a dryer -- they go round and round, spinning recklessly, circulating randomly, never getting anywhere. As a result, the things we say -- the things that tumble out of our mouths -- have about as much sequential order as shredded lettuce on a taco.

Many of our verbalizations are convoluted, over-explained or expositional — thus another reason why it's difficult to thread information together in a meaningful and easy-to-assimilate fashion. Many people take a long time to say very little. And we hardly ever know where they are in terms of the evolution of a scene; they jerk back and forth within that trilogy like an old person trying to parallel park.

In listening to others, very often we have had to hand pick or second guess strategic places where we think the beginning stops and the middle begins. We know it's the end only when the dialogue stops or someone makes an exit. Many people offer up information like stir fry; it's all mixed up and dialogue is just plopped down in spoonfuls. We have to pick through it if we want to separate one specific from the next. No wonder, then, that there is wasted time, little substance, and minds that are left confused and bewildered.

Before ever taking to the stage, improv actors know exactly what it takes to make a scene whole. When I teach improv classes, I place great emphasis in the first few weeks on beginning, middle and end. For instance, we do scenes and dissect them into these three parts. We may spend an entire evening just on the beginnings of scenes. Very often we re-do a scene, presenting several alternate endings to the piece, just to demonstrate how many workable choices could resolve ány particular situation. I wish we could take meetings and re-run them this way for the benefit of study — or just for laughs!

Improv students soon learn there is a road map that guides their verbal journey, that gets them to a logical destination. I would like you to begin to think in those terms, too. Then keep a lookout for all the posted signs.

Let's delve into scene-making further. Let's take a closer look at what constitutes each of these basics: a beginning, middle and an end.

At the beginning of a scene, the improv actors always do what we call situate the audience. They cleverly introduce us to the who, what, why, where and when. If we were watching TV, it's as though when the scene starts, we switched on a channel and instantly got an entire glimpse of who the characters are, where they are, what they're doing, when they're doing it — and why. Improv players create all this in a flash. For them, it can happen in a matter of seconds. For us, we need to think about situating our audiences and acclimating them to who we are, why we're engaged in dialogue with them, and where we are, literally or figuratively. This simple process makes people comfortable; it helps them to settle in to what's coming next.

After this has been accomplished –- the beginning –- most improv players then begin to get to the point, or, as one of my favorite directors and writers, Tom Maxwell, who served as Artistic Director for the L.A. Groundlings says, "get to the car crash." In other words, now they begin to deal with the issue or conflict, the matter at hand, the reason for the communication in the first place. That process fulfills the requirement of the middle. In the process of any dialogue, we know we're at the end when we solve the problem, bring it to resolution or find closure. The end for the improv player and the business professional should come swiftly and simply, although I have noticed in many communications that people take forever to wind things up. This is a common problem for the beginner improv player. They exhaust a piece by running laps around their final remarks.

Can you see how much we have in common with the improv player? The way in which they learn to perfect their communication on stage is no different from the way in which we can master it — by awareness, practice and repetition.

Now, there are other improv-comedy-player rules and guidelines that assist us in fleshing out each integral portion of a scene. There are variables that will aid in transitioning us along from the scene's beginning to its middle to its end. We'll cover those later in the book.

For now, though, pay close attention to your communications and whether or not you are making reasonable transitions. Also, pay close attention to the moments your communications don't progress — what I call the dog-chasing-its-tail syndrome. Watch the people around you and their interrelating with others. I always tell my students: A great actor is a great observer. I think awareness is the first assignment in becoming a stronger communicator. Watch how other people formulate and execute their communications.

If you're the one calling the meeting or you're instigating the communication, you actually have one up on the improv player when it comes to the beginning, middle and end. You know going in the reason you're approaching the person or persons. You know what you want or need to accomplish. To that extent, you can prepare yourself a basic outline for beginning, middle and end. Granted, there are times we engage in communication when we didn't introduce it, when we didn't prepare the agenda. And at those times we need to roll with it. Still, pay close attention to what stage the communication is in; you may be a great help in moving a piece of communication along and making the scene more complete.

The following homework assignments will help you recognize a beginning, middle and an end — and achieve all three in your day-to-day scenes.

1. Start by listening to other people communicate. Take notes on what you thought was the beginning, what they said to indicate they were at the middle, and what conclusive remarks were made, or problem resolved, to demonstrate a strong ending. If the scenes you are observing are not complete, jot down where they seem to fail. Is there no beginning? Did someone forget to handle the middle -- really tackle the need or problem? Or did people simply depart from one another with no closure?

2. Next, take a piece of paper and draw vertical lines in three columns. Head the columns "Beginning," "Middle" and "End." As you talk on the phone to a colleague or client, take notes. Write down key words or phrases that indicate you're off to a strong beginning. After that, record important moments that illustrate you've reached the middle. Finally, switch to your third column with final remarks, or the ultimate solution that was agreed upon. Just writing this down in compartmentalized fashion helps delineate the three parts of a scene and provides greater clarity as to how and when one part leads to another.

3. Make certain you take the time to situate every audience. Set them up with the who, what, why, where and when. Don't be too eager to rush right into the middle, leaving the other person or persons confused and disoriented because they aren't quite sure what you're talking about. Similarly, make sure your middle is specifically addressing the reason or purpose for the get-together. Is it muddled? Not clearly identified? If so, clarify. Finally, always bring each scene you're in to completion, even if it's a remark such as, "I don't know what the answer is, but I'll get back to tomorrow by noon with some solution."

4. Study films, plays or books and take notes. Identify at what point the piece left the beginning and segued into the middle. Notice how some films milk the endings to death, while others have sharp, quick and surprise endings. A good example of the former would be the movie "Speed," while the second might be the abrupt ending of "Wag The Dog".

5. Anything that tends to have a beginning, middle and end is what you want to study. This could include a song. For instance, there is the softer beginning of a Whitney Houston tune, then the bridge (middle) and the final note or notes. Things that are complete are satisfying. What other things can you think of that have a distinct beginning, middle and end. How about your washing machine cycle? A meal that features a salad, entree and desert? The gradual slope of a swimming pool? The entrance and exit of a room with two doors? There are so many things around us that complete this all-important trilogy. Start thinking in those three separate terms in all your communications. You'll be a pleasure to communicate with and people around you will always feel a sense of security. That's how complete and entire communication translates.

6. Another fun exercise, if you're industrious, is to write some short stories or accounts of personal experiences. Tell them from the vantage point of thoroughly covering a beginning, middle and end. Not only is this great practice. It stimulates your ability to improvise freely.

Now for a look at "Take Two" of our opening scene. You're about to see an illustration of how much clearer, tighter and more meaningful the communication becomes when structure and order is a consideration. Remember: You can only come upon a sequential scene when you focus on the framework of a beginning, a middle and an end.

One more note: When you begin to think like the improv actor, and go into scenes watching for the important segues, you'll save yourself time, be more efficient, better understand those with whom you communicate, and impress your clients and colleagues. There is just something that conveys confidence when we flesh out our scenes and don't stay in any one part of them any longer than need be.

Now let's return to that conversation with Mr. Spacey and his crew. See if you can detect the precise and pivotal moments when the scene moves from beginning to middle to end.

TAKE TWO: "We Get Letters"

(**Int. conference room. Three people are seated, playing with prototype containers and boxes, writing notes. A fourth person enters, sits himself down, reaches for his day planner, produces one piece of paper and begins to speak**)

MR. SPACEY

(**Clears his throat**) Well, welcome everyone. Our goal this morning is to put out another fire here at Hair-On-End -– to find more efficient ways to ship our products. With that in mind, I thought we could discuss the benefits of taking the M from the U cases and packing those Ms in the F cases.

MS. SWEETNIZ

(**Timidly**) M from U?

MR. SPACEY

(**Kindly**) Yes, M from U and tucking them right into the F cases.

MR. TRYARD

(Looking about the room at his colleagues. Helpfully) Sure. I can see it now. If we put the Moko-Soako Mousse in with the Pants-On-Fire Perm solution, then mix in the Frizz-Off/Flip-You-Off Gel, everything would be more compact.

MR. SPACEY

(Upbeat) And secure.

MR. BRAUNOS

Hey, why don't we just tuck in the P and XY products while we're at it? It would keep the Frizz-Off from flaking.

MR. SPACEY

Why, yes, if we wedged the Pipe-Down Toner around the sides of the corrugated cardboard and packed the Frizz-Off inside the Bongo-Brush silos, we could ship more in fewer containers.

MS. SWEETNIZ

I'll pack them all myself.

MR. BRAUNOS

(Trying to impress Spacey again) Oh, I'll do it.

MR. SPACEY

(Diplomatically) Well, why don't you take turns.
(Sweetniz and Braunos look at one another and assent)

MR. SPACEY

Well, then, it looks like together we've found a work-able solution to the packaging problem. Thank you all very much. (**Stands to exit**) Well, I'm off to my next meeting. (**Confidentially**) The creative team and I are trying to come up with a new name for the (**Pause**) Crapola Curling Iron.

-Lights-

Chapter 7

Scene-ing Is Believing
Trust

TAKE ONE: "Going Up?"

(**Int. elevator in downtown high-rise building. Two people have entered at lobby floor, one man, one woman. They don't know each other. They turn and smile perfunctorily**)

MS. RAWTREET

(**Standing nearest button panel, she pushes button for ninth floor. Looks up, eyes fixed on area just above the metal doors**) Boy, this thing is slow today.

MR. WITHEN

(**Reaches in front of her to push his button**) 'Scuse me.

MS. RAWTREET

I can get that. What floor?

MR. WITHEN

(**Reluctantly**) Tenth.

MS. RAWTREET

(She pushes ten) Ten it is.

MR. WITHEN

'Scuse me. (He reaches in front of her)

MS. RAWTREET

Huh?

MR. WITHEN

Just want to make sure … (He re-pushes the button two times, smiles apologetically)

MS. RAWTREET

(A little hurt) Well … .

(They stop at five. Man enters. He offers an obligatory smile. Stands between the two)

MS. RAWTREET

(Helpfully) Floor?

MAN

Oh, I'll get it. Thank you. (He pushes number eight)

MR. WITHEN

'Scuse me. (**Reaches across the woman to push his tenth floor button again. He pushes it four times**)

MAN
(**Ms. Rawtreet stays fixed, eyes upward. Man going to eight shoots his glance at the same target**) Nice day.

MR. WITHEN

(**Has eyes glued to elevator button panel. He's sweating**) Yeah.

MS. RAWTREET

Uh-huh.

(**Elevator stops at eight. Man in center departs. Doors close**)

MR. WITHEN

(**Reaches Across**) 'Scuse me. (**Pushes his button again three times**)

MS. RAWTREET

(**They reach ninth floor. Ms. Rawtreet departs**) 'Nice day. (**She's hurt**)

MR. WITHEN

(**Door closes. He pushes his button again frantically, doors close, elevator rises. Elevator stops at tenth floor. His finger is still on button when he realizes** he's arrived at his destination. Doors open. Young woman gets in. Shoves rudely past her, afraid she'll push her button before he can depart). 'Scuse me.

-Lights-

Chapter 7

═══════════════

Scene-ing Is Believing
Trust

Most of us don't realize how distrusting we are, and how negatively such feelings impact our day-to-day business communications. If you were to closely examine the manner in which you communicate with many people, even those you've known and worked with for a long period of time, you would probably, honestly, own up to the fact that you're not very trusting. During the course of that same examination, you might also come to realize that you don't exactly create fertile ground for others to trust you, either.

We hedge, we pull back, we withdraw, we scrutinize, we hold out. We don't send a strong beacon of light that says "safety right here — just pull yourself into my harbor." As a result, distrust builds and accumulates like mold on high school yearbooks. It cakes on, and it's hard to scrape off. It eats away at things.

Distrust also creates something else: distance. You can't have strong relationships when you perpetuate distance; being close while you're far away is an oxymoron.

We saw the distance that was created between strangers when distrust overtook the elevator scene. These three people could have had a cordial, if brief, relationship — had there been trust. They could have also experienced the optimum: They could have networked with each other for a few floors. I once opened the way for a large account in an elevator ride with,

"Hey, can I help with some of those things? That briefcase alone must weigh a ton." The gentleman and I struck up a conversation; I held a handful of files for him while he got organized. We exchanged cards. He called about a week later. I met with him and his boss and they hired me to train their sales teams.

I certainly haven't gotten all my business leads in elevators, but the point is, you never know where opportunity awaits. We need to trust enough to open up and converse with others. Whether it's business or just kindness, we all need more of both.

True, we live in a damaged world, and with the preponderance of car jackings, murders and assaults permeating the media airwaves, it's hard to trust. For many, it's impossible.

But we must trust, and, if we want to maximize our business relations, simultaneously we must demonstrate that we are trustworthy. We can't cop to what's gone before, or what we see out there, what we read, what the media focus on. The vast majority of people in your everyday dealings are people you come to count on. So, we have to trust that we can trust, no matter how much our personal histories or world activities tell us otherwise. I'm not suggesting that you not exercise a good measure of caution as you go about your life. I don't recommend running in front of a truck and believing that it will stop. The idea of the kind of trust I'm referring to is different. The idea is this: to proceed in each new-business related encounter without fear or misgiving and to project a sense of confidence and reliability about ourselves to others.

On stage, improv players perform with this mindset every second of every scene. In fact, it's the first thing we teach improv actors. To them, the premise of trust is as fundamental as a key is to starting a car. Each actor serves as a safety net for the other, and trust is always expected and absolute.

Believe it or not, it takes discipline and focus to develop trust. As directors and teachers, we instill this in our casts and students in every drill. Their natural tendency is to resist. I don't know a beginning improv student who hasn't had some difficulty fully trusting. It has to do with control. Students feel that if they're not taking care of the scene — not running it, not in charge of it — it won't work. It's a natural human behavioral quirk. We, as business people, feel the same need to control in our daily scenes, too. But here's the problem with control: If everyone has to have it, there can be no real communication. Everyone's too busy guarding the Alamo. My deep personal belief is that great relationships always embody unbridled trust. When you think about the long-standing business relationships you have, I'm certain you can tag each one of them with a common identifying factor: You have a great sense of trust with one another.

There is no margin of distrust among a troupe of improv players. They take to the stage with the idea that they will demonstrate their trustworthiness throughout the scene by allowing and inviting the others to rely on them. In turn, they blindly and willingly acquiesce to their partners' every word and action. In both these forms of trust, they let go, go with, give in and give way. Each player is both the care-giver and care-taker. They have the rhythm of trapeze artists, the buddy system of a SWAT team, and the faith of a crowd at Lourdes. They believe in the process; they believe in one another. This fundamental element is never questioned on stage; it's a given. It's the basic principle that guides every single piece of their work together. Interestingly, giving away control actually provides these actors more control. More on that in our chapter on "Give and Take."

Goody for them, but what about me?, you might be asking. I can't control other people's trust levels, you might be thinking. And I certainly can't go forth into the good day or night with no trepidation.

Well. I'm not buying that because, for starters, you can begin to place more trust in yourself and you can make a greater effort to illustrate to others that you are worthy of being trusted. You can send those signals. That's where this whole trust thing starts.

Next, you can sell yourself on the idea that you will go forward and trust everyone until they prove to you that they cannot be trusted. You would be very surprised what a bond of trust you can establish with someone if you take the first step. If you let them know you're to be counted on, then proceed with your communication as though they can be trusted, you suddenly have rapport. Good rapport starts with a sense of trust. In the work environment, we should always, without exception, begin our relationships with that attitude, that mindset, that intent. Far too often, though, we begin our relations with cynicism, skepticism, tentativeness, and sometimes downright paranoia. For many, it's a matter of cowboys and Indians. We think of the people in the office in terms of who has the arrows and who has the guns. We're afraid of getting ambushed. We must hide out or someone might get in. Getting in means we're vulnerable. Being vulnerable means we're destructible.

But so what?! That's what the improv player says. Better to take that outside chance of possible annihilation (which never happens in improv because everyone's in the trust zone). Because in the end, if you don't take a chance, if you don't trust, you can guarantee yourself you'll probably end up with nothing. That's the improv philosophy. If the players can't take to their work with unrestrained trust, they can't do the job. The job is everything to them. It should be to us, too. Remember, it's all about relationships. Business relationships can feed us literally and figuratively for the long term if trust is the foundation.

So then, good business communication begins with trust — the manner, the attitude in which we approach those with whom we come in contact. Ask yourself what your attitude is with those you meet for the first time. Then measure the trust factor with those you work with every day. Are you trusting? Trustworthy? You might be very surprised when taking an objective assessment.

We tend to think of trust in terms of personal relationships, but trust at work is just as critical. Your sense of trust with business colleagues should be the same with each group and each encounter. I know improv players who are suddenly thrown on stage with actors they've never worked with before — with people they haven't had the benefit of building a chemistry with. Nonetheless, they proceed with bold trust from the get-go, and that becomes contagious to the others.

I often hear conversations like this one. They're short and seemingly meaningless, but a lot is revealed about trust if you read between the lines:

Guy #1: Hey, what's up?
Guy #2: What do you mean?
Guy #1: What's goin' on?
Guy #2: What's goin' on?
Guy #1: Yeah.
Guy #2: Nothing.
Guy #1: Nothing?
Guy #2: Yeah.
Guy #1: Oh.

Obviously, not a lot of trust by either party; therefore, not a good deal of opportunity to further their relationship. But don't you see these kind of exchanges every day in one office or another?

I say, take a chance with trust! You'll get far more out of your relationships with peers, subordinates, customers and bosses if you approach your communication from a posture of trust.

I understand that the business world is competitive. Even treacherous at times. I understand the urge to cover our backs. But it's important not to overreact. How sad, how counterproductive our business lives would be if we were to establish atmospheres polluted with our own distrust. Even if you have had bad experiences, why let them sour new encounters?

Okay. Let's say you've bought into the idea of "trust and be trusted." How do you go about doing it?

Well, as we instruct the improv player: First, you must learn to trust yourself, to know that you can count on yourself. Next, you want to send the message — give the signals — that others can count on you. You do this with consistency both as care-giver and care-taker. Whether it's one encounter or many, people should come to always expect the same from you. You should be right there for them and, conversely, let them take care of you. That builds trust.

Next, you want to approach others with an open sense of trust as you begin any conversation, whether you're meeting with them once or you've worked with them for 20 years. Always give people the benefit of the doubt. Treat each situation with renewed optimism. Have as much faith in other people as you do in yourself. Don't question someone's integrity; don't make anyone prove anything to you. Instead, come to expect it. Most people in the workplace come through for us when we approach them from that angle of thought. There's a certain amount of dignity in that approach.

I really believe that if we went about our work tasks with an emphasis on trust, trust is what we would get back. I've experimented with this idea. I've found that when I'm the least bit distrustful of someone, they pick up that vibe and begin to mirror me. Pretty soon we're not only distrustful and uncomfortable with one another, we begin to attack, sometimes covertly, sometimes directly. Can you imagine, knowing how delicate scene work is on stage among improv players, what would happen if this atmosphere prevailed with them? Their scenes would have little, if any, chance of working. They'd disintegrate. Knowing that, can you now understand why so many of our on-the-job communications — in the office or in the field — don't work? Trust! Make it a habit!

For homework, here are some exercises that will increase your self-trust, your ability to show you can be trusted, and your ability to trust others:

1. Take a candid assessment of your ability to trust yourself. If you make a commitment to take some time for yourself, do you do it? Do you honor your declaration to swear off chocolate? Do you stick with that physical workout regime? Do you return phone calls when you say you will? Do you meet your deadlines at work? If you say "yes" to all of these, your ability to depend on yourself is excellent; if, however, you slide on commitments to yourself, your first assignment is to build better trust within. You can start by choosing one obligation. Maybe it's 30 minutes a day to

indulge yourself — some alone-time to recharge your batteries. The more you honor your own commitments to yourself, the stronger your level of self-trust. And, again, that's where trust starts. If you can't rely on yourself, no one else can, either. One last note: Don't overtax yourself, or beat yourself up for not being able to handle this area all at once. Remember, you obviously must have *some* reliability; you get yourself up and go to work every day. So, make a list of the commitments you're already coming through on, and get ready to go from there.

No matter how good you are at self-trust, see if you can elevate it to a higher level. For instance, you may be one of those people you can really count on, for everything. I'm one of those. (But in the process people like us often try to control everything and everyone. Watch for that danger.) Now, even though you think you can totally rely on yourself, take an additional step and commit to something you haven't conquered yet. Maybe it's trusting that you will keep to that physical exercise program; maybe it's that promise you've been making to get, and keep, your Rolodex updated.

2. Start demonstrating ways in which you can convey to others that you can be trusted. Being on time for meetings, conference calls or business appointments is one of the first steps (whenever people are late, we tend not to trust them). Next, honor your deadlines to customers and peers. If you say you're going to have those samples to your client on such and such date, have them there. If you agree to meet with a subordinate about an issue, be prepared for that meeting. If you told your secretary she could have a particular afternoon off, honor that, no matter how busy you get. A promise is a promise. We need to keep them.

3. Make a list of how many commitments you make each day, then make a list of how many you keep. This is a great reality check. It's good for the soul and probably your karma, too.

4. Listen to your conversation when meeting both strangers and conversing with the people in your work environment. Do your statements send trust signals? Do you give the other person the benefit of the doubt? Begin to take a reading on your trust factor. Listening to how you phrase requests and responses will serve as a great barometer for where you rank and rate yourself on the trust scale.

5. Be willing to let go more often. I'm not asking you to subjugate your common sense and intelligence. I'm simply asking you to relinquish the need to retain control of everything around you. When the people around us see too much control, they can't trust that their ideas and feelings will be regarded. Therefore, we can't gain their trust. In order to have trust from others, we need to give way and accede to the idea that their suggestions have potential and merit.

6. Go out of your way at least once a day to abandon all fear about something you've been avoiding and handle that situation with aplomb. You will build trust all the way around. Maybe it's approaching your boss for a raise; maybe it's talking to a stranger in an elevator. Remember, engage in at least one trust-building effort a day.

7. Last, remember that once you violate trust with someone, it's hard to retrieve it. Trust can topple like a stack of badly arranged melon balls. Getting it back is as painstaking and arduous as rebuilding an Egyptian pyramid. So be careful about the impressions you make from the outset and don't forget that when you're willing to trust, people automatically respond positively. Again, our associations at work are all about relationships. And building relationships start with a foundation of trust.

Now, let's play back that elevator scene and see what happens when everyone ascends with the trust factor.

TAKE TWO: "Going Up?"

(Int. elevator in downtown high-rise building. Two people have entered at lobby floor, one man, one woman. They don't know each other. They turn and smile warmly)

MS. RAWTREET

(Standing nearest button panel, she pushes button for ninth floor. Looks up, eyes swipe past area just above metal doors. She turns to make eye contact with man next to her) Boy, this thing is slow today, don't you think?

MR. WITHEN

(Reaches in front of her to push button. His button) 'Scuse me.

MS. RAWTREET

I can get that for you. What floor?

MR. WITHEN

(Appreciatively) Why, thank you! Tenth. Yeah, it's always slow!

MS. RAWTREET

(Pushes ten) Ten it is. Your office there?

MR. WITHEN

Yes, I work at Farkbonics. Sales manager for the western region.

MS. RAWTREET

Oh, then I'd like to get your card. We need some farks
for our flurrels.

MR. WITHEN

(Pulls card out of coat pocket. Hands it to her)
Oh, are you with a farkernaut concern?

**(They stop at five. Man enters. He smiles broadly.
Stands between the two)**

MAN

Hey, how's everybody doin' today?

MR. WITHEN

Fine, thanks.

MS. RAWTREET

Fine, and you? Which floor do you need?

MAN

Eight.

MS. RAWTREET

**(She pushes button for newcomer. Pushes eight,
nine and ten just to be sure. Smiles at Withen
to offer reassurance. He returns the smile)** Yes,
I am Farkernauts R Us, as a matter of fact.

MAN

(**Makes eye contact with her for brief time. Nods toward button panel**) Thanks so much. (**Directing his attention now to Withen**) Hey, aren't you with Farkbonics?

MR. WITHEN

Yes, I am. (**Looks at Rawtreet**) Can I get your card? My department needs a new Fark system. I'd like to see what you've got.

MAN

(**Elevator stops at his floor**) Hey, can I get a card, too? We're looking at farkers for our Farkports.

(**Ms. Rawtreet hands him one**)

MAN

(**Exits. Turns to each of them before doors close**) ... Good one! (**Waves card above his head**) I'll call you!

(**Doors close. Ms. Rawtreet pushes both buttons again. Smiles and nods reassuringly to Withen once again**)

MR. WITHEN

If you have time later, how 'bout stopping in for coffee and walking me and my boss, Snortlewhip, through your new brochure? In fact, I'll show you ours.

(**Doors open. It's the tenth floor**)

MS. RAWTREET

Sure. How 'bout after lunch?

MR. WITHEN

(Exits) One, one-thirty is fine. **(Doors begin to close)**

MS. RAWTREET

I'll be there! **(Doors close. Elevator ascends
to next floor. Doors open. She stays in elevator.
Pushes down button to lobby and says outloud as
doors close)** These elevator rides are great for
business.   **(Looks at wristwatch)** I have time for
at least two more! **(She gets her business cards
ready)**

-Lights-

Chapter 8

Part Of The Scene
Commitment

TAKE ONE: "Who Can Budge-It?"

(Two women, one guy are walking briskly down an office corridor on their way to a meeting. It's a big one. They're going to present a report to a few members of the board of directors on next year's budget additions. They're embroiled in intense conversation as they scurry)

MS. UHLHOUT

(Head high, marching forward boldly)
This is it. The big day.

MR. RISKETT

(Confident and sure) Oh, boy! Is it ever.

MS. MAIBHEE

(Out of step with the other two and somewhat hesitant) I don't know, you guys. We don't know what we're walking into. If it doesn't start out well, I think I'll feign E. coli.

MS. UHLHOUT

(**Pauses. Reconfirms her resolve and blurts**)
It doesn't matter what happens in there. We'll find a
way to make it work.

MR. RISKETT

(**From deep within**) We'll give it all we've got.

MS. MAIBHEE

(**Hedging**) But our butts will be on the line.

MS. UHLHOUT

(**Knowingly**) A butt on the line …

MR. RISKETT

(**Finishing her sentence without missing a beat**)
… is a butt that can shine!

MS. MAIBHEE

(**Even more reluctant**) I don't know …

MR. RISKETT

(**Patriotically**) Maibhee, did you ever see "A Few Good
Men"?

MS. UHLHOUT

(**Finishing his thought**) … Read "The Little
Engine That Could"?

**(Maibhee seems to indicate "yes" with her facial
animation, yet follows that with a look of skepticism)**

MR. RISKETT

(Sternly) Ever hear of Dorothy and Toto … ?

MS. UHLHOUT

(With power) Mr. Smith and Washington?

**(Riskett and Uhlhout exchange a brisk verbal volley with
precision and momentum. Maibhee follows the repartee
like a tennis match)**

MR. RISKETT

Helen Keller, Evel Knievel?

MS. UHLHOUT

Florence Chadwick, Bucky Fuller, Tina Turner?

MR. RISKETT

Horatio Alger, Richard Kimble?

MS. UHLHOUT

Oliver Twist? Forrest Gump?

MR. RISKETT

Rocky?

MS. UHLHOUT

Scarlett?

MS. MAIBHEE

(**Semi-playing along**) As in "Gone With the Wind"?

MS. UHLHOUT

(**Screeches to a halt. Inquires suspiciously**)
Is that a bad E. coli joke?

(**Riskett turns the knob to the conference room door**)

MR. RISKETT

Let's take this room!

MS. UHLHOUT

(**Profoundly**) I'm there!

MS. MAIBHEE

(**Tentatively**) I'll see.

-Lights-

Chapter 8

Part of The Scene
Commitment

I dislike nothing more than to be in a business situation where most of the people are willing but one or more are straddling the fence. The people in the latter category aren't necessarily naysayers or grumps; they simply don't care to commit. They just play it somewhere in nowhere; they're there but only in theory; they torment us with maybe-I-will, maybe-I-won't. So as we attempt to progress in the communication game, we're taunted and teased like experimental rats in a lab. While we run toward the surf and plunge into it, they submit one toe at a time.

The absence of commitment can be the most damaging missing link in the act of communication. Ms. Maibhee, in our last skit, wasn't willing to throw herself behind the other two with intent and zeal. With pledge or passion. So in their quest to persuade that board to go for the budget additions, their zip surely lost some zap.

Had we the opportunity of watching this trio perform before that board of directors, we would have clearly felt the subtextual reluctance of Ms. Maibhee. A great deal would have been lost. We may not have been consciously aware of why we felt her non-verbal undertow, but we would have reacted to it. In fact, we could have drowned because of it.

The much-missed television and film personality, Phil Hartman, whom I had the pleasure of knowing (and who graciously wrote the Foreword to my first ExecuProv book), always used to tell his Groundlings students: "If you believe it, they'll believe it." However, belief cannot be present without commitment. When we really believe something, we're pretty adamant about it, and that push only comes from a base level of commitment to some idea or value.

Far too often, though, we ourselves, or others, are not quite sure, or not quite willing to go for "it," whatever "it" may be.

I was in a meeting not long ago. Seven people. Not one of them was committed to the proposal they had put on the table. Their half-hearted dialogue pitches moved around the table like Jell-O cubes on a slip and slide. The prevailing atmosphere was an unspoken "uhhhh, I don't know," and it wasn't long before the substance of their basic selling point disintegrated, like gelatin in a sauna.

Now here's a way of looking at this improv principle called commitment: An improv player cannot enter into a scene without full and uncensored commitment. It's just a given that any actor will take the stage and participate in a scene with no reserve, no hesitation and no reluctance. And it doesn't matter what conditions the audience impose upon the players; whatever they're asked to do, they do it.

I remember being in an improv show one night when the audience was behaving like something out of "Animal House." One of the patrons assigned me the task of barking like a frog. I repeated the request because I thought the person must have meant "barking like a dog" or "croaking like a frog." But no, this Belushi-like smart-aleck meant what he said. "Bark like a frog," he challenged. Without reservation, I resolved to do just that. Granted, I thought I sounded like a sea lion with PMS, but no matter, I did my job. I was fully committed to the process. And I presented a very "can do" attitude as I threw a confident smile back, even though animal sounds are not my strong suit. What mattered was my unwavering resolve to carry out my mission, while risking the possibility of self-destruction. That's right. I'm not big on public humiliation. And I'm a terrible sport when it comes to losing. But none of those notions could interfere with my level of professionalism. And so it goes with all improv players. Making scenes work is initially solely dependent upon each participant's level of commitment. Nothing else. When a scene starts, everyone has mentally bellied up to the bar, and they're ready to order!

When you decide to enlist as an improv actor, there is no such thing as the luxury of choice. Our code is that you take the first thing you're given.

I wish we could adopt the same "belief system" when it comes to performing in our everyday business scenes: full-on commitment. Notice though, how you and those around you pick and choose what scenes you'll commit to. Some you embrace with all your heart. Others, you play half-assed.

I believe that none of us should participate partially; instead, I feel we should always play full-out — whether we like the scene or not. A pro is a pro, and the show must go on! And while it's going, we should be into it up to our necks, not just to our waistlines.

Now, if we could adapt yet another mindset of the improv player — "this is it!" — and play every scene like it's our only scene, we would probably tend to be a bit more willing. We would pledge to do our very best because we would take our obligation more seriously. But we as business-persons don't tend to take each "scene" that importantly. Our commitment depends on our mood, how important the client is, the impression we wish to make, and perhaps the level of our blood sugar.

Well, forget that! It's my wish to get you thinking and functioning like an improv player.

Here's something else to consider: Most of the scenes in which an improv player engages include other people. There is a buddy system in place. Where there is joint commitment, there is teamwork. Where there is teamwork, there is power. Where there is power, anything is possible.

I'm sure you've had at least one experience where you were part of a group whose collective desire impelled you with a momentum that was unflappable. That's what happens when commitment is the cornerstone of a scene. And when everyone is committed, trust builds — and good things always come from that.

Before we take a second look at Ms. Maibhee and her friends, take on a couple of the following homework assignments to increase the consistency of your commitment:

1. Do another one of those personal assessments. Ask yourself if you are as fully committed to every work task no matter your interest or enthusiasm. Try to rank your commitment levels: are you committed 20 percent of the time, 90 percent? Determining where your general level of commitment falls is your starting point.

2. Take any given business day and keep a running tab on how many tasks you had to perform. Write them down. Next to each, give yourself a score, from one to ten, that grades your level of commitment. If you're scoring high, good for you. If you're scoring way below "giving it all you've got," then there's work to do. Naturally, we can't feel 100 percent committed to every single thing we do all day (making the coffee is a tough one for me), but what about those meetings and interactions with others? Are you in the game, or sitting on the bench? Keeping score is a great way to lay the groundwork for increasing your sense of commitment on the job.

3. Get that full-speed-ahead mind-set going by making yourself play at the hundred-percent level at some work activity at least once a day. This could be anything from making the coffee (even though you don't want to) to becoming fully participative in a meeting you really don't want to attend. Like a good improv player, soon you'll turn the switch to tell yourself, "It's Showtime," each time your sense of commitment is required. We need and rely on commitment all day. The challenge is to be and stay committed those times we least want to.

4. Keep a weekly journal recording which "scenes" you didn't want to "perform" in, and which you did. Give yourself

points for committing when you didn't really want to. Next, reward yourself in some way. I'm big on pay-backs. I think they motivate us to continue to do better and more.

5. Watch those around you, like a good Director, and notice who is and who is not committed. Ask yourself how you feel when someone doesn't commit. Keep notes in your journal. Reviewing these from time to time will help you see things more clearly and will also show you how far you've come.

6. At least once a week, make yourself do something, anything, you really don't want to do (for me, it's learning something else about computers). When you do this particular activity, do it with all your heart. The idea is to make commitment a habit. It takes practice. It's simply a matter of re-conditioning our subconscious to accept the idea that we will perform with the same level of intent no matter what is asked, or required of us, on the job. That's exactly what the programming becomes for the improv player who's been at it long enough. They are no different than the rest of us: Sometimes they get assignments they don't want to do, but they do them with courage and resolve — with a fabulous attitude. I have such respect for people who "play hard" no matter what they're asked to do. Work at being counted among that group; it will pay off throughout your professional career.

Now let's take a peek at that previous scene.

TAKE TWO: "Who Can Budge-It?"

(Two women and one man are walking briskly down an office corridor on their way to a meeting. It's a big one. They're going to present a report to a few members of the board of directors on next year's budget additions. They're embroiled in intense conversation as they scurry)

MS. UHLHOUT

(Head high, marching boldly forward) This is it!
The big day!

MR. RISKETT

(Confident and sure) Oh, boy! Is it ever.

MS. MAIBHEE

(In step with them and not the least bit resistant)
I don't know what exactly we're walking into — what
may happen — but, hey, I'm there ... .

MS. UHLHOUT

(Pauses. Reconfirms her resolve and blurts) It
doesn't matter what happens. We'll find a
way to make it work.

MR. RISKETT

(From deep within) We'll give it all we've got.

MS. MAIBHEE

(Seconding that idea) Yep, our butts will be on the
line. **(Pausing to look at her colleagues)** By the way,
I'm proud to line my butt up along side the two of
yours ... .

MS. UHLHOUT

(Knowingly) Indeed, three butts on the line ...

MR. RISKETT

(Finishing her thought without missing a beat) …
are butts that can shine.

MS. MAIBHEE

(Affirming their notion) And a butt that doth shine
is a very good sign.

MS. UHLHOUT

(With a look of recognition) Ahhh, yes, I believe those
were the immortal words of Ralph Waldo Emerson in
his fit of determination to see the reflection of his
back-end in that pond … not many people know he
uttered that.

MR. RISKETT

(Recollecting) Yes, indeed. And I'll never forget
the words of Ben Franklin on the subject.

(Maibhee and Uhlhout look at him inquisitively)

MR. RISKETT

"A butt in time saves nine."

MS. MAIBHEE

(With recognition) Ah yes, if I'm not mistaken,
those were the words he spoke as he hurriedly put
his pen to the Declaration of Independence.

MS. UHLHOUT

(Shooting one back at the two) Ah, uh-huh.   And

what about Mark Twain in his quest to unify humanity: "I never met a butt I didn't like."

MR. RISKETT

Oh, and Lincoln recalling the will of our ancestors: "Four score and seven butts ago ... ."

MS. MAIBHEE

Benedict Arnold holding steady: "Don't shoot till you see the butts of their eyes."

MS. UHLHOUT

Henry VIII: "Off with their butts ... !"

MR. RISKETT

"To butt, or not to butt ... ."

MS. UHLHOUT

And my favorite: Yogi Berra ...

(They abruptly stop, trade high fives as they whisper in unison)

ALL

"It ain't over till the butt lady sings."

MR. RISKETT

Let's take this room.

MS. UHLHOUT

(**Profoundly**) I'm there!

MS. MAIBHEE

(**With great purpose**) Count me in!

-Lights-

Chapter 9

Scene One, Scene 'Em All
Attending To

TAKE ONE: "Lookee Here"

(Five people are seated at a round table in the office of Mr. Raspecht, a VP of business affairs for a major company. It's the weekly staff meeting)

MR. RASPECHT

Well, then, I wanted to ask that we discuss the tracking report for the sales department. Mr. Roode, let's start with you.

(All four of the attendees, including Mr. Roode, are seemingly busy with other things. None of them has an eye on Raspecht. Roode is scribbling notes, Ms. Enanhout is looking back and forth between Raspecht, and her watch, Mr. Flytee is reading the newspaper, and Mr. Helseware is staring dreamily out the window)

MR. RASPECHT

Mr. Roode ... excuse me ... Mr. Roode ...

MR. ROODE

**(Shoots a fleeting glance at Raspecht, waves his hand
upward, still writing. Never looks up)** Yes, we tracked
14 new customers just last night.

MS. ENANHOUT

**(Tapping the face of her watch, eyes fixed on it, as it
seems broken)** Yes, 14, I counted them myself.

MR. HELSEWARE

(Watching a Porsche cruise by) Wow, 14's a lot.

MR. FLYTEE

(Flips to the business section) That's four more than ten.

MR. RASPECHT

**(Frustrated and feeling all alone. He continues,
although the others remain inattentive)** I wanted to
show you what the bonus structure looks like. **(He turns
to the flip chart and begins to write, scribbling a large
number "13" on the chart)** This is all you need to get
$10,000 each.

**(The foursome have their eyes elsewhere. Each is still
involved in his or her own individual activity. Raspecht looks
at each of them, hoping — striving — for some eye contact.
He points again at the chart. They never look his way)**

MR. ROODE

I'll be plugging.

MR. FLYTEE

Sounds like a plan.

MR. HELSEWARE

I could use the money.

MS. ENANHOUT

I'll sure work at it.

(They stand, one after the other, and begin to exit without ever looking at Raspecht or the chart. Almost simultaneously, they utter their "goodbyes," "good days," etc.)

MR. RASPECHT

(Demoralized, then angry. Mumbles to himself as the door closes behind them) Finders, keepers …

-Lights-

Chapter 9

Scene One, Scene 'Em All
Attending To

When we're not looking, we often miss a lot. I know that's true for me. I recently ran into a post at the car wash and knocked down a cabana. People ran like hell. (Some of them were sitting underneath it at the time.) Obviously, I'm not the only one. Others miss a lot, too. Such was the case with the bonehead contingency sales department in our last sketch. Boy, talk about out to lunch! I'd say dinner, too, and then some!

I've been to meetings where no one is paying attention — where, instead of looking at the person speaking, everyone is busy with note-taking, daydreaming and other non-attendant behaviors. Nothing unusual. Yet something so seemingly innocent as looking in a direction other than that of the speaking person can disrupt and dismantle rapport. It also precludes meaningful connections between those who come together for discussion.

I feel strongly that it's downright rude to be looking anywhere but at the person who is speaking. (I was schooled by Dominican nuns.) If I had my way, I would make it part of a company's policy to be more polite. The handbook might read: "Make certain you're on time each day; do not make personal phone calls; park in the designated parking spaces only; and at all times, look at the person who is speaking to you, whether you feel like it or not."

"Pay attention" is an admonishment many of us were given as youngsters; however, we have come to ignore it in our adult years. It's just not an idea we find easy to honor. I suppose it's not intentional; rather, we seem to become so wrapped up in ourselves, we forget to pay attention — not only to those who seem to be center stage in the meeting, but to those on the sidelines. If we're the central character in a meeting, for instance, we often tend to blow off the peripheral few (like a rock star does with background singers). I think our rationale is that we have to stay focused on "our thing." That being the case, we look only at others when it's important to us.

If we have the proper workplace etiquette, however — whether we're a rock star or a business professional — we should be looking, as much as possible, at each person speaking. Whether or not we realize it consciously, we feel bad when people look elsewhere when we speak, so we certainly don't want to be guilty of doing that to ourselves. I've shuffled out from many meetings dragging my self esteem behind me like a rusty file cabinet. The atmosphere felt isolated and lonely, but I couldn't exactly put my finger on why. Later, when I recalled the scene, I remembered that people were visually preoccupied while I was talking. That can make anyone feel slightly or totally worthless. What we should all be aware of is that it can take just one person lost in his world to shatter ours.

The improv player's handbook has a wonderful stipulation regarding consideration of others. It's known as the "Attending To" rule. "Attending To" means simply that you look at whomever is speaking when they are speaking. This applies to all actors on stage whether there are two or five of them. And what a great concept to promote teamwork and close communication.

This basic "Attending To" rule works for both actors and business people for several reasons. First, if you're not "Attending To," you may miss a terribly important visual cue. In improv, very often the evolution of a piece hinges on physical changes made by an actor with his body, his facial expressions, or the handling of what we term space objects (pantomiming the use of things that aren't really there). For the actor, missing a visual cue might mean missing a facial expression that spells out a vital sub-textual attitude. For a business person, it could mean missing a hand raised in response to a query. Whatever it is, you can't play off of what you don't see.

Improv players subscribe to the "Attending To" rule because it makes us appear unified when we're on stage in a scene; it makes it look as though each piece was pre-written. This is because each time someone delivers a line, the actors' heads snap simultaneously -- all eyes shifting in the same direction at the same time toward the person speaking.

This suggests another important reason for following the "Attending To" precept. It provides the opportunity to make eye contact with others in the scene. It is through eye contact that we make the human connection. And, I continue to point out, connecting to others, no matter who you are and what you're doing, is vital in terms of selling ideas and products. Without engaging the other person, we may as well turn our back and speak to the wall. (I've actually seen people do this!)

One more valid reason "Attending To" works is that it keeps you from doing what we term "stepping on the other guy's lines." We sometimes interrupt someone's dialogue or cut them off, very often because we are not looking at them when they speak. As improv players, we use this tenet on stage to prevent us from treading on the other person. ("Don't tread on me" is so Corporate America, isn't it?)

"Attending To" also enhances your ability to listen more intently and carefully to the spoken word. As a Director, I don't want my actors to miss any critical verbal or physical cues. The better my troupes hear and focus on what they're hearing or seeing, the more appropriate and quicker their responses. Can you see how wonderfully this can work for the business professional?

Lastly, and most importantly, "Attending To" builds trust and rapport. It is a wonderful feeling to work with a team of improv players who follow the "Attending To" rule because you can be sure that whenever it's your turn to speak, you'll be given everybody else's full attention. "It makes me feel regal," an improv actor once said. And when everyone on a team reacts instantly not only to what they hear, but to what they see, communication volleys like a well-thrust badminton birdie. Remember, many of the scenes on the improv stage are short-lived. Without "Attending To," one could miss an important turning point, leaving a team member behind like a slow cop in a high-speed chase.

I get a considerable amount of complaints from beginner students about the violation of the "Attending To" rule because the failure to "Attend To" makes them feel detached and left out. To be ignored visually creates uneasiness in all of us. In that situation, whether you're an actor or a business person, trust begins to crumble, the synergy breaks down, people start doing their own thing, and, before you know it, the scene is out of sync. Soon it falls apart. And this dynamic builds on itself too. People who get together frequently establish counter-productive habits — one of which is looking anywhere but at the person talking. And once we get set in our ways ... .

Though "Attending To" is a discipline that must be adhered to, that's not to say you must be looking at the person speaking 100 percent of the time. That would be nearly impossible. There are moments on the improv stage, for instance, when the unfolding of a scene calls for the breaking of eye contact. One such example might be a couple having a fight in the kitchen. Words are spoken as they face-off, looking right at one another, but then they turn away, each caught up in their own snit. One actor's visual focus might shift as she begins looking for a can of tuna, while the other actor might be jamming bread in the toaster. But they are still "Attending To" in an audio sense listening intently to verbal cues such as a heavy sigh or a "tsk" sound. And it is through that listening that they are able to keep the "Attending To" principle in place. For, quite frequently, in direct response to the vibes in the room, something important will transpire. So, the tuna-seeker will not only listen intently, but randomly "Attend To" by throwing angry glances toward the toast-maker. This keeps them on the same page. But ordinarily, when it comes time to deliver dialogue, they return to looking directly at each other as they speak. If there are others in the scene, they, too, will keep their eyes fixed on whoever is talking — because they might be able to seize an appropriate moment to throw in a line of dialogue of their own. In the kitchen-fight scene, maybe it's the teenage son who stands by witnessing the discord and finally says: "You guys!"

I'm suggesting that as a business person you are no different from any of the actors I just mentioned. You're simply in a different scene with different circumstances. Sure, you may be operating your PowerPoint or flipping your pages on a chart, but when it comes to delivering your "lines," it's far more effective to do so "Attending To" the others in the room. In turn, it will ensure better odds that they continue to attend to you!

After a while, actors instinctively know when to "Attend To" and when they can briefly look away. What is most important for all of us is to *develop* that instinct for knowing when to look and when you can manage without it. If you're following along the lines of "Be Here Now" you will quickly feel your way around – soon you'll know the "when" of "Attending To." We often see this with the seasoned improv actor. He or she fully understands when to attend to and when it's okay to take a break. But for them the visual cues are critical, so they don't look away very often. They know that it is their responsibility to look at who is speaking, because one fleeting moment may be "the moment." For instance, let's say an actor is at a ballgame with his wife. She is not happy being there. When she speaks, she may throw off some visual cue such as a snarled lip. The other actor can use that with his next response: "Your lip is up to your nostril, Hortense. Go ahead, inhale deeply, I dare ya!"

The process is similar in a business setting. Someone may be fiddling with a pen while explaining a concept. By "Attending To" — watching them fidget — you've not only made a better connection, you've also picked up on their nervousness. As you begin to respond to their statements, you may want to comment on that noticeable visual cue with something like, "Don't sweat it, Barrington, the idea is a good one." "Attending To" gives us a chance to show some sensitivity, understanding — appropriate responses that go beyond the obvious spoken word.

Again, I realize that "Attending To" is not possible in every meeting, every encounter, throughout your business day. You have logical things to do such as take notes or reach for papers. But here's my request: Attend to as much as possible. I'm willing to bet that you currently attend to most people in your work environment only a small percentage of the time; or that you are inconsistent in following this rule, depending on the importance of the person or persons in your meeting. I say, make "Attending To" a habit. Spend more time looking at whoever is speaking; refer to your notes and engage in other activities only when absolutely necessary. Sure, it's easy to look when something is appealing (I for one can't take my eyes off a guy in a pink oxford shirt), but we must discipline ourselves to be consistent.

Bottom line: "Attending To" is just good etiquette. There is clearly something impressive about those who have good manners. We all like people who are polite, respectful and considerate. In one of my favorite movies, "Get Shorty," John Travolta's character insists on such respect each time he speaks to one of his protagonists. He continually demands, "Look at me. *Look* at me!" (I'm not suggesting you behave like that — I just want you to keep the idea in mind.)

Before I get to your "Attending To" workout, I want to share a story concerning a female colleague. She was presiding over a meeting at a major law firm one day with five male business executives, all of them potential clients. She was making a sales pitch. She had an easel with a flipchart on it and began writing down key, bulleted phrases to illustrate her verbal points. She got so caught up in her scribbling that she kept her back to the audience, rambling as she wrote. As they asked questions, she answered them, but with her back turned. When she finally swung around, she was surprised to see two of them had fallen asleep. The other three were preoccupied — one was doodling, one was updating his electronic day planner, and the other was reading *Sports Illustrated.* She laughed and cried when she told me this story. The lesson is this: It's pretty easy for people to check out on you if you don't attend to them. When you leave, even figuratively, they probably will, too.

These following homework tasks are geared to aid you in restructuring and/or bolstering the way in which you "Attend To."

1. Take time out at least once each business day to stay focused on the "Attending To" rule. Find at least two others with whom to have a conversation (the bigger the group, the better) and discipline yourself to stay riveted on whoever is speaking. Follow

the dialogue like a tennis ball; where it goes, let your eyes go with it. If you're officiating in a meeting, make sure you attend to those you ask questions of and keep your eye contact consistent.

2. I've said earlier that a great actor is a great observer, so I want you to take time out just to sit in a meeting and watch everyone else. Notice who is "Attending To" and who isn't. Assess the dynamics of the room. See if you can get a feel for who is bonding and who isn't — who is showing respect and consideration, and who isn't. What's the rapport like between the different parties? I predict you'll soon come to understand how powerful "Attending To" is.

3. As you go about "Attending To," see if you can gain more insight into the people with whom you're dealing. Make notes after meetings. Keep a journal of your discoveries; this is a wonderful thing to revisit before your next encounter with them. It's like having a cheat sheet, especially in terms of how people react and respond to others. But if you don't attend to others, you won't have this edge.

4. Take an opportunity during one of your assignments to work on your eye contact when someone else is speaking to you. Notice the change in the rapport and connection between the two of you because of your eye contact. Don't stare them down, just demonstrate good "Attending To." If they direct you to look at a report or chart, do so. But your main job in this assignment is to become very aware of the benefit of eye contact.

5. Think about your own sense of etiquette. Make a small list of all the things your mother said to you when she wanted you to pay attention. "Be polite," "Lookee here," "Heads up," and "Look at me when I'm talking to you," are just a few I can recall from my mom. How about you? Whatever they are it's good to write them down, then post them in places you frequently attend to! They'll serve as constant, wonderful

reminders to mind your manners. After all, that's all "Attending To" is.

Now, for a second look at that staff meeting — this time with everyone "looking" good!

TAKE TWO: "Lookee Here"

(Five people are seated at a round table in the office of Mr. Raspecht, a VP of business affairs for a major company. It's the weekly staff meeting)

MR. RASPECHT

(Clears his throat) Well then, I wanted to ask that we discuss the tracking report for the sales department. Mr. Roode, let's start with you.

(All four of the attendees, including Mr. Roode, are alert, perky and ready to respond. Sitting straight and tall and facing Raspecht, all eyes are on him now)

MR. RASPECHT

Mr. Roode …

(All eyes shift to Mr. Roode)

MR. ROODE

(Nods appreciatively and begins) Yes, we tracked 14 new customers just last night, didn't we, Gladys?

(All eyes shift to Gladys Enanhout)

MS. ENANHOUT

(Smiling brightly and making eye contact around the table as she speaks) Yep, I counted 14 myself.

(As Helsewhere pipes in, all eyes shift his way)

MR. HELSEWHERE

Wow, 14's a lot.

(Flytee begins to speak and with his first words, everyone turns his way)

MR. FLYTEE

That's four more than ten.

(All eyes report back to Raspecht; they appear to be begging for intervention based on Flytee's last remark)

MR. RASPECHT

(Laughing nervously, trying to save the day) Yes, Mr. Flytee, and pay attention because we have even more math stumpers. You see, now I'm going to explain the bonus structure.

(Eyes stay fixed)

MR. RASPECHT

(As he turns the flip chart, he maintains eye contact with his staff. As he speaks, he looks meaningfully from one person to the next, making worthwhile eye contact. He writes the number "13" on the chart. He smiles largely) This is all you need to get $10,000 each.

(The foursome look at one another, then back at Raspecht in unison. As Roode begins to speak, all eyes go to him)

MR. ROODE

Cool.

(Flytee butts in. Eyes follow there)

MR. FLYTEE

I believe we're one under par ... but, actually, I'm not sure ... well, uh ... I'd have to do the math.

(Looking him square in the eye, they all smile faintly. Elsewhere looks at the chart, the rest of the eyes go there with him)

MR. HELSEWHERE

I could use the money!

(They all nod at him affirmatively with a "me, too." Then Enanhout speaks. Though suspicious, they all turn to eye her)

MS. ENANHOUT

(She makes eye contact with all of them as she says)
I'll sure work at it! Or maybe I already have??!

(The remaining three look to Raspecht again for assistance. He throws a glance over his shoulder, still looking at everyone as he exits)

MR. RASPECHT

That's the spirit. **(Turning around completely he stops,**

and contacting them with his eyes, one at a time) Now, **(pauses and lowers his voice)** who wants to follow me to accounting to cash in?

-Lights-

Chapter 10

Cut From the Scene
Division of Responsibility

TAKE ONE: "It's Not My Job"

(Int. library in a law office. Three attorneys are seated at the table. They're doing research on a big case)

HUGH DEWIT

(Shoving the books toward the other two) I think you folks can handle the rest of this.

LEAH ZEE

(Shoving the books out of her way and toward the others) I'm tapped out, dudes.

TRYNE ARD

Hey, you two, come on. I need help. The Brockport case is a zillion-dollar contingency number and if we don't get these briefs handled, we're toast.

LEAH ZEE

(Folds her arms on top of the table and lays her head

down) Well, butter me on both sides cuz I don't have the energy.

(Enter: Mr. Burden Onmi, a senior partner with tattered shirt and whimpering associate hanging on his suit coat sleeve. Onmi drags him along, reluctantly)

BURDEN ONMI

(Tries to shake the guy loose. Wyner releases his boss and slides into a chair. He's fallen silent) Well, what did you get done?

TRYNE ARD

Well, this morning while you were doing all the billing sheets, trying the Litwer case and meeting with two Fortune 500 companies and interviewing seven paralegal candidates, we were just … um … .

HUGH DEWIT

We were putting the books on the table.

LEAH ZEE

(Head still resting on conference table top) 'Cept me. I think I have a cold.

BURDEN ONMI

Well, what do you think? Talk to me. I need to hear from everyone.

HUGH DEWIT

Leah, go ahead.

LEAH ZEE

I think I'm getting laryngitis.

TRYNE ARD

(Dusting off the book covers with her scarf and straightening the books in the center of the table) Well, as you can see, sir, I did line the books up nicely. They're in numerical order. Okay, (pondering his request) you want me to say something … um … .

BURDEN ONMI

(Discouraged but undaunted) I need to know what all you have done to prepare for tomorrow?

(All four, including Wyner, look at him uncertainly. They shrug their shoulders; they shake their heads)

BURDEN ONMI

Well, say something, damn it! You've been in here all morning!

HUGH DEWIT

(Points to Leah) Go ahead. You first.

LEAH ZEE

(Gestures to Burden) Nice tie.

TRYNE ARD

Looks really nice with that shirt, sir.

WYNER

(**Looking hopeless**) Uh ... uh ... .

BURDEN ONMI

(**Exasperated**) Okay, okay, here's the plan, I guess. We'll plead the Dugger Defense, and I'll prepare the briefs along with exhibits, then we'll collect at least ten declarations, take the Morton and Martin depositions, then file a motion for ... .

-Fade to Black-

Chapter 10

===========

Cut From The Scene
Division of Responsibilty

Talk about a lack of accountability! Poor Burden Onmi, he may as well have been a sole practitioner. I know people like the ones in that group, and for me, trying to get folks like that to rally round the "Project is like wearing ankle weights to the company picnic: Who wants to play anything? As you can see, Burden got minimal, if any, assistance from his team. It looked like he was doing all of the work, all of the time. Though this scene may seem like an exaggeration, I encounter the same dynamic in many companies as I go about teaching my corporate executives on a weekly basis. I sit through their work-related get-togethers and am astounded as I watch the interaction. Some people just expect everyone else to do all the work.

But here again, we have an improv rule that calls for every group participating in a scene to divide the responsibility for its success equally. If there are four people, each person in the scene is 25 percent responsible for making it work. If there are five, 20 percent; two, fifty-fifty, and so on.

I don't know about you, but I've been in scenes where, if I hadn't talked there would have been no conversation at all. I've also felt like the burden was on me to solve the problem — to make things happen, to find resolution. It's neither productive nor comfortable to be in that fix. It's like going out on a blind date with someone who's had a lobotomy.

Every scene needs balance. If the dialogue isn't somewhat even between the participants, equality can't exist. Without balance, synergy suffers. What I notice, and what I hear from most people who have to do all the work in any scene, is that they begin to feel resentful, just as they would in anything else where the weight is misplaced and mainly on them.

As for Mr. Onmi, he had to feel a great deal of stress working with such a lackluster team. There is nothing harder than having to carry the ball, not just for yourself, but for everyone in a scene.

Sometimes people "lay out" (a term we use when people pull back on stage in dialogue or action intentionally or unintentionally) simply because they're shy. But more often I think people lay out because they aren't willing to be accountable for the conversational results. Kind of a passive-aggressive thing. Either the scene they're in isn't one they want to be in, or it's a scene that doesn't interest them. Well, too bad. If you recall, when we talked about commitment, there is no sabbatical in scenework. We all need to do our job, to become an integral part of the discussion. That includes good days, bad days and all those other in-between days.

What if someone tramples you, verbally, you ask? Well, though I'll cover that more in the following chapter, let me just say here and now that you can still assert yourself; you can still take your portion of the responsibility and adroitly wedge yourself in there. Letting someone garrulously topple you is a great excuse for not having to kick in your verbal percentage. Some will argue this point with me, but I've tested the theory of even-steven in the toughest of meetings, and if you push to be heard, you can get your due. Though I don't wish to show any cultural bias, I suggest watching either a Jewish or Italian family scene. If you'll just sit back and listen, quite often you'll note that they're all in there slugging it out equally with word play. I know. I grew up in an Italian household. It became an art form at our dinner table. Fact is: You can begin to notice a rhythm in the banter among those who are "scene-ing" together frequently. So, though it's tempting, don't cop to the "can't get a word in edgewise" mentality. We all can if we make our move. Rare is the person who just won't shut up, at least in the business setting.

Here's what I tell my improv actors when trying to pound this principle into them: If you're not participating in the scene, you don't belong in it. How often do you sit through meetings where some people do just that: sit there? How often do you do it yourself?

I firmly believe that if everyone approached each communication task with a sense of doing their part — if they were conscious of offering up their proportional helping — group conversations would not only be much more interesting, they'd be a hell of a lot more productive. Most companies spend at least 10 percent (that's a low estimate) in staff meetings weekly. Most of those companies achieve very little at meeting's end. Now, if everyone were to participate, fully, the results in terms of productivity would be dramatically different. There's a very distinct reason for that: It has to do with dynamics and the shift of energy.

Keep in mind that when anyone enters or exits a room (or the stage), the dynamics instantly change; so does the responsibility of the performers who are in the scene. We all must be acutely aware of the chemistry as a result of the change in the room and readily adapt. When we do — when we have that single-minded purpose, the sole intent of seeing to it that a scene works no matter how many times it's reinvented beyond our control — it's easy to think, and genuinely support, the concept: "Division of Responsibility." When, however, we put the emphasis just on ourselves, it's hard to get behind the idea of dividing up the verbal pie. Because after all, the focus is very "self" oriented. And if everyone else in the scene is coming from that same vantage point, it's hard for any group scene to function smoothly. Remember the "Serve and Support" theory I discussed earlier? It all ties together. Hopefully, these two improv rules should start to come together for you, to make a little more sense now. (See how all these rules blend together and layer?)

I went to a meeting recently where I was asked to observe the interaction among a marketing team. They were working on a rather difficult problem. They had to redesign a print ad campaign for a computer chip and had pretty much run out of ideas. Over the prior seven weeks, they'd pitched six different programs. Each was rejected. The Creative Director was trying desperately to solicit comments from his comrades but they seemed to just sit there waiting for him to go on; they were spent. At that point, they were collectively demoralized, so it was understandable when they laid back.

Sal kept tossing out creative bait, but they would take to it as eagerly as a salmon to caviar. I felt really sorry for him, and his team. They would mutter, but most of their retorts were as understandable and enthusiastic as the Latin responses I remember hearing at Mass as a young girl.

We took a short nutrition break and Sal and I were left alone in the room. We conferred. I handed him a football. We huddled. I gave him some instructions. When the team returned, Sal said, "Okay, here's the deal: whoever gets the ball thrown at them must catch it and speak for as long as it's in their possession. Now, you must give at least two solutions to the problem we're here to address before you're allowed to pass the ball to someone else. The ball has to move fast, too." This exercise forced each team member to be just that — a team player. Like it or not, each person in that room had to take responsibility for the solution to the problem, to ante up and kick in their fair share. Each also had to be alert and ready to catch that ball at all times because they never knew when it would come their way.

The dynamics in that room changed faster than a quarterback faking a pass. People were eager. People began to pick up on the idea that if they didn't chip in, who else would? I will have to admit that some of the guys did get a little out of hand in this exercise. While trying to impress a few of their female counterparts, one angled a long pass down the center of the conference table. When the pitcher of water went flying, so did one woman's temper. It splattered her shiny, silk blue top. Some guy yelled something about a wet blouse contest and that's when I blew the whistle, so to speak. But at least they all got involved. Rather someone a little off-sides, than only one player on the field! And by the way, the team did come up with a solution for an ad campaign. Something about a "chip off the old block." When they all got involved, the energy was impossible to ignore. It built on itself. What I most enjoyed watching was how vital every person in that meeting began to feel as the dialogue proceeded. After the water-fall incident, they settled down once again and, without the benefit of the football, continued in the "pass the ball" mode.

I mentioned "shift in energy" a moment ago, when I was talking about dynamics. We are, I believe, masses of energy housed in physical bodies. What we emit creates a reaction. What we don't emit also has an effect. We've all certainly had high energy days and low energy days. We've also been in a room when a new person enters. Sometimes the person picks up the tempo and feel of the room by his or her mere upbeat presence. Other times, they bring a dirge-like residue that clings like wet cement. We can either be energized by someone's presence, or made to go retrograde. Both reactions to the undercurrent in the atmosphere tend to redefine the nature of the scene. Perhaps we will be more vocal, or perhaps we'll shut down. The point is this: You can't let the energies that be, or the energies that shift, change your level of willingness to stay at par. No matter what the energy, you must take your share of the responsibility.

There is something about the energy that changes, too, in a wonderful way, when everyone comes together with an eager concern, knowing that they are to be accountable for the ultimate outcome of that particular piece of communication. The more energy that is released in a room, the more inviting it is for others to participate. You've heard such a dynamic referred to as momentum. And that's what happens; the more energy, the greater the "mo." I may be putting myself on the line now, but I've yet to see any scene that *didn't* work when the energy was strong and **equally placed,** be it on the stage of business or the stage of theater.

Maybe you're the one who has to take the lead to stimulate participation during one scene or another, but that's okay. That's a confident and powerful position to put yourself in. If a scene needs a kick start, take responsibility to provide one. Just don't let others lean on you too much to make communication continue to "happen." Throw others the ball.

If you've had the good fortune to be in a meeting with a facilitator present, you know that he or she is equivalent to a good improv Director, steering the scene quietly from the sidelines, while the participants actually create it. Unfortunately, though, we don't always have a facilitator around to keep the players equally involved or to keep the "scene" on course. Sometimes we're on our own and very dependent on one another. It is then that the "Division of Responsibility" rule is so critical.

I realize that not everyone you come in contact with will know this rule. Surely you can't hand out the rulebook as people walk through the door. But a simple awareness — remaining conscious of its importance on your end — is a great start. Just like a seasoned improv player, you'll become adroit at helping others on stage subtly. You'll learn to maneuver them gracefully, as well as entice and jolt them into doing their fair share.

The Orange County Crazies (a sketch and improvisational comedy group I direct) is known for its bravado when it comes to putting audience members in its all-improv scenes. Sometimes the team consists of only one actor and one audience member. Our actors are asked not to dominate the scene, but rather to strive for a sense of fifty-fifty. Sticking closely and credibly to the audience's set-up (initial suggestions for the premise of the scene), the actors make the scene appear balanced and even. Without exception, the audience is always pleased during the course of the scene, not to mention delighted at the conclusion. I know I've said this before, but I'll say it again: It's not that veteran improv players are smarter at conversing; it's just that they approach it differently. They process and share information differently. They are always aware of each improv rule, and "Division of Responsibility" is no exception.

A word about lack of balance in a scene: Most of the participants, conscious of it or not, (as well as audience members) will always feel a direct or underlying sense of discomfort when the dialogue is not evenly doled out. How many times have you been witness to a scene where you felt uneasy because the dynamics were out of sync?

When there is parity, there is harmony. I've mentioned this before. So, you must do your part. Always. Without exception. That may mean becoming more involved or less. It depends on your personality, your approach to conversing with others, your current state of mind and the nature of the scene you're engaged in.

As you work on "Division of Responsibility," see if you can begin to look at the group settings you're in a bit differently. Do you do your part? If not, get on the ball! Can you help others to do their fair share? Try the following homework tasks to master this communication rule.

1. At your next meeting that includes a minimum of three or more — you and at least two others — make sure that you offer as much dialogue as your percentage requires. If others sit silent, see if you can elicit responses or input by asking them questions, and most importantly, their opinions. Everyone is more apt to participate when we ask for their points of view or their advice. It's a great way to create a more inviting atmosphere.

2. Take time out to simply observe meetings. Watch the dynamics. Do you like what you see? Pretend you're the Director. Take notes on what you would change in the scene if you could re-run the piece.

3. When doing the above exercise, see if you can score each participant; give them a percentage total for their participation.

4. As you're observing and note-taking, see if you can write down responses that may have served as valuable input — dialogue opportunities that were missed. In other words, record what you would have said had you been an active participant in the scene. These observations can take place in an elevator, on a bus, in the office cubicle next door, the coffee room — wherever people gather, take note of just this one principle: "Division of Responsibility." Who's doing their part, who isn't.

5. On one of those days when you just don't feel up to participating, do it anyway. Soon you will begin to make a habit of digging in and doing your part even when you'd rather be napping. Remember that each group opportunity provides great

rehearsal time for you, so take advantage of such situations.

6. Practice "Division of Responsibility" at home with family. Observe those dynamics, too.

Now let's take another look at the library law scene and how differently it plays when everyone is slicing up the verbal responsibility in equal servings.

TAKE TWO: "It's Not My Job"

(Int. of library law office. Three attorneys are seated at the table. They're doing research on a big case)

HUGH DEWIT

(Dividing the books among the group) Here's one for each of us.

LEAH ZEE

(Taking hers in hand and opening it) I'm a little tired but I've got input.

TRYNE ARD

Great. Me, too. The Brockport case is a zillion-dollar contingency number and I know I can count on both of you to help me get these briefs handled.

LEAH ZEE

(Eager to speak) You bet, Tryne. What I'll do is prepare the points and authorities … **(She coughs)**

HUGH DEWIT

Feeling okay, Leah?

LEAH ZEE

Got a cold, but that's okay, focusing on this makes me forget ... .

HUGH DEWIT

(Hands her a tissue) Well, I have an idea. Why don't we —

(Burden Onmi enters, looking sharp and perky. His assistant, Wyner, walks beside him)

BURDEN ONMI

(Offers Wyner a chair. Wyner begins to sit as he greets everyone individually, then changes his mind and gets up to pour coffee) Hi, everyone!

WYNER

Who needs coffee? (They all raise a hand) Great, I got it. Coffee all around!

BURDEN ONMI

Well, what did we get done?

TRYNE ARD

Well, while you were busy this morning, we found various citations we thought we could use in the brief.

LEAH ZEE

Yes, Burd, I'm going to prepare the points and authorities.

HUGH DEWIT

And I'll do the research.

WYNER

(Passing out coffee mugs) Count on me for word processing.

BURDEN ONMI

Well, don't forget the Dugger defense.

HUGH DEWIT

And the Morton and Martin depositions.

LEAH ZEE

And I've got exhibits A through P.

BURDEN ONMI

Maybe we can divide those ten declarations among the five of us.

(He begins to exit. They nod in sound agreement)

TRYNE ARD

Where ya goin', Burd?

BURDEN ONMI

Tee time! You guys have this case in such great shape,
I'm shootin' all 18 this afternoon. Same time tomorrow?

ALL

Same time … tomorrow …

WYNER

Hope you shoot a bird, Burd!! **(He laughs until the rest,
including Burd, groan evenly)**

-Fade to Black-

Chapter 11

═══════════

Stealing The Scene
Give and Take

Take One: "The Lower Lobby"

(Int. company lobby. Two salespersons are seated, waiting for their respective meetings to be called. They have appointments with customers. One is from a stationers, the other a printing firm. They begin to chat while they wait)

TIM IDATED

(Softly) Hi, my name is Tim. I'm from Lowesteem Stationers and I'm waiting to see —

TAY KOVER

(Extends hand for a shake only to shove a business card in Tim's hand instead) Kover, Tay Kover. How 'do! I'm from BS Image Printing and I'm waiting to see Case S. Hass. **(Proudly)** He's the vice president, and, hey we go back a long way —

TIM IDATED

(Timidly) Oh, I went to school with Case. In fact —

TAY KOVER

Well, hey, I guess it was during our fraternity days when
Case and I were —

TIM IDATED

I —

TAY KOVER

Well, we were having one of those toga parties and I
papered him in Charmin and ever since then —

TIM IDATED

When I met him —

TAY KOVER

(Laughs a big belly one) Since then, he kept calling me
"Paper Tiger." So, hell, I took that on faith that I should
be in paper, ya know the paper biz, in some way. Then
after college at Me U, I began to work for every big paper
company in the country, Boise Cascade —

TIM IDATED

(Hoping to be heard) I worked for Boise about five
years ago —

TAY KOVER

(Not even pausing to take a breath) Then it was
Weyerhauser. Fact, when I worked for them I was also
working for Pizza Hut, see, I had to work two jobs. My
mother became a widow — stepfather died — tripped on a

curb and beaned his head on a mailbox — being the old-
est, I had to support two little brothers, along with my
mother. I also had an uncle who dropped a kidney in
'Nam and I had to pay his medical bills, too. So it was
then I got a third job. For a paper company, too. **(Big
breath and sigh)** See, I worked —

TIM IDATED

(Trying to get a word in) My mother ... **(Louder, now)**
My mother was a wid —

TAY KOVER

See, that's where I got the experience ... I think that was —

TIM IDATED

Here's your customer.

TAY KOVER

Huh? What?

TIM IDATED

(Flatly) Case S. Hass.

TAY KOVER

**(Gets up to greet his customer, Case. They walk away
together)** Did I ever tell you 'bout my mother, Case?
Geez, she was a great gal, raising me and my two brothers.
See I had four jobs at a time, having to support ... .

(Case tries to get a word in. Impossible)

-Lights-

Chapter 11

Stealing the Scene
Give and Take

Dealing with a Tay of the business world is like trying to traverse an avalanche. In Tim's case, he no sooner found a pocket of air to sneak a word through when he was crushed with yet more weighty verbiage.

As I mentioned in Chapter Ten, "Division of Responsibility" means that everyone gets equal time and takes equal accountability for making a scene work. The only way to get there is through a wonderful sense of "Give and Take" — another very basic rule all improv comedy actors are mandated to follow when they take to the stage. Without "Give and Take" there is chaos and pandemonium, a verbal brawl of sorts. Inevitably, at least one person gets trampled in the foray.

The work environment is full of people like Tay — people who tend to dominate and control the conversation. You can always tell who they are — they're the ones doing all the talking or interrupting everyone. Typically, they're the ones who never let you or anyone else get a word in edgewise. When I come upon these people, I think only one thing: How great a strip of duct tape would look pressed against their lips. It's frustrating and infuriating to try to converse with someone who has little regard for the others engaged in the conversation process.

For anyone sitting in, watching such communication, it's irritating as hell. I have seen audiences boo improv students who won't let the other players participate. Unfortunately, though, in business meetings, most of us would seem out of place booing a verbal bulldozer — especially if it's our boss!

Trying to cut off someone who plows ahead sometimes works to gain equality, but I contend that once a dynamic is set in motion, it usually prevails. The person who just won't shut up or who tries to intercede at every verbal turn will usually try to reclaim center stage at everyone else's expense.

There is nothing worse for a qualified improv player to deal with than someone who hogs the scene. The take-over artists are the people no one wants to work with during class. And if they're graduates of an improv school, they're branded for the rest of their improv lives as people who should know the rules, but don't follow them because they're selfish and arrogant. There were several of us working at The Comedy Store in Hollywood who had to share the stage with such an individual. I won't name him. Not because you'd recognize his name. You wouldn't — and that's my point. Thanks to his penchant for scene-stealing, this guy never made a name for himself. He gained a reputation as a self-centered, inconsiderate jerk, and the word spread faster than an open casting call. No one wanted to work with him. It wasn't long before he was doing standup — a form of comedy you do all alone.

To dominate in the presence of others when they are brought together for mutual discussion is to be overbearing. There is just no room for that in improvisational comedy — or the business arena. On the contrary. Everyone should think of themselves as a team player. Whether two are on the team or ten. That means everyone shares. If not, there is no equilibrium. No equilibrium, no harmony. Without harmony, no scene can work — whether the setting is a theater or a conference room. Ideally, everyone in any scene or meeting should get the chance to lead but be willing to follow — that always constitutes a great piece of communication — but if it can't be even-steven, we at least can strive to get as close to that as possible.

Here's the opposite problem: When another player opts to be the "submissive" one in the scene, that too, can be unnerving. So, staying at parity — balancing out the "Give and Take" — means that while letting go of the lead here and there, no one can just sit idly by and make everyone else do all the work. To lay back — to do nothing, or very little — is to invite someone else's dominance. But this is rare in improv work, because everyone is taught to "Give and Take" from the very first night of class. I only wish business people were taught the same thing as part of their training and orientation sessions before performing on the job. Maybe you've been in a situation where your only logical choice has been to "take" in order to keep the communication rolling. I've had students break down and cry in class over this. Too much conversational responsibility can be scary.

When you communicate with others, you don't want one person to play the role of the leader and the other the follower throughout the entire scene. I've seen this happen: The actors take to the stage, and from the very first opening lines, one person takes the leadership role while the other just follows along. Instead, the principle behind "Give and Take" is to trade off. One person takes the lead from another who acquiesces, graciously giving the lead away until an appropriate time to reclaim it. No one steps on anybody's lines — meaning no one speaks while another person is speaking.

One of the most vivid metaphors for describing the theory of "Give and Take" is to say that it's like a dance. In improv, both "dancers" take turns leading and following. (Naturally, if there are more than two people in a scene, they all take equal turns on the verbal dance floor.) For an audience, this is wonderful to watch. And, in the business meeting, nothing is more powerful for those in attendance than to see how the dance moves the communication along productively. The reason the dance always works is that the people doing it get the overall sense that they are unified and equal. That's an extremely fertile atmosphere for effective communication — whether people are in agreement or not. That's right — even arguments, when they're handled properly, can foster this concept of leading and following — following and leading.

Another phrase that's frequently used in describing the "Give and Take" principle is "advance and retreat" — which I think is a wonderful way to define the whole idea. You go forward; you step backwards; and so on. The idea of simply taking turns is all any of us have to remember. (Didn't we all learn that even before kindergarten?)

So, then, when it comes to "Give and Take" here are some questions to answer: Are you conscious of it? How often do you do it? Are you aware of it as you observe others? Are you typically a leader or a follower? Does it depend on who you're with? Think about these things as you go about your daily communication. If you need work in some of these areas, get busy! I guarantee, just a simple awareness will make a huge difference in how you interface with others.

Here's something I want you to consider as you increase your awareness level: In most instances, dynamics get firmly planted in a company culture, but that doesn't preclude the possibility of change. So don't be hard on yourself if you tend to exhibit characteristics of one over the other, if you seem to be mostly giver or mostly taker. The idea is to work at learning to behave appropriately at appropriate times — usually with an equal measure of "Give and Take" in any and all your work "scenes." It's something you can strive for.

I've often wondered what would happen if every business professional had to take a few improv classes on the "Give and Take" lesson alone. I am absolutely convinced that working people would view their participation in every piece of communication quite differently. The implementation of this one improv comedy principle alone would make a vast difference in how people get along, not to mention how much more productive everyone would be.

By now, you're probably ready for some practical advice — things you can do to become better at "Give and Take." First off, what do you do if someone is trying to dominate a scene — how do you take back the control and equality for the sake of everyone involved? There are a few options. You can interrupt someone, making sure you do get your two cents in. You can overpower them, which will probably make them shift to the submissive role very quickly without realizing it. You can turn and walk away (in improv there is no more final way to end a scene, or to make a strong statement, than to make an exit). Or, you can honestly and openly approach them with a comment like: "I get the feeling we need to communicate, but so far I feel you're the only one doing the talking. Mind if I have a say?" Most reasonable people will suddenly become aware that they weren't being very considerate and apologize or welcome your remarks. That will set a definitive tone for the rest of the "scene." It's great when we're honest in a kind way. Personally, I think it beats turning and walking away, because once you bail from a scene, it's hard to jump back in assertively. Too, when we're open and genuine, it helps build rapport. And when it comes to people, there is nothing more sacred than establishing, maintaining and building rapport. That's the underlying message of this book.

Sometimes people aren't aware that they're dominating the "scene." By pointing out dominance — kindly — you can begin to change the dynamic. Even better, you can be a role model in the "Give and Take" mode. People often follow our example when it comes to communication. If you master the concept, then practice it, you may find that it's not so hard to entice everyone else to enlist in the "take turns" process.

What if you're on the other end of the spectrum — what if you tend to "lay out," pull back? You'll want to keep reminding yourself that it's your responsibility to take part — remember "Division of Responsibility"? — no matter how shy you might be, how disinterested you are in the "scene," or how much you just might feel like not talking. If you encounter others who play this "part," try to elicit responses from them, get them involved, ask questions. Most people will come forward to communicate if we make an overture. If they don't, just do your best to carry the scene without it looking like you're taking over. For instance, while you're forced to do all the talking, you might say things like: "I think the Johnson report is lacking in its impact. Well, it looks like you might think so, too. I didn't hear any response to the contrary." With that — subtly speaking for the other person — they may pipe up with their own opinion. Just remember to make eye contact, to nudge them in various ways to become a part of the "scene." Sometimes that's all anyone needs to take an active part.

Pure and simple: I think the "Give and Take" rule just goes back to good manners. If we're thinking along the lines of being gracious, polite, supportive and personally very generous, we can't go wrong. We will sense when it is time to lead and when we should follow. But again, this starts with awareness.

The last thing I want you to realize about "Give and Take" is that when this tenet is firmly in place in any "scene," more information is given and gathered. Participants are quicker to get a hint of what is needed and wanted to progress the scene further. If we as business professionals could open our initial conversations with an awareness of taking turns, of shared, all-hands-on-deck participation, we would get so much more out of every business day.

Before we return to the lobby and the scene between Tay and Tim, here are some assignments that will help you increase your sense of "Give and Take."

1. As in your other observation exercises, sit back and watch the back-and-forth dynamics of others. You can do this in meetings, business social events like mixers and association luncheons, in the airport lounge while you wait for your plane, and at home between family members. You will be astounded at what comes to light.

2. Take at least one interaction a day with a business associate and practice. One day you may have to stop the leader from getting too carried away, while another day you may have to pull teeth to get the other or others to participate. This is challenging because you never know how you'll have to maneuver the scene to get it to parity. Make this assignment a conscious effort at least once a day. Pat yourself on the back when you notice that you've gotten to parity with the other person or persons in your "scene." Soon this will become more of a habit.

3. Notice how many times you step on people's lines. Or, how many times they step on yours. Handle those situations appropriately. Remember, it's all about good manners.

4. If it's necessary for you to lay out because your boss or a client is dominating the scene, go with it. There are those times when being more submissive is the right role to play. If you think it's right to even the communication, go with your instincts. If you

need to take a dominant position because the "scene" requires it, take over. In the end, it's whatever it takes to make a "scene" work. Your job, however, is to strive for a great sense of "Give and Take" as often as possible.

5. Take a few minutes to remember some of those admonishments your mother gave you in order to be considerate of others, like: "Do unto others … ," "Don't forget to share," "Take turns." We all have several we can remember from childhood, I'm sure. Write some of these down and keep them posted nearby -- on your desk, by the phone, inside your briefcase, car dashboard. These subliminal reminders will seep into your subconscious and help you further develop and lock in the "Give and Take" principle.

6. Take in an improv comedy show if you can. Watching the pros "Give and Take" is one more reinforcement. Also, this assignment allows you to see how scenes progress effectively. The task can be a very enjoyable experience.

Now, let's revisit the lobby of that office facility and see what happens when those characters "Give and Take"!

TAKE TWO: "The Lower Lobby"

(Int. company lobby. Two salespersons are seated, waiting for their respective meetings to be called. They have appointments with customers. One is from a stationers; the other a printing firm. They begin to chat while they wait)

TIM IDATED

(Softly) Hi, my name is Tim. I'm from Lowesteem Stationers and I'm waiting to see Brownose Benson.

TAY KOVER

(**Extends hand for a shake**) Hi, the name is Kover. Tay Kover. How do! I'm from BS Image Printing and I'm waiting to see Case S. Hass. (**Proudly**) He's the vice president, and, hey, we go back a long way.

TIM IDATED

(**Timidly**) Oh, I went to school with Case. In fact, we were on the chess team together.

TAY KOVER

Were ya? Well, Case and I were in the same fraternity together. What a small world. Did he ever talk about those toga parties?

TIM IDATED

I don't recall.

TAY KOVER

Well, he got crazy at one of 'em and papered me in Charmin. Ever since then he kept calling me "Paper Tiger." That's what got me into the paper business.

TIM IDATED

Well, when I met him, he got so frustrated during a match with me he took a pawn and pressed it into my forehead. (**Gestures to forehead**) I've had this imprint there ever since.

TAY KOVER

Embossing looks good on you. Guess he had quite an influence on you, too, huh?

TIM IDATED

Yes, he did. I skipped college and went to work for Rubber Duckie Stamp Press. Testing department. Got tendinitis and eczema so I switched to the printing of stationery supplies.

TAY KOVER

Well, that's interesting. I, too, followed Case's lead. Went to Me U and, gee, I think I've worked for every big paper company in the country since, Boise Cascade...

TIM IDATED

I worked for Boise.

TAY KOVER

Did ya?

TIM IDATED

Yeah, in their pencil department.

TAY KOVER

Ah, challenging. Well, then I went to Weyerhauser. Also worked for Pizza Hut at the same time. Then I had a lot of family problems. My mother was a widow so I had to get a third job. Actually, it too was for another paper company.

TIM IDATED

That's funny, my mother was a widow, too.

TAY KOVER

Ah, sorry. But ya know — working for all those paper companies really gave me the experience I needed.

TIM IDATED

Oh, hey, there's your customer.

TAY KOVER

Huh, what?

TIM IDATED

Our mutual friend, Case S. Hass.

TAY KOVER

(Rises to greet Case. Pauses) Case, guess who's here? (Gestures to Tim) Your old pal, Tim Idated.

(The two shake. Exchange a few pleasantries while Tay looks on. Then ...)

TAY KOVER

Case, did you know that both our mothers are widows?

CASE S. HASS

That's funny. So's mine. Or, at least that's why she told

me I never met my father.

(They offer mutual condolences. Case and Tay bid farewell to Tim. They walk on continuing to share dialogue of personal stories)

-Lights-

Chapter 12

Crashing the Scene
Refusal and Denial

TAKE ONE: "Dishing"

(Int. lunch room at the offices of a large computer company. Two women, trays in hand, are working their way down the cafeteria line. They're dishing more than just the food d'jour)

REA FOOSE

(Weary of the same old fair) The goulash looks good.

DEE NYE

(Fed up) No, it doesn't. I hate goulash. What do think about the chop suey?

REA FOOSE

I can't hold it back anymore. I think Martha Pearlstein is lousy at the postage machine. Hell, she'd be better licking stamps. God knows she has the tongue for it … wag, wag, wag... .

DEE NYE

I think she does a fine job. I mean who else can lick and weigh?

REA FOOSE

Maybe I'll just have a salad. I'm trying to diet.

DEE NYE

(Snarly) Diets are stupid. Everyone knows they never work. (Same breath) Hell, I was born on a diet. I hear they're moving Martha to word processing.

REA FOOSE

Would you look at that stroganoff. (Getting aggravated) How slow can this line go? It's slower than Althorp trying to get the words together for the weekly wrap-up.

DEE NYE

No it's slower than Althorp demonstrating PowerPoint. Martha'll get fired if they put her on a computer. Just watch.

REA FOOSE

Forget it. I'll just have the Microchip soup.

DEE NYE

That sounds about as filling as Johnson's Christmas stocking.

REA FOOSE

Wonder if that comes with megabite crackers?

-Lights-

Chapter 12

Crashing The Scene
Refusal and Denial

After witnessing the last scene, you're probably saying to yourself, "So, what's the big deal? That conversation seemed pretty ordinary to me." Unfortunately, you're right. Scenes like that are pretty normal — not only in the Corporate-America lunch room, but the board room as well.

Usually when we find ourselves in a verbal "Dee/Rea" exchange, we tend to walk away from it feeling confused, resentful, unsettled or frustrated. Sometimes all of the above! I always harbor a "he bugs me" feeling. Many of us also feel the other person wasn't listening at all (the Rea syndrome at work) or that everything we said wasn't valid (Dee's malady). Oddly enough, often we can't even label these feelings; we just sense something is amiss. We characterize such conversations with remarks such as: "We just didn't click," "We weren't in the same groove," "We didn't jell," or "So-and-so was on a different page."

All of those are accurate assessments, and here's why: With conversations like the one we just witnessed, there's no real communication. In fact, there is a total lack of communication. In order to have communication, two or more people have to be *sharing* information — they have to be exchanging sentiments, observations, opinions or ideas. In Rea and Dee's case, they were exchanging all right but not necessarily the same things at the same time. Instead, one had an observation while the other expressed a sentiment. Again, this is typical of how most of us operate in the scope of a conversation at some point (or many points) during the business day. For instance, someone may say, "I'm hungry," while the person they're talking to may in response say, "I can't get my briefcase locked." Oh how we talk to each other! Mostly in non-sequiturs.

Communication also requires that people involved in it transmit information, thought, or feeling so that it is satisfactorily received and understood. That, in a soundbite, is the key: Information must be easily taken in and assimilated. If only we all could remember that, if only we could focus on just that one simple idea! Ask yourself now: Just today, for instance, did the receiver(s) of your information seem sated? Did all of them send back signals that in some way let you know that what you had imparted, they understood? Did you do the same for them? If not, it's time to check your refusal/denial barometer and make some appropriate changes to the way in which you converse.

Let's define our terms: Refusal occurs in the course of a conversation when you ignore something someone says. Denial happens when you change or undercut what someone says. Rea was ignoring (refusing) almost everything Dee said, while Dee was putting down, or negating, everything Rea said. For instance, when Dee said, "I think she does a fine job. I mean who else can lick and weigh?" Rea responded with, "Maybe I'll just have a salad." In other words, Rea completely **ignored** what Dee said. But Dee was no better. When Rea finished her remarks with, "I'm trying to diet," Dee **denied** her by saying, "Diets are stupid." She negated her.

Though these two women wanted to express their very own ideas, and had every right to do so, they had absolutely no regard for one another in the process. The same thoughts and feelings could have been expressed, but differently — without ignoring or negating the other person. For example, when Dee said, "I think she does a fine job. I mean who else can lick and weigh?" Rea could have first replied: "I can't think of anyone else in our department, that's for sure." That remark would have illustrated that Rea had "received and understood" what was said to her. It also would have validated Dee's opinion. Rea then could have gone on to add, "Maybe I'll just have a salad. I'm trying to diet," to which Dee might have replied: "Dieting is good if you believe in it. Hell, I was born on a diet, but frankly I think they're stupid." You'll note the first words out of Dee's mouth paid some respect to Rea's attempt to diet. Dee was still able to vocalize her opinion about her experience with dieting, and subsequently how she also felt about diets in general — yet when she did so it was after responding and giving credence to Rea. Too, going this last route, you'll notice neither of Dee's follow-up remarks was inconsiderate of Rea.

As you can see in this last go-around, the same ideas, observations, thoughts and feelings were expressed, but because the dialogue was handled in a different way, it provided for a real conversation between the two women. They were connecting one thought and idea to the next. In improv parlance we call it "going with." We follow along and acquiesce to the other actor, always. But don't misunderstand — this doesn't mean you can't have differing opinions. To avoid "Refusal and Denial" doesn't mean that those engaged in dialogue have to agree. They don't. In real life, agreement in every conversation just isn't realistic. But as I illustrated with the follow-up choices of dialogue between Rea and Dee, even in disagreement there are more positive and powerful ways to respond to one another — to stay in tune, move along together — in order to have a continuous flow during any verbal volley.

In the world of improv, when you choose not to ignore or negate anything someone says, you have guaranteed success with every single "scene." Pieces always work.

The improv comedy actor is taught in the very beginning stages of instruction that the evil twins of "Refusal and Denial" are the two things that will kill a scene. Instant death! If the actors opt to communicate in either of these modes, without question, every scene will have problems. With denial, the scene will automatically come to a screeching halt. With refusal the same can happen, but more frequently a scene rife with refusal will simply go round and round, like a dog chasing its tail. If either of these problems occur then someone will have to, out of necessity, create the communication all over again, from scratch. Stop and start, stop and start — there's no continuity in that! Scenes that travel the path of "Refusal and Denial" will always end up nowhere. Such scenes have no integrity. And, from an audience's point of view — whether the audience is in the theater or in the workplace — this is really uncomfortable to watch. You know how you feel when you witness two people arguing. It's like a tug of war. Same thing. Same reaction.

So, the improv student runs drills when first taking to the stage — drills that repeatedly engrain in them a permanent "red flag" that stops them short of falling into bad habits. (It also helps them detect "Refusal and Denial" in others — and deal with it adroitly.)

A truly refined improv actor will tell you he or she fears only one thing: working with another actor who doesn't know or abide by the rules. To them, it's not the least bit scary to take audience suggestions and make something wonderful out of them. Instead, it's frightful to be on stage with those who poison conversations with "Refusal and Denial." You may have already noticed what the improv actor notices: People who communicate from a vantage point of constant refusal and denial can be downright obnoxious.

Here's something to consider: When refusal and denial, or both, are present between two people, two conversations are actually taking place rather than one. Under those circumstances, how can you possibly make any communication headway? Is this perhaps something you do? I know I do at times!

If you want to perform your own diagnostic test to check your level of "Refusal and Denial," here are some clues. Are you frequently saying "no," "don't," "can't," "won't," "shouldn't," "oughtn't"? If so, you're probably leaning heavily toward chronic denial. Here's an example:

Person one: "Let's call a meeting."
Person two: "No, I don't want to call a meeting."
As you can see, the scene has stopped. Or it will simply continue down a "you say tomato/ I say tomahto" trail.
What would have worked better is:
Person one: "Let's call a meeting."
Person two: "Okay, let's. Though I'd rather finish this report."
Same result, perhaps, but the method of communicating the

information doesn't deny person number one.

Now, let's take this conversation a few words down the line and see how it could have progressed without denial.

Person one: "I know you want to finish that report, and I'm hellbent on calling a meeting."

Person two: "Well, if you're set on calling that meeting, it looks like we're at an impasse."

Person one: "Yeah, we sure are, so that means we need to resolve our conflict."

Person two: "Yes, a resolution is in order. I suggest we split the difference. You have a meeting and I'll work on my report."

This banter could conceivably continue until the speakers find a way to negotiate a reasonable solution to their differences. But they at least work through the dilemma without denying one another.

In addition to words that denote "no" messages, the word "but" is another indicator that you're digging a negative hole. Example: "Yes, the sky is blue, but I see a lot of gray." That's a more subtle denial, but it's still a denial. It would be better to say "Yes, the sky is blue and I seem to notice a lot of gray, too." This choice of words and phrasing expresses an opinion without changing or undercutting the other person.

Now here's a way to check your refusal dipstick: Are you responding directly to things people are saying to you, or are you peddling your own agenda? One clue would be if you find yourself saying "Huh?" a lot. That tells you you're not listening very well. And, if you're not listening you can't possibly respond directly to what anyone says. Tuning someone out is the way in which most people fall into the refusal trap. They inadvertently "ignore" because they're in their own heads.

Good conversations always have a sequential flow to them, and they always come to completion. Remember how much I stressed the importance of a beginning, middle and end? This would be virtually impossible to achieve with a preponderance of "Refusal and Denial." Again, these are two pits you don't want to fall into. It's too hard to claw your way out. "Refusal and Denial," by the way, not only create disharmony and misunderstandings, they also deplete energy; they're not only emotionally taxing, they can drain you physically as well. If you have a rebellious teenager, or a cohort who is always competitive, you'll probably find yourself wanting to take frequent naps.

That happened to me recently when I was in a sales pitch one day. The person being pitched to had a sidekick, and every time the pitchee expressed approval, his Tonto disagreed. It went something like this:

Pitcher: "We can produce this ad in color, too."
Pitchee: "Color? Oh, that sounds interesting."
Sidekick: "No, not color. I think that ad would only work if it was in black and white."

From there, at every verbal turn, the Sidekick kept taking the opposite point of view, which caused the Pitchee to become increasingly uncomfortable. As the pattern progressed, everyone else standing by was also becoming irritated and fidgety. Finally, though, the Pitcher began to catch on. Rather than get into the denial mode with the guy riding shotgun, he simply used reverse psychology to get the client to do what he really wanted him to do — sign off on a full series of ads. Here's how:

Pitcher: "I think you should only commission the one ad, not the series of three."
Sidekick: "Nah, I think we should do all three."

Getting out of that meeting was like getting off the teacups at Disneyland. I was dizzy. Parched and tipsy. I wanted a Dramamine to go with my Evian.

Though what I've just described may seem like an exaggeration, it's not. Such conversations take place all day, every day, from the panoramic corner office suite to the smallest of cubicles, all over Workplace-America. Maybe some are more subtle, but still in all, people go round and round, refusing, denying, then doing it some more. Scenes stop, then go. Stop, then go. I've often thought this is what "getting jerked around" really means. And we yank each other around mercilessly, although most of the time many of us don't realize we're even doing it.

"But," you might ask, "how can you express differing opinions or ideas without going into a state of refusal or denial?" Well, to avoid denial, you first give credence to the other person's idea before expressing your own. In terms of refusal, you simply address or answer someone's statement before you express your own.

These new ways of dialoguing are minor adjustments, really, but they make a world of difference in terms of whether your communication is tight or sloppy, meaningful or meaningless. If it's tight, you'll eventually reach a reasonable ending to your scene. If it's not, you'll wind up like Rea and Dee in the first take. Their scene spun in circles and their conversation never crossed the finish line. One was talking crackers, the other stockings.

The following assignments will aid you in testing your "Refusal and Denial" status. After your personal assessment, I'll prescribe some tips to help you steer clear of the land of "Refusal and Denial" while managing to work with those who call it home.

THE TEST

Denial

1. Beyond the use of words like "no," "don't," "but," do you often say "maybe," "whatever," "oh, well" or other noncommittal phrases in response to what is being said to you? These responses also serve as denials, albeit subtle passive-aggressive ones.

2. Do you respond to statements or questions by opposing a stated view or question?

3. Do you enjoy playing devil's advocate? Doing so can be helpful to people who need to bounce things around to find solutions, but you risk raining on too many parades.

4. Do you have a tendency to want to take an opposite point of view to whatever is being expressed? Often people do this because their sense of competitiveness is getting in the way, or because it doesn't know reasonable boundaries. Using a com-

bative approach is fine when you're on the battlefield fighting for the sale, but to use that stance as a means of everyday communication can be counter-productive.

5. When your day isn't going the way you want it to, do you find yourself projecting a negative mood at meetings, during one-on-one communications with superiors or subordinates, or with clients and customers? Our moods often color our communications in very dark hues, which can lead to an atmosphere of denial, even subtextually.

Refusal

1. Do you frequently find it necessary to have someone repeat what they just said? If so, that's a big refusal! That means you weren't even listening, in which case how could you possibly repsond? Listen to everything being said to you.

2. Do your replies have everything to do with what was just said to you, or are you verbalizing your own agenda? Remember the "React and Respond" rule. Do you respond to the last thing said or last idea held?

3. Do you cut people off in mid-sentence and begin talking about something else entirely? That's a big time refusal, not to mention downright rude! It's one thing to interrupt someone, kindly, making sure your dialogue is reasonably connected to theirs. It's another to barge in without even saying, "Excuse me." (Don't you hate it when people don't knock?)

4. Do you stare out the window, look at your shoes, doodle on your note pad, or otherwise semi-tune-out the person you're having a conversation with? Though this marks a subtle refusal, it's a refusal nonetheless, a way of ignoring someone.

I think all of us are guilty of at least one, if not most, of the above! It's human nature to behave in patterns of "Refusal and

Denial." But we can change old habits and try new ways of taking better care of our communications. Here's how:

1. Start by observing the conversations surrounding you. Great places to do this are meetings, one-on-one communications where there is boredom (refusal) or tension (denial), people having confrontations, and people at those networking mixers. Wherever there's conversation, there is refusal and denial. Watching from the outside is a great way to start to making corrections for yourself on the inside.

2. Take at least one conversation a day and pay attention to how many times you refuse the other person. Next, do the same assignment with denial. If you're on the phone, grab pencil and paper and write "Refusal" at the top of one column, "Denial" atop another. Keep score as you dialogue, busting yourself for each transgression. I was told by one student that this was the most helpful homework assignment of all. He could see in black and white how many times he broke the rules — sometimes during the course of even a short two-minute phone call.

3. Practice keeping eye contact with people you're talking to; there is something about doing so that forces you to take in more of what is being said. It's hard to focus on yourself when you're literally focusing on the other guy.

4. A subtle means of breaking the denial habit is to occasionally nod in affirmation when someone is talking to you. It's a great way to prepare yourself for a more "go with" approach when it's your turn to speak.

5. See if you can think in a more "go with" mentality. Sometimes denial stems from a disjointed thought pattern. The same goes for refusal. Do your thoughts connect, or are they all over the place? I realize that we all think in fragmented ways, but it's good discipline to go quietly within and let your mind run with one thought appropriately connected to the next.

6. Write out some dialogue (great way to prepare for meetings), making certain that each "player's" remarks stay out of the refusal/denial trap. Now, rehearse different responses, having a two-way conversation with yourself. In other words, play both parts. This a great way to have an exercise session — an invigorating verbal workout.

7. If you're sitting through a meeting (with not a lot to do, which isn't uncommon), take notes on what refusals and denials are taking place with the others. See if you can write out more appropriate responses than what you're hearing.

8. Reward yourself in some way for catching yourself prior to making an obvious refusal/denial goof. It's a wonderful way to reinforce positive behavior.

9. Make your own list of reasons why refusal and denial don't work in the scope of your work experience. This exercise forces you to do an honest appraisal of what might be hindering your communications with specific people in your work environment. Don't skip this one. The answers can be very revealing.

10. Don't forget the credo of the improvisational comedy player: "Go with!" This means that whatever direction the dialogue is taking, the actors stay firmly grounded in the flow of it. No matter the circumstance, they make all their communications work. You are no different from an improv player, for you, too, are improvising during each and every scene.

Take a few minutes to design your own refusal/denial homework, such as practicing on your children, tackling the tensions between you and your ex-spouse, screwing up the courage to make headway with a difficult co-worker. There are lots of things you can do. Get creative!

Now, let's return to the company cafeteria and our friends Dee and Rea.

TAKE TWO: "Dishing"

(Int. cafeteria at the offices of a large computer company. Two women, trays in hand, are working their way down the chow line. They're dishing more than just the food d'jour)

REA FOOSE

(Weary of the same old fair) The goulash looks good.

DEE NYE

Looks good to you alright, although I, myself, hate goulash. What do you think about the chop suey?

REA FOOSE

It's messy and it's hard to swallow, which brings me to what I just can't hold back anymore. I think Martha Pearlstein is lousy at the postage machine. Hell, she'd be better licking stamps. God knows she has the tongue for it … wag, wag, wag … .

DEE NYE

Oh, and what a wag. It never stops. I'm surprised to hear you say that about the postage machine. She does a great job. I mean, come on, Rea, who else can lick and weigh?

REA FOOSE

Probably her boss, Tonlik. Hell, that's who taught her. Oh, lookee there, maybe I'll just have a salad. I'm trying to diet.

DEE NYE

Good for you. I hope dieting works for you. I'll tell you, I think diets are stupid and I don't know too many people who say they work. Hell, I was born on a diet. Speaking of losing things, I hear they're moving Martha to word processing.

REA FOOSE

I heard that, too. God help ComputerTech Hardsoft! Would you look at that stroganoff. How slow can this line go? It's slower than Althorp trying to get the words together for the weekly wrap-up.

DEE NYE

Yeah, and nothing could be worse than that except Althorp demonstrating PowerPoint. Martha'll get fired if they put her on a computer. Just watch.

REA FOOSE

Boy, I hope you're right. Ah, forget this "should I have this or should I have that." I'll just have the Microchip soup.

DEE NYE

Oh, do. It's almost as good as the Hard-drive Hamburger. The only problem is that soup is about as filling as Johnson's Christmas stocking.

REA FOOSE

Oh, not again — those short, puny stockings. This year I

hope he doesn't fill them with Hershey covered floppies. (**They mirror a snarl**) Do you think the soup comes with Megabite crackers?

-Lights-

Chapter 13

A Pleasant Scene
Yes, and ...

TAKE ONE: "Words At Wango Chorale"

(Int. Human Resources office at a belt buckle plant. The Director is giving a review to a Quality Control Supervisor)

NOAH BUTT

(Confrontational) Well, Mr. Isle, it appears that the prongs on the last forty dozen Western Wangos were crooked. I believe the Beer-Belly Wrap-Around is your department.

DENNY ISLE

(Defensive) No, it's not all my department. Other people work there.

NOAH BUTT

We have belts that won't buckle, Isle. I have no choice but to write you up for lack of coordination.

DENNY ISLE

You could handle this some other way. You don't have to pick on me.

NOAH BUTT

Mr. Isle, we have redneck truckers who are going to tie up traffic in half the western United States because they won't be able to get their pants together.

DENNY ISLE

But —

NOAH BUTT

It's Mr. Butt to you.

DENNY ISLE

This sucks. I don't know why you don't write up a few of the other guys. Give them the five second Fasten/Loosen test.

NOAH BUTT

(**Sarcastically**) If I was doing an F & L drill, you wouldn't be here by yourself. Look here, Mr. Isle, you've got your head so far up your ten gallon you're not seeing my point.

DENNY ISLE

No, I'm not, because there is no point.

NOAH BUTT

No?

DENNY ISLE

No.

NOAH BUTT

(Incredulous) No?!!

DENNY ISLE

(Emphatically) No!

NOAH BUTT

(Challenging) Did I hear you say "no"?

DENNY ISLE

(Rethinking his position) No.

NOAH BUTT

What are you saying, then?

DENNY ISLE

Never mind. **(A faint cow bell clangs in the background. Suddenly there is the sound of a thundering buffalo stampede)** Oh! It's lunch time. I gotta get to the Oscar Meyer wiener before all the dogs are gone. **(He rises to exit)**

NOAH BUTT

But, no, uh … **(too late, he's gone).** I hate talking to myself!

-Lights-

Chapter 13

A Pleasant Scene
Yes, and ...

Holy cow, are there lessons to be learned from Denny and Noah! Lessons about how to maneuver wayward conversations, or reroute faulty ones. Though I won't be covering ways in which to stay alive as you work your way through the lunch line in this chapter, I will offer ways in which you can steer clear of any similar negative communications. Actually, this chapter will be a continuation of the last chapter, delving more deeply into ways you can successfully lick the refusal/denial dilemma — ways to re-program yourself as you respond and react to others.

As I begin to focus more sharply on refusal and denial, I first want to point out that the last scene was yet another example of how a piece of communication gets undermined by way of word choices and attitudes. As we take the scene apart, you will begin to understand more fully the importance of sticking to the precepts behind the refusal/denial rule.

Let's take a look -- and a good listen — to the dialogue that was exchanged between the two characters. As you could plainly see, both Denny and Noah were committing the two mortal sins of improv comedy. They openly denied one another, and, yes, there were refusals along the way, as well. As such, they got absolutely nowhere with each other. Neither did they complete their scene. True, Isle's exit ended the conversation, but that's very different from the notion of *completing* a piece of communication.

Now, it would have been perfectly fine for the Human Resource Director to confront his belt-maker, and vice versa —they could have disagreed — but the way in which they went about it pre-cluded their communication from being just that: communication. Without really knowing it, they chose not to communicate at all. Thanks to the choices they made with regard to exchanging ideas and feelings, their verbal trade had little substantive content and therefore little meaning, and of course, as I already pointed out, no concrete resolution.

Now, I realize it's not uncommon to be headstrong in the business arena where pressures are often so great. What regularly happens is that each of us has a point of view — or a strong opinion or idea — and to make our point, we dig in our heels, drilling as we go a deeper hole in order to stand our ground. Unfortunately, by doing so we spin many a conversation in a circle. We just keep going round and round, back and forth, like a taffy making machine; we spin, they yank. They tug, we pull. And all the while, of course, we're creating a very frustrating atmosphere for ourselves and those around us. In the end, there is no end, because when we continue to refuse and deny, our exchange of words doesn't really accomplish anything. Quite the opposite: we continually find ourselves at a stalemate. Ergo — communication rut.

If you're a person who often finds yourself at an impasse or deadlocked on an issue, you can be relatively certain you're operating in a state of refusal and denial, the state which occurs when two people are going in two different directions while engaged in the same conversation. This isn't to say that you can't have opposing views on an issue; it just means that as you disagree, you should follow a format, a flow that keeps the argument intact.

Fortunately, for all of us there are more tricks in the improv actor's bag — tricks you as a business professional can use to keep from getting caught in the traps of refusal and denial. As I explained earlier, it's not that we train improv actors to think differently. Instead, we train them to process information differently. And one of our processing tricks — for the improv player, it's a hard-and-fast rule from day one — is the use of what we call the "Yes, and … " theory.

Ah, yes, the "Yes, and … " theory. It means we go *with* whatever is happening. It means we travel along the same verbal path as that of our partner (or partners). We react and respond. We serve and support. We stay clearly in the moment. By so doing, we can still have different ideas and express true feelings that don't always coincide with our speaking counterpart — but each conversation will be threaded together tightly. The result: Each piece of communication has meaning and, nearly always, resolution.

Here's how the "Yes, and ... "theory works: You simply think in terms of "Yes, and ... " prior to expressing any sentiment. In improv class, when first grasping this rule, you're instructed during each scene to begin each and every sentence with the words "Yes, and ... ." Doing this makes it impossible for anyone to remain in a state of refusal and/or (especially) denial. It safeguards all communication among the actors. It assures that no matter someone's opinion or feeling, the other actor (or actors) will automatically go with each and every idea expressed.

In order to illustrate the validity of the concept, let's revisit a bit of dialogue in our last scene. When Mr. Butt was confronting Mr. Isle with "I believe the Beer-Belly Wrap-Around is your department," Mr. Isle responded with "No, it's not all my department. Other people work there." Now, what if Isle had followed Butt's remark with the "Yes, and ... " principle? Imagine if he had said something like: "Yes, and in that department there are other people, as well." He would still have been stating his point of view — only without denying Butt. Butt could have then countered with, "Yes, and I want you and the others in your department to know we have belts that won't buckle. I have no choice but to write you up for lack of coordination." Isle, then: "Yes, and I believe you could handle this some other way. You don't have to pick on me." Again, the same ideas are put forth. They're just put forth differently. By using the "Yes, and ... " theory, you can handle disagreements smoothly.

It's strange at first for the improv player to try this theory. People resist the idea because they don't feel like it will work. Yet once they do try it and see how splendidly it works, they wouldn't think of communicating in any other way. They know from experience, in a relatively short period of time, that using "Yes, and ..." keeps conversationalists on the same path.   They may not know exactly where they'll end up, but they know they'll get there together.

The same holds true for the business professional. We, too, can use the "Yes, and ... " idea as we engage in each and every one of our daily communications.

You're probably thinking: "I can't go around saying 'Yes, and ... all the time." And, in fact, you're right. You can't. But if you practice using the rule for a time, it will become a part of you as it does for the accomplished improv actor. If you practice saying "Yes, and ... " repeatedly, you eventually change the way you process information. This is because as you follow the "Yes, and ..." train of thought, you soon develop a "Yes, and ... " mentality. Eventually, you shed the phrase "Yes, and ... " and simply react with responses that bolster the philosophy. So, while the words "Yes, and ... " don't precede every sentence, the "Yes, and ... " mindset does.

If you doubt that it's possible to challenge, disagree, confront or argue using the "Yes, and ... " principle, let me prove to you otherwise. Let's consider an example. Let's say two women are having a conversation about artichokes. Ethel and Mabel, we'll call them. Two women who disagree.

Take One:

ETHEL

We'll just serve artichokes. If they don't like them, the heck with them.

MABEL

No, I think we should serve stewed tomatoes.

ETHEL

Gross. No one wants to dip those in mayonnaise and butter.

MABEL

I say nix the condiments. Tomatoes are cheaper.

ETHEL

No. They're not. Not this time of year.

MABEL

You're wrong. They're five times less expensive.

Get the picture? Okay, now let's run that same snippet of conversation implementing the "Yes, and … "theory – using it like the improv player would.

Take Two:

ETHEL

Yes, and we'll just serve artichokes. If they don't like them, to heck with them.

MABEL

Yes, and if they don't like artichokes, I suggest we serve stewed tomatoes.

ETHEL

Yes, and the problem with serving stewed tomatoes is they're gross. I doubt anyone would want to dip those in mayonnaise and butter.

MABEL

Yes, and they probably won't, so let's nix the condiments

and simply serve the tomatoes. After all, they're cheaper.

ETHEL

Yes, and I see that's your understanding — that the price of tomatoes this time of year is cheaper. I'm rather certain they're five times as much as you think they are.

MABEL

Yes, and I know you're certain in your own mind of that, and I know I'm right. They are cheaper.

Though the two women were polarized on what vegetable to serve and what it cost, they still went down the same communication trail with one another; their discussion had a flow. Also, if you noticed, with each and every response, they continued to acknowledge and consider the other's ideas and opinions though they strongly disagreed. This kept their communication much tighter than it had been in Take One.

What happens when you use the "Yes, and ... " theory is that it tends to put a more positive spin on any conversation, whether you're in accord with the others or not. It's nearly impossible to set up bad vibes when conversations are approached from a "Yes, and ... " mode. The reason: there is no refusal or denial present.

You might be thinking: "Habits are so hard to break. How can I change the way I talk to people?" And it's true that much of our behavior is knee-jerk -- habitual and programmed — but you simply re-program, that's all. It won't take long, either, if you focus on it. And practice, practice, practice. You'll begin to notice that you no longer butt up against people; instead, you go with the flow of wherever they go. When you get really proficient at implementing the rule, you'll get others to go with *your* flow. It's a wonderfully powerful tool, this "Yes, and ... " thing; it actually gives you more control over the outcome of each "scene." If you're going where "they're" going, you're not in a constant tug of war over who's got the upper hand. Good improv players know this. They know that no matter how much their scene-partner may deny or refuse them, if they simply go along for the ride, they're still in the driver's seat.

Of course, those times when you're in accord with the people you're speaking with, using the "Yes, and ... " rule simply makes your dialogue wonderfully tighter. In these situations, we implement yet another improv rule -- the "adding information" principle. This I'll cover in the next chapter. For now, here are some assignments to aid you in using and reaping the rewards of "Yes, and ....".

1. Start by saying "Yes, and ... " during your self-appointed rehearsal times. If, at first, you're a bit reluctant to burst into the office pronouncing "yes, and ... " you can always start your practice sessions at home with an obstinate teenager (I do this!) or someone who doesn't impact your work environment. It will get you in the spirit. Soon enough, you will take the tool to work and, when you do, I'm absolutely certain you will find a marked difference in how others react to you. Eventually, you'll use the principle everywhere!

2. Prepare for crucial meetings (or other important "scene" moments where you think you're liable to encounter some conflict) by writing out a script of what you think the other person will say. Write your answers and retorts in the "Yes, and ... " mode. This is just one more way to reinforce the use of the principle and to focus on how well it works.

3. Keep a journal or log that tracks how often, in any given business day, you opted for the "Yes, and ... " principle. Give yourself points for the times you know your use of the rule helped keep the conversation on course, or avoided bad vibes. Also give points for times you didn't fall into the refusal/denial pit. As you design your point system, plan some type of reward program to go with it. We all need pay-offs for a job well done. I do chocolate!

4. Keep your eye on others when they converse. Notice when they seem to be going with and against their "scene" partner.

Take notes if you can, jotting down explicit instances where the "Yes, and … " rule could have been used. This will help you reinforce the rule.

5. Don't think ahead. Don't, as I tell my students, think globally. Don't try to project where you think the conversation should be going. Just stay in the moment, as I discussed before, and trust that the "Yes, and … " of it all will get you to where you need to go. Planning ahead is dangerous; it tempts you to want to control what the other person is saying and that's something you just can't do. If you react and respond to the last thing said, the last idea held, with "Yes, and … ," you can't fail.

6. If you can tape any of your conversations or communications, do so. The ability to play back conversations is one more way to see where they bog down and where they worked. You can also take the liberty of re-writing such "scenes," fully using the "Yes, and … " principle.

Now, let's return to the Mr. Isle and Mr. Butt discourse and approach it from the "Yes, and … " mindset.

TAKE TWO: "Words At Wango Chorale"

(Int. Human Resources office at a belt buckle plant. The director is giving a review to a Quality Control Supervisor)

NOAH BUTT

(In his face) Yes, and Mr. Isle, it appears that the prongs on the last forty dozen Western Wangos were crooked. I believe the Beer-Belly Wrap-Around is your department.

DENNY ISLE

(Standing tall) Yes, and it is, though it's not *all* my department. Other people work there, too.

NOAH BUTT

Yes, and whoever's responsible, we now have belts that won't buckle, Isle. I have no choice but to write you up for lack of coordination.

DENNY ISLE

Yes, and I believe you could handle this some other way. Maybe pick on some of the other guys besides me.

NOAH BUTT

Yes, and, Mr. Isle, I could. By the way, did you know we have redneck truckers who are going to tie up traffic in half the western United States because they won't be able to get their pants together?

DENNY ISLE

Yes, and …

NOAH BUTT

(Upset) Yes, and that's a rotund of a problem.

DENNY ISLE

(Upset, too) Yes, and it is, and the whole thing sucks. The pants, the belts — and I don't know why you don't write up a few of the other guys while you're at it and maybe give them the five-second Fasten/Loosen test.

NOAH BUTT

(**Sarcastically**) Yes, and if I was doing an F& L drill you wouldn't be here by yourself. That alone tells me you've got your head so far up your ten gallon, you're not seeing my point.

DENNY ISLE

Yes, and that's true. I'm not because there is no point.

NOAH BUTT

Yes, and it sounds like you think there really isn't.

DENNY ISLE

Yes, and I think there isn't.

NOAH BUTT

(**Matter of fact**) Yes, and then I suppose you think something else.

DENNY ISLE

(**Sure of himself**) Yes, and I do, and I was going to say I think everything's okay, though you see it differently.

NOAH BUTT

(**On task**) Yes, and here we are, Isle, talking about our differences.

DENNY ISLE

Yes, and I'd love to talk more about them. (**A faint cow**

bell clangs in the background — then the sound of a thundering buffalo stampede) So I suggest we do that over an Oscar Meyer wiener. **(He rises to exit)** I'm going to get one before they're all gone.

NOAH BUTT

Yes, and get me one, too — with mustard, relish ... .

DENNY ISLE

(Exiting, we hear him faintly yell) Yes, and I'll get you the usual amount of onions!

-Lights-

Chapter 14

Making More of A Scene
Adding Information

TAKE ONE: "After The Bored Meeting"

(Two guys at a posh marble conference table, slumped over, tuckered out, spent. They've just completed a 12-hour meeting with what seemed like the grand jury of stockholders)

MR. BINAIRE

(Arms spread straight out, head resting with chin planted on top of table. Staring blankly. He's monotone) Well, that was sweet.

MR. DUNATT

(Fetal position, curled up in his chair) Yes, that was sweet.

MR. BINAIRE

It seemed like forever.

MR. DUNATT

It sure did.

MR. BINAIRE

I want a beer.

MR. DUNATT

Me, too.

MR. BINAIRE

(Teeth clinking, they're so close together) I'm glad they liked the So-What deal.

MR. DUNATT

Yeah, So-What.

MR. BINAIRE

I bet it takes another eight hours to get them off the fence on the Now-What deal.

MR. DUNATT

(Curling tighter) Touché. Now what?

MR. BINAIRE

If I ever get the energy to move again, I'm going to swallow down the entire drinking fountain.

MR. DUNATT

(Parched) Sounds like a plan.

(The two remain silent and motionless. Their eyes occasionally blink as the sun sets)

-Lights-

Chapter 14

Making More Of A Scene
Adding Information

As I pointed out in the last chapter, it's almost impossible to have a piece of communication falter when you operate from the "Yes, and ... " theory. And indeed, the theory was in place in our scene with the two guys in the board room. They were "going with" each other — "Yes, and-ing" all the way. In other words, no refusal or denial. Thus they had a smooth piece of communication.

But in the improv player's manual, there is yet another idea — an adjunct to the basic "Yes, and ... " theory — an additional principle that further strengthens and unifies communication. We call it the principle of "Adding Information" and here's how it goes: You simply add to — expound on — the very last thing said or last idea held. We've already covered the "last thing said, last idea held" concept, but as a reminder, I just want to reiterate that we as improv actors are mandated to "React and Respond" to *only* the very last thing we hear or see.

The way in which we are able to uphold that very precious principle is, first, to go with the notion of "Yes, and ... ." After establishing that, we paint a broader picture by extending or embellishing upon the idea, thought or feeling expressed. We are constantly conscious of making more out of what is presented — we are instinctively aware of the need to continually develop what the other actor or actors have laid before us. In theory, simple. But not always easy.

"Adding Information" requires that we listen intently and that we be disciplined to stay in the moment. Never anywhere else. If we add something new — something that ties to or expands on what has most recently transpired — we're home free. Let's say, for example, that one actor initiates a scene not in words but in action. He slams a door. In keeping with the "Adding Information" tenet, the other actor might slam two doors and several drawers. Adhering to the "Yes, and … " principle and that of "Adding Information," the first actor might then knock over a table. In response to that, the second actor throws a lamp against the wall. Now, as he throws that lamp, the other actor might catch it. There the dialogue might begin, with the lamp-thrower saying something like "Nice catch." The other actor might respond, as he hurls the sofa toward the door, "Well, catch this!" The scene would then continue along those lines, threading nicely, each actor playing off the other as they add information.

In the real world of business, the theory functions as beautifully as it does in an improv comedy scene. It's important to "React and Respond." It's important to "Yes, and … ." But only when we add information is in-depth communication developed. By "Adding Information," more and more is revealed and shared, providing greater insight and understanding. Scenes are more productive, more interesting and, in the end, far more results-oriented. It's one more way to get somewhere with the business associate with whom you're talking. Simply focus on expanding or expounding upon what the other person or persons are saying or doing.

This way of going about communication is especially helpful to creative teams, to those who convene to solve problems, and to planning committees, to name but a few. It's also helpful during a Q &A session at a talk, during a seminar, or at a sales pitch. And it would have been very helpful to our friends Dunatt and Binaire. In Take One: "After The Bored Meeting," Dunatt and Binaire were certainly in the "Yes, and … " mode. They were definitely on the same page, so in my book they were halfway there. But because they weren't adding much information, their conversation didn't cover a whole lot of ground. They were in accord — in agreement, true — but they could have gotten far more out of their exchange if each had made more out of the other's remarks.

For example, when Binaire said, "I want a beer," Dunatt, instead of saying only "Me, too," could have replied, "I, too, want a beer, and a pizza and a large fruit basket." In response to that, Binaire could have said, "Yes, and in that fruit basket I hope there's three pomegranates and four kiwis." Now, if Dunatt continued to "Add Information" to Binaire's remarks, he might have said, "I pray for not only those two special fruits, but I also hope for bananas. Lots of them. I'm deplete in potassium." Dunatt: "Yeah? Sorry to hear that. Well, I'm low in blood sugar," and so on. By tagging on more information, their conversation could have continued to get tighter and tighter as they stitched their responses together, sewing one idea to the next. As they proceeded it would not have mattered where exactly the conversation led; wherever it traveled, the twosome would have gone there together. As the song says: *"Wherever we go/whatever we do/we're going to go through it together...."* That's all that matters. That's what makes for good, strong communication — that people talking to one another are mentally aligned — that they are closely linked as they express and share their thoughts, ideas and feelings.

As I've mentioned, as improv players in the improv setting, we know that when we "Yes, and ... " and subsequently "Add Information," we can't possibly fail. It's absolutely, positively impossible. Granted, I have seen many scenes end up far removed from the ideas that actually opened them, but just as in our day-to-day business communications, that doesn't really matter. What does count is that all the players are moving along together, in theory and context, every step of the way. For improv players, playing to and off of one another's thoughts, feelings and ideas ensures that they will all end up in the same place. They will reach the finish line in a unified manner simply because their communication has been neatly tied together.

In our work on stage, we never project ahead. To us it makes no difference whatsoever where a scene ends up. Instead, we focus on staying closely knit through each piece of dialogue (or action). We know that doing so will make each scene complete and whole. When you step back and think through how some of your business scenes could have benefited from this approach, I'm sure you'll agree that this method of discourse builds far more rapport. But business professionals tend to jump ahead, to anticipate. We are obsessively conscious of the need to control the communication. We think things like: What if the conversation gets off course? What if they change the subject? Well, I say so what? When partners in communication, you can always steer the "scene" back toward a certain goal. Why threaten an entire piece of communication by responding to what hasn't even happened?

Many business executives tell me that they fear their conversations will go awry or out of control if they "Add Information." Ironically, though, "Adding Information" is the very tenet that removes any reason for such fear. "Adding Information" is the cement that holds dialogue together and helps it build on itself. You have much more control when you use the rule — not less. If you stay fully in tune with the other person or persons in the course of any conversation, you'll have an excellent chance of assuring communication that has meaning and substance, not to mention positive results. So then, stop spending so much time thinking ahead — planning where and how you think your communications should go. It's only when each communicator tries to control and maneuver the conversation the way he or she *thinks* it should go that things fall apart or end inconclusively. The following snippets of conversations — business in nature — illustrate the effectiveness — before and after — of "Adding Information":

TAKE ONE: "Once Around The Water Cooler"

(Int. lunch room. Two guys standing, slumped, facing the water cooler, cups in hand, just staring and lost in thought. One of them breaks the silence)

CARLISLE

(Noticeably burned out and bored with the same routine. Subtly tries to get his colleague on board with the possibility of something different) I feel like putting Kool-Aid in this cooler. I'm tired of water.

BENNETT

(**Feeling just as hopeless**) Yeah, me, too.

CARLISLE

(**A bit inspired hearing he's not alone. Decides to share some possibilities, hoping to get Bennett on board**) Maybe besides some flavor, some ice cubes, too.

BENNETT

(**Hoping Carlisle will expound, so he doesn't have to come up with any creative answers besides the Kool-Aid**) Good idea.

CARLISLE

(**Waiting to see if Bennett has any suggestions. Nothing. So now he tries to get Bennett as an ally regarding the flimsy paper cup dilemma**) These damn little cheap cups keep folding up on me.

BENNETT

(**Well aware of having the same problem. But offering no help. Suddenly, his cup folds up and he spills water on his tie, again**) Bummer … .

TAKE TWO: "Once Around The Water Cooler"

(**Same visual**)

CARLISLE

(**Noticeably burned out and bored with the same after-noon water break. Subtly tries to get his colleague on**

board with something different) I feel like putting Kool-Aid in this cooler. I'm tired of water.

                    BENNETT

(Hopeless, but goes along with that idea) Yeah, water's gettin' real old, man.

                    CARLISLE

(Leads him on) *Real* old, man. I was thinking something tart or tangy.

                    BENNETT

(That thought triggers a brainstorm. He shares it) Cherry flavor sounds good.

                    CARLISLE

(He likes the idea of cherry. Takes that idea a step further) Maybe cherry with grape ice cubes.

                    BENNETT

(Bennett likes what he hears. He offers an additional solution) Yeah. Cubes that taste like grape — with little peelings hidden inside them.

                    CARLISLE

(He's overwhelmed at the possibility. He lets his mind travel that trail) Yeah, if I could collect enough peelings I could pack them into the bottom of this cheap cup so it'd stop folding up on me.

BENNETT

(**Wiping the water off his tie, again. That remark reminds Bennett of his desk chair**) Only thing worse than a folding cup folding up on ya is a folding chair folding up on ya.

CARLISLE

(**Stays on the same page as Bennett**) Yeah, especially when you're sittin' in it.

You can easily see how much tighter and more productive this short passage of conversation was when the two added information to the other's remarks.

Here's one more.

TAKE ONE: "Fed Up At Lunch"

(**Int. upscale restaurant. Two co-workers from the marketing department seated at a linen-covered table, waiting for the check. Connors can't wait any longer. He wants the scoop on the rumor that Flanders is changing departments**)

CONNERS

(**Digging for the story behind Flanders' sudden occupational in-house company move**) So, Barnes tells me you're moving from marketing to purchasing.

FLANDERS

(**Holding back. Reluctant to reveal anything**) Yep, I'm moving.

CONNNERS

(Growing more curious. Subtly trying to get Flanders to spill his guts) Purchasing must have something particularly intriguing for you to make that shift.

FLANDERS

(Still playing cloak and dagger) Boy, I'll say it does.

CONNERS

(Getting exasperated but not letting it show. Instead, hoping to nudge him into telling him why he's changing positions) Yeah?

FLANDERS

(Taking that remark no further) Yeah!

Talk about a conversation going nowhere! So let's run that one more time, only this time let's use the "Adding Information" principle.

TAKE TWO: "Fed Up At Lunch"

(Same visual)

CONNERS

(Digging for the story behind Flanders' sudden occupational in-house company move) So, Barnes tells me you're moving from marketing to purchasing.

FLANDERS

(Being up front and direct about it) Yep, tomorrow I

make that historic move and someday I hope to head the department.

CONNERS

(Fascinated at this revelation. Hopes to learn more. Maybe Flanders will consider taking him with him) Wow! For you to want to be in charge must mean that you find something particularly intriguing about making such a shift.

FLANDERS

(Proud of sharing what makes him tick) Yep. What fascinates me is the money. I get to count the money all day. I love money.

CONNERS

(Realizing they share common ground. Decides to share his innermost feelings) I, too, love money — money that's my own, that is.

FLANDERS

(Feeling a real kinship with Connors, now) Hey, nothing like your own money. I'll have much more of my own money when I head the department because I intend to fire everyone else and bag their salaries.

(Connors lunges for the check. Flanders quickly notices)

FLANDERS

Well, I'll still a need a few good men, Connors.

There is a sense of closure with this conversation the second time around. Granted, in both the above snippets there was a "Yes, and ... " mentality, but again, it's hard to move communication forward — it's hard for anything substantial to develop — when you don't "Add Information."

Here's what else you'll begin to experience when you use the "Adding Information" principle in conjunction with the "Yes, and ... " theory: You'll actually have a sense of safety and comfort, consistently, in every verbal exchange. No conversation will ever make you feel uneasy again. Because, you see, if you're not projecting ahead, if you're not trying to control the outcome, if you're not trying to "direct and instruct," if you're not glued to your own agenda — the dialogue between you and others will probably just flow. And it's in that flow that you get somewhere. Let go the idea that conversations have to unravel the way you pictured they would. Don't predict. Just follow the rules, step by step, and watch the amazing results. Knowing that you're safe and secure helps to boost your confidence no matter who you're talking to. And as any Director will tell you, confidence sells any audience. (Note to all you men: a recent survey in a major women's magazine cited confidence as the number-one sexiest thing women found in men.)

Your follow-up assignments depend on your staying conscious of what the other person or persons are saying, and doing your very best not only to "go with" — to "Yes, and ... ," but also to add something meaningful to the last thing said or last idea held.

1. Start by noticing how many work-related conversations you feel you need to control while in the midst of them. Are you constantly trying to reorient, maneuver, manipulate, steer, direct, or otherwise take over? A great actor is a great observer, so a conscious awareness of how often you don't listen is the best way to begin to reprogram your communication behavior.

2. During one conversation a day, practice on a colleague — someone you trust and are familiar with — by adding information to whatever they say. Try to listen carefully to the last thing they say or last idea they express. Make sure your comments are direct responses only to the last thing said and not to

what they expressed a few sentences ago. Keep a journal of your feelings about how you think these conversations went. Were they productive? Were they tight? What did you accomplish by adding information? Were there reasonable "endings" — conclusions?

3. Sit in on conversations where you're not an active participant. Just listen. Are those who purport to be conversing really communicating? Who adds information and who doesn't? What are the results? Do the scenes you witness have closure? `Is anything meaningful being accomplished? Even if they're on the same page, are the participants moving the communication forward? I often tell my students that watching those on stage is far more valuable in terms of getting the lesson than actually doing it. So, if you choose one conversation a day, do this exercise diligently. Soon you'll be rewriting those scenes in your head (do it on paper, too) and you'll see the value of the "Adding Information" rule.

4. Vow to add information to more than one conversation a day. Build that number steadily until every conversation you engage in includes the use of the "Adding Information" tenet. Give yourself points every time you score big in terms of rapport, a sale, or just good, clear and tight communication. Now reward yourself for those efforts. You deserve it.

5. Actually write out the responses you wish you had given in certain conversations that you missed or overlooked. Writing things out so that you can rewrite them is a wonderful training tool. People who write for a living will tell you their thoughts are much more clearly expressed when they put them down on paper, then revise them. Don't be afraid to take one "scene" and rewrite it several ways using the "Adding Information" rule. The good news is there are always options; there are many ways a "scene" can go. So long as you're adding information, you can't go wrong.

Now for kicks, let's go back to that marble-top conference table with our two jelled-out execs and run their scene one more time.

TAKE TWO: "After The Bored Meeting"

(Two guys at a posh marble conference table, slumped over, tuckered out, spent. They've just completed a 12-hour meeting with what seemed like the grand jury of stockholders)

MR. BINAIRE

(Arms spread straight out, head resting with chin planted on top of table. Staring blankly. He's monotone) Well, that was sweet.

MR. DUNATT

(Fetal position curled up in his chair) Yes, sweet and long, real long, like longer than eternity.

MR. BINAIRE

It did seem like forever.

MR. DUNATT

Forever and a day.

MR. BINAIRE

I think it's been that long since I had something to drink. I want a beer.

MR. DUNATT

Yeah, a beer with some beer nuts.

MR. BINAIRE

Speaking of nuts, they went crazy for the So-What deal, huh?

MR. DUNATT

So-What! Yeah, those so and so's were flippin.' They even bit on the That's-What deal.

MR BINAIRE

That's-What and What's-What look promising, yes. Wish we could get them to buy off on the Now-What deal. It's going to take at least another eight hours to get them off the fence on that one.

MR. DUNATT

Nothing worse than a bunch of ol' farts sitting on a fence 'cause you never know which way a fart will go.

MR. BINAIRE

Or if it will go at all. **(Reflective)** Now-What. That one is a bugger!

MR. DUNATT

What now?

MR. BINAIRE

If I ever get the energy to move again, I'm going to swallow the entire drinking fountain.

MR. DUNATT

Me, I'm taking on the atrium waterfall in the central courtyard.

(The two remain silent and motionless. Their eyes occasionally blink as the sun sets)

-Lights-

Chapter 15

Scene Cues
Listening: Surface and Subtext

TAKE ONE: "Hear Say!"

(**Two corporate intern trainees are on hand for a briefing with the company's Human Resource Director on Project Hear Say. They're seated at a small table in the Director's office suite, each preoccupied with their own stuff. The Director enters)**

LIL LOWDER

(She's fidgeting with her starched Peter-Pan collar. As she comes upon the interns she appears irritated. Sarcastically) Well, I see you two are ready for the briefing on the Hear Say project.

CEY WHA

(Still into the doodle on his pad) Huh? Oh, yes. Hear Say. Sounds intriguing.

GUS AERYA

(Checking a sudden incoming page. Responding halfheartedly) Sounds, uh, what?

LIL LOWDER

(**Getting really annoyed and raising her voice**) Hear
Say, damn it, everybody's talking about someone and
somebody's talking about everyone and now it's gotten to
the point where anybody's telling anyone anything. I'm
not sure what the dirt is around here — I just want to
know what's going on or if what they're saying is just
what people think they're hearing or if what they're hearing is … oh, never mind. I just want to get to
the bottom of it.

(**Lil awaits a response for what seems like an eternity**)

CEY WHA

(**Folding his doodled page into a cootie catcher**) I'm
sorry, did you say something?

GUS AERYA

Could you repeat that?

LIL LOWDER

(**Her volume rising with her obvious inner tension**) I
said, people are gossiping all over this facility and I don't
know fact from fiction. It's up to you two to find out
what's going on here!

GUS AERYA

(**Fogged out from reading his pager again**) Maybe we
should find out what's going on here.

CEY WHA

(**Constructing a paper airplane. Begins to sing**) Fly
Me To The Moon/And Let Me Play Among ... (**Suddenly
stops with a bright idea**) I don't know if you've gotten to
this, but I think Gus and I should get to the bottom of this
Hear Say thing.

GUS AERYA

Hmm? Did somebody call me?

LIL LOWDER

(**In total exasperation, she rips the collar off her dress.
Between clinched teeth**) I'm going to say it one more
time ...

GUS AERYA

(**Squinting hard to read the incoming number on his
pager**) Excuse me, Miss Lowder. Were you going to say
something?

CEY WHA

(**Directing his remark at Gus**) Did you say something?

LIL LOWDER

(**Shrieking with rage**) Yes, I did — I was — going to say
something. (**Imploding with a heated snarl**) I was going
to say what a wonderful meeting this is and what a wonderful time I'm having with you two interns.

CEY WHA

I'm sorry, you said … ?

GUS AERYA

Could you repeat that?

**(Lowder lets go a groan that deflates all her air. She crumples
to the floor)**

CEY WHA

(To Gus) Wow, did you hear that?

GUS AYERA

Hear what?

-Lights-

Chapter 15

Scene Cues
Listening: Surface and Subtext

I don't know about you but I have wanted to rip off more than my collar at some meetings. I've wanted to rip off people's heads! To hell with the consequences of aggravated assault — I'd rather do ten years in federal prison than have someone blow off my important dialogue. I hate it when people don't listen to me! But it happens all the time. Everyday. Everywhere.

If it happens to you, too — and I'd bet both my ears it does — you don't have the luxury of losing your cool like Lil Lowder did. Instead, we business professionals have to keep ourselves together. We don't really do ourselves any favors by lashing out at the wrong person at the wrong time. Unfortunately, to avoid lashing out, we often internalize our anger at being ignored. That internalization can lead to a slew of physical repercussions, from hives to heart attacks.

My unconscious reaction to the frustration of people not listening to me is to burn up loads of Seratonin. My brain becomes open season for Prozac. I remember the time I was asked to speak impromptu on the scope of my ExecuProv classes in front of a group of mechanical engineers. They had just been given handout materials by the person who preceded me. While I talked, they perused. When I finished, I asked, "Anyone have any questions?" Only one raised his hand. "Yes," he said, "Do you have any classes?" I went home and slept for 12 hours.

I don't think there is anything more frustrating or demoralizing than to have people tune you out. Not being listened to is painful and tiring. Nothing makes us feel less important or more insignificant than when someone doesn't seem to hear us — especially when we have something important to say (and most of us think everything we say is important). The irony is, as much as we hate being ignored, we ignore others all the time.

Incidentally, when I talk about ignoring — not listening — tuning out — I'm not talking only about the spoken word. I'm also talking about what isn't spoken. The subtext: what is not verbally said but expressed nonetheless. It's depressing when people don't pick up on our nuances and subtleties, our body language, our tone of voice. It's a humiliating kind of rejection that we feel in a very deep place.

So, just a little pop quiz here; how much do you really hear from the people who are speaking to you everyday?

If I were to list communication-skill deficiencies among the people who interact in the American workplace, I would put lack-of-listening at the very top of the page. I'd classify it first among the communication shortcomings of American business professionals, no matter their rank and file.

If you're completely honest, I'm sure you're ready to admit that you don't always listen to what others are saying. In fact, I believe the only time any of us really listens to everything being said is when someone is complimenting us. Unless, of course, you're the type who tends to be super-hard on yourself in which case you may listen most when someone is criticizing you. Me? Forget the criticism; I beat myself up really well. I listen more carefully to the good stuff. I love hearing it.

Why don't we listen? We might be bored with what is being presented to us. Something someone says might trigger ideas in our head, sending our mind spinning off in other directions. We might suddenly remember something we must take care of. The person we're with might be so attractive that we fantasize instead of focusing. Or, on the contrary, the person we're with might be so repulsive to us that we're escaping to more pleasant places. And sometimes we tune out for physical reasons: low blood sugar, anxiety, exhaustion or just plain not feeling good. But in communication, no excuses, we have to listen.

When it comes to listening, it's really very simple: Follow the "Golden Rule." Do unto others, in other words — though I realize that doing so consistently is difficult. It takes discipline, and most of us, myself included, didn't start out on the workplace trail with that in mind. No, most us had our focus on making the sale, whatever it was.

Yet, like so many other communications skills outlined in this book, it's never too late to get better at listening. It's just going to take some awareness and some re-programming. And the training regimen is something the whole corporate family can play. To listen more intently is to have the edge over all your competition, by the way, because listening to what someone is saying gives you ammo for more interesting and persuasive dialogue when it's time for you to do the talking.

In my ExecuProv program, increasing your listening abilities is termed "keening up your ear." It's very simple, really. We just teach people how to hear things they actually hear everyday but don't really listen to. Spoken or unspoken. Homework lessons might include the serious checking out of the variety of sounds a dishwasher makes. On a more advanced plane, students might be asked to pick up on the hidden meaning behind someone's tone of voice.

Now, as exaggerated as you may think Lil Lowder's meeting was, it was not. We're all in similar conversations every day, and we've been on both sides. Most of us know when people aren't listening to us, but we're not as proficient at detecting the moments we actively or subconsciously decide not to listen to someone else. I'm willing to bet that if you carried a tape recorder and taped your various "scenes," come playback time you'd flip over how many people you blatantly ignored (without really meaning to, of course).

I'm going to ask you to refer back to Chapter 12 for just a moment to recall one of its messages: When you don't listen, you're in the "Refusal" trap. Remember? And to refuse is to lose.

There is no way, in the work-world as we all know it, to maximize communications with others without continuous listening.

Indeed, when consistent listening is lacking, most of our conversations sooner or later reach a stalemate status. They simply can't grow or move forward, because there is no real connection. Without listening, people cut each other off.

Again, it takes tremendous discipline to hear everything being said around you, but hear you must if you want to play improv with the pros. And whether you're an actor or a business professional, you are playing improv every day.

So, in revisiting the improv comedy player's manual, it's interesting to note that a great deal of emphasis in the first few weeks of training is always placed on learning the drills for better listening. Until students acquire impeccable listening skills, they can't go on to master the other disciplines. Listening, for them, is not just intermittent, either. They don't engage in the practice of listening only when something piques their interest. They're not in and out of their listening; they're fully engaged in the process every single moment. They're trained well to listen to the good, the bad and the boring. And during the intense early-stages of listening drills, they are trained to take in not only every verbal cue but those other things — those loud and clear messages that have no words attached to them at all. Facial expressions, attitude shifts, distinctive body language, subtle idiosyncrasies. Until my students master this, I won't take them further — not because I'm being difficult, but because I know they can't possibly survive on stage without near-perfect listening skills.

For improv performers, there is no margin for error when it comes to listening onstage in a scene setting. The step-by-step development of a scene and the scene's ultimate outcome depend on it. Your business meetings — whether by phone or in person — are the same as the improv actor's stage scenes. They entail the same skills — skills which take time to grasp and lots of due diligence to become habit.

One of the tricks improv players use to listen constantly is to remember the "Be Here Now" principle. Always stay in the moment — if you do this, you will always be current with what is being said. There is no way your mind can tune out or wander. But again, first you develop discipline, then it becomes second nature.

One more reason improv comedy players place such emphasis on listening is that very often they may not be a starting player in a scene. They may be off-stage, looking for opportunities to jump in, to make themselves part of the goings-on. As business professionals, are we any different? Of course not. You know how it goes: A meeting starts; two people are talking; you're on the sidelines. Now, if you've not been listening to everything, you may enter that "scene" awkwardly or never at all. So, think the way the improv actor does: "I'm listening to everything so I can become part of the piece in a meaningful way at the right moment in time."

What I'm saying here is: Be ready to play off someone. As we already discussed, it's virtually impossible to play off someone if you haven't been listening to them every step of the way. Most of us listen partially and respond appropriately, sometimes, but a premier listener will listen to everything.

Though I'm not asking you to become as multi-dimensional in your listening as the improv player, I do want to point out that because they train so rigorously, they can actually hear several things simultaneously. For instance, the ring of the phone, the surprise statement of another actor, a third actor making an entrance, a fourth one expressing a subtle body-language message. In nanosecond succession, all are heard in the improv actor's ear as quickly as they happen. Because the listening is so intent, the actor can translate the information and respond to it with no hesitation. This comes only as a result of a tremendous sense of alertness, constant awareness and a commitment to stay attentive to the goings-on of the moment. "Quick" is what we call people who can do it. And we can all become expeditious if we work at it.

Now it's time to share the improv actor's secrets for listening boot-camp. As you can imagine, all the drills are mental ones.

1. First, as I alluded to earlier, improv actors are forced to be more cognizant of their surroundings. Next, they find themselves more focused on the smallest of details. You can do the same. For instance, turn on some music and listen to select parts of a recording — maybe the violin section of a symphony orchestra. Now get a little more advanced; listen to the not-so-obvious:

the rhythm of dripping faucets; jackhammers, footsteps. Basic things — silly things you may think at first. But my rule for my actors is, everything is fair game. If you can hear *something*, you're listening. So consider this: Everything can be listened to, even silence. Sitting very still and communing with what's around you is a wonderful way to kick off your program — to start increasing the listen-ability of your ear! Next, you can begin to listen to people — if only one conversation a day to begin with — until listening all of the time becomes routine.

2. Focus on the "surface" stuff when you first do your listening. You want to master the obvious. Take your time. Several weeks of listening every day to something you never "heard" before (a chirping bird, a whirling fan, a creaking floor board) builds listening strength. Soon your ear will signal your brain that it heard something new — something you ordinarily wouldn't catch.

3. Remember what I stated earlier. A good actor is a good observer. Take in everything around you — this time in the audio sense. Close your eyes when you first begin to warm up your ear; it's always easier to focus on your hearing with your eyes shut. My theory is, your eyes and ears compete for center stage, so let those lids fall for at least the time being. Later you'll get better at integrating what you see and what you hear.

4. Listen to newscasts, other people's conversations, talking that doesn't pertain to or involve you. Notice how much you do and don't hear. Watch how your listening is in and out. Anchor your ear to hear it all. When you start to drift, make an effort to pull yourself back. This will get easier each time.

5. As you go about building your listening acumen, spend some time just focusing or concentrating intently on something or someone. Do an activity in slow motion — no speeding up as you go along. This forces you to deepen your ability to concentrate. Focus and listening are inseparable!

6. The next step in the listening workout is to hear what is not said — in other words, the undercurrent. I'm of the belief that most people rarely say what they really mean or feel. Instead, they hedge — they beat around the bush hinting at what they really wish to express. So then, "listening" to body language, being more perceptive about what you hear in someone's tone of voice, becoming proficient at listening to the beneath-the-surface, between-the-lines messages — all of this will qualify you as a master listener. When it comes to body language, notice if someone is open and free or cross-armed and cross-legged. If they're folded up — pretzel-like, they're protecting themselves; if they keep turning their back as you speak, they're avoiding you. There are hundreds of screaming messages in a person's body language; you just need to learn how to read such signals. There are wonderful books out on the subject. Pick up a few and learn about listening to what someone's movements and posture are saying. Again, gaining such insight provides great fuel for something meaningful to say when it's your turn to speak. I often tell my ExecuProv students to just listen to subtext at certain meetings. They will get more of what is really going on by doing that than by just listening to the spoken word. So don't forget to spend as much time listening to subtext; it's critical. I maintain that more of your training time should go toward subtext because it's harder to "hear." People who are good at subtext are called perceptive. I believe we're all perceptive; we just don't tune in as often as we could. When you begin to communicate from the vantage point of someone's subtext you bond like you do in no other way. I'll cover this philosophy more in Part Two of the book.

7. Make a point of listening to at least one conversation, in total, every day. Your job is to hear everything that is being said the entire time. This includes any nonverbal messages, by the way. Now, see if you can extend that goal to two, and so forth. Soon you'll find yourself completely immersed in the conversation at hand. Eventually, this will become habitual. You'll simply get on the phone or enter a meeting and immediately lock in your

listening — both in regard to the spoken and unspoken messages.

One final note: In the workplace, we have a great deal to contend with. So listen we must in order to succeed. Listening promotes better relationships; relationships promote sales.

Once your listening skills are at Olympian levels, you will run circles around your competitors. Because remember — when you listen, you can play off the others; when you play off them, your communication becomes tight and cohesive. As a result, your exchanges build rapport. And in the end, once again, rapport is all that ever matters.

Now, let's return to the Hear Say briefing and see what happens when everyone is all ears!

TAKE TWO: "Hear Say!"

(Two corporate intern trainees are on hand for a briefing by the company's Human Resource Director on Project Hear Say. They're seated at a small table in the Director's office suite, each attending to one another and listening carefully to what the other is saying. The Director enters. They shift their eyes and ears to her)

LIL LOWDER

(She's fidgeting with her starched Peter Pan collar. As she comes upon the interns she returns their smiles)
Well, how nice, I see you two are ready for the briefing on the Hear Say Project.

CEY AND GUS

(In unison) We are!

CEY WHA

Boy, Hear Say. That sounds really intriguing.

LIL LOWDER

(Pleased at their attentiveness and interest) It is more than intriguing, gentlemen. It's sensational!

GUS AERYA

Oh, goodie, nothing like tabloid material.

LIL LOWDER

(Getting caught up in Gus' enthusiasm) Ah, yes! See, everybody's talking about someone and somebody's talking about everyone and now it's gotten to the point where anybody's telling anyone anything. I'm not sure what the dirt is around here — I just want to know what's going on or if what they're saying is **(laughs carelessly)** just what people think they're hearing or if what they're hearing is **(struggling for the right word)** —

CEY WHA

Hear Say?

LIL LOWDER

Precisely! And, boy, do I want to get to the bottom of it.

GUS AERYA

And so do we. So we intend to start at the top!

LIL LOWDER

At the top? Aha! That may mean the president is gossiping!

CEY WHA

(Starts singing to the tune of "Fly Me To The Moon")
Fly Me To The Top/And Let Me Peek In On the Brass —

GUS AERYA

(Continuing the song parody) If He's Taking Part/We're
Going To Have Him By The —

LIL LOWDER

Asssss-tronomical odds that that's the case, gentlemen! I
don't care if it's fact or fiction. I just want to find out! I
want to find out what everyone's saying! **(Shrieking with
such joy she rips off her collar and flings it into the air)**
Whoopee, what a wonderful meeting this has been. I'm
having a fabulous time with you two interns.

CEY WHA

**(Catching her collar on the way down and giving it
another Frisbee toss)** I've had a marvelous time myself.

GUS AERYA

**(Jumping to catch the collar, then aiming it toward Lil.
It ends up around her neck where it started)**
I've had the time of my life!

LIL LOWDER

**(She gestures to have them lean in. Then, confidential-
ly)** Say, did you hear about … .

(They listen intently)

-Lights-

Chapter 16

When It's Not What It Scenes To Be
Creating Into Certainty

TAKE ONE: "These and Those"
(Int. This-N-That Cargo Company warehouse facility. A female supervisor is barking instructions at two guys — ostensibly particulars on their next delivery. They're waiting for a directive on what to load onto the truck)

CONNIE FUSING

(Clipboard in hand, she begins to gesture toward several identical cardboard cartons within view) 'Kay guys. Let's move those there.

UNSER TIN

(Overall-clad, heavy-set longshoreman type nods, but eyes aren't registering any understanding as he looks from one stack of boxes to the next) Oh, yeah. You mean this one?

VAY GUH

(Hulk Hogan type, booming voice. Condescending) No, Unser, that one.

CONNIE FUSING

**(Slightly disgusted that they're both overlooking the
obvious. Pointing to rows of boxes)** That one over
there, you dudes!

**(They both step forward in the direction she has indicated.
They stop, look at the boxes, then look at one another)**

VAY GUH

She means this one, dork!

UNSER TIN

No, duh! I coulda told you that.

CONNIE FUSING

(Perusing her clipboard and half listening) Told who
what?

VAY GUH

**(Thinking momentarily as he takes in her question. He
points)** *I* told him that.

UNSER TIN

(Pause) You told me what?

VAY GUH

(Points) That.

CONNIE FUSING

(**A sweeping gesture with her clipboard**) Yes, get those there.

VAY GUH

(**Points recklessly**) Yeah, you get those, I'll get these.

UNSER TIN

No, I'll get these and you get those!

CONNIE FUSING

Gentlemen, I'll be back in a — whatever. (**As she exits she randomly points at hundreds of boxes**) Just make sure you put all those things back in the whatchamacallit.

(**Unser and Vay do a double take. They're lost**)

-Lights-

Chapter 16

When It's Not What It Scenes To Be
Creating Into Certainty

That last scene reminds me of many a conversation with my mother. My mother playing the part of Connie, of course. Always well-intended, for sure, but, oh, what hell if you needed to communicate something really important to her!

If your mother is not like Connie, is there someone else in your life who is? Do you know at least one person at work who seems to talk from the planet of Obscurity? I'm sure you know the types to whom I'm referring; they're talking, all right, but in some form of verbal shorthand. As though we're all supposed to understand what the heck they're trying to say! With regard to my late mother (who I adored), it became a contest for those of us around her to guess what she meant. My favorite of all her mystery comments was: "Oh, just put the thing in the thing."

That last scene may have made you laugh, as we often did at my mother. Or perhaps you found the scene ludicrous, if you work in the same world I do, it's not so far fetched. People try to communicate like that all the time. It's an everyday thing. And, ohmygod, the frustration it causes. I'd rather make my way up-river whitewater-rafting without a boat than be in on one of those conversations. Talk about swimming upstream! (Let's hear it for the salmon of the world!)

I've thought a lot about why people talk in obscure and cryptic terms. Often when we do it, we actually have a perfect picture in our head of what we mean, we just can't seem to connect that picture with the right photo caption. I've deduced that this is because we're distracted by other thoughts. Or we're simply uncomfortable. Or totally into our own head — our own point of view. Whatever it is, our thinking gets fragmented. So out of our mouths come vague descriptions rather than concrete examples; we refer to things with terminology like "this" and "that," "them" and "those," even grunts and groans. We offer up inexplicable communication by delivering phrases like: "Yeah, sure … whenever." One of the more contemporary and arcane responses I constantly hear is: "Whatever."

I'm guessing we also talk in inscrutable terms because we're hiding our feelings or afraid to express our innermost thoughts. That's kind of an unconscious thing. But more often than not, we speak vaguely because we're preoccupied or we're so self-centered (and I don't mean this in a selfish way) that we think the person will automatically understand what we're trying to communicate. So while we're in mental reorganization, or "over there," for whatever reason, we open our mouths and warm up on the other guy's ear until we get to the point of it all. Sadly, some of us never come forth with "it," ever. This can actually destroy relationships. You know how it goes: You have a falling out with someone over something that was said. You took what they said to mean something other than what they thought they were conveying. If you're lucky, years down the road you make amends. You begin discussing what caused the rift in the first place, only to learn with great chagrin that one of you misinterpreted what the other said. There is only one reason that can happen: lack of clarity.

For now, let's forget the psychological aspect of why these things happen — why we talk obscurely with fuzzy dialogue. Rather, let's focus on the damage caused when we truly do want to get something across to the other person and very innocently don't. And let's look at how we can prevent ourselves from getting caught in the trap of ambiguity.

As you couldn't help but notice in the last scene, Connie was sincere in getting her guys on track to load that truck. She wasn't openly trying to sabotage the communication, but that's what was happening. And, too, let's give credit to Vay and Unser, as well.

They intended to be cooperative — they wanted to communicate with Connie and one another. Sure, they were sarcastic, but sarcasm is, for many people, a knee-jerk response to frustration. Vay and Unser were willing, but it was virtually impossible to create any meaningful talk because each of the characters spoke in vague terms. Most of us are not mind readers (although I confess I did become one with my mother, out of sheer necessity), so we have to be explicit. We have to be articulate in order to be understood; we need others to be so as well. Providing others with what is wanted and needed in communication comes only from the clarity of the words that bounce back and forth between us.

If we're abstract, we miss one another. What I've noticed with many of my clients is that some of our ambiguities are so subtle in nature that the other person *thinks* she knows what is intended, when in fact, she doesn't at all. (Bottom line: we're exiled to live in a world of inferences when what we say is not exactly expressed.)

I was sitting in on a meeting one afternoon, taking notes, observing a team of quality-control managers. It was my job to determine what I thought they might want to cover in their upcoming ExecuProv communication-skills workshop. Here's how the conversation went: One of these guys said: "I think we ought to cover the basis for our system." Another one responded: "Well, if that's the case, why not evaluate the system itself?" Guy number three said: "Well, the system is the system; I think we all know that." This kind of parallel-speak went on for about ten minutes. The final comment in the going-nowhere-circle was, "Well the nature of system is the system itself." Metaphorically speaking, I felt like I was on a mental exercise bike. Everyone was peddling but going nowhere. I was as tired as if we had just cycled to the top of the Matterhorn all the way from Mexico City. I broke into a sweat. I could restrain myself no longer. I blurted accusingly: "System? What system? What the hell *is* the system, anyway? Somebody tell me, please." They looked puzzled.

As you can imagine, it was useless trying to talk about making "the system" more effective until we first came to an understanding of what each guy thought the term meant. Guy Number One thought the system was the philosophy behind their way of conducting their quality-control activities; Guy Two understood "system" to mean each incremental step they were required to take to complete their inspections; Guy Three thought the system was some kind of reference to the structure that made up the consistency of management. Talk about three people not being on the same page! They weren't even reading the same book! There was a brief moment during it all when I thought they were heading for a real Abbott and Costello "Who's On First" routine. Of course, in my frustrated state of mind at that time in corporate history, I couldn't seem to find the humor in it all.

I think it's safe to assume that those three guys are no different than most of us. Each of us mis-communicates at some point during our day-to-day business dealings. We too often tend to assume that the other person knows what we're talking about. Truth is, when we're not definitive, the outcome of our conversations depends on sheer luck, in terms of the other person grasping what we're really trying to get across. And that's dangerous. In business, that could cost business, so we can't afford to be vague and ambiguous. We have to be precise.

Well, you knew it was coming. The improv lesson in this chapter. The one that addresses this problem.

In improv, we call the need to be explicit "Creating Into Certainty." What that means is, we can never talk in **generalities** or ambiguities; we must always speak in **specifics**. It's a hard-and-fast rule.

Remember what I explained earlier: When improv players take to the stage, they realize they have a very short period of time to create, develop and complete a scene. If they were to speak in generalities it would take too much time to even get the scene off the ground, much less accomplish anything else. Their rule is to start the first line of dialogue with a specific statement. For example, let's say two people are decorating a Christmas tree; let's assume that's the set-up the audience has ordered. Here's what doesn't work as they begin to converse:

Player One: Well, do you want to put these on it this year, or those?
Player Two: I was thinking we could put the other ones on it.

As you can see, we have no clarity whatsoever as to what these two people are referring to. Just what is "this" and "these" and "the other ones"? Going this route in the normal course of conversation, it might take up to four or five minutes to finally clear up precisely what is being discussed. In the improv world, we don't have that kind of time. Like a race car driver, we have to bolt off the starting line with precision. Each maneuver and turn must be ever so exact. We have to get to the point immediately if our goal is to get to the finish line as soon as possible.

Again, there is no opportunity to beat around the bush. First of all, the audience becomes quickly bored. And next, they become confused. (If the actors become confused, you can be damn sure the audience will be, too.) If one actor begins with a non-specific statement, the other has no real jumping-off point. That person has to begin to guess — fish around — play in the world of inferences — to determine what the other person really *means*. After that, he or she has to say something meaningful and substantial. But if it's murky from the start, how is this possible? Sure, he or she can ask questions. But getting answers to questions means more downtime. Improv players don't have margin for downtime. No audience can sit still for that.

Improv work is designed to be slick and quick — that's why "Creating into Certainty" is so vital to the rulebook. The idea is to start all scenes with exact, clear, plain, simple and easy-to-understand dialogue that the other person can quickly and easily tag onto. It's the only way a scene can move forward. And each line of dialogue should do just that: move the scene forward. Also, when the actors are definitive, the audience gets a stronger understanding of the relationship between the characters, the actual scenery, and the feelings that are present.

Are we as business professionals any different from the improv actor? I don't think so!

With this in mind, let's go back and re-run those two lines of opening dialogue between the Christmas tree decorators:
Player One: Well, we've got six feet of tree to decorate. Do you want to use the blue bulbs that Aunt Martha gave us for our anniversary, or the red ones that your brother Clyde bought us at Pic 'N' Save?

Player Two: I was thinking we could hang the green ones with the pictures of the Beatles on them. Nothing like the fab four on a six-foot Douglas fir.

As you can see, we have a much clearer understanding of what they're talking about. In just two lines of dialogue, we know what they're considering hanging on the tree, and what that tree looks like. And in this last verbal go-around it was cake for each actor to play off the other. No guessing game involved. They quickly and spontaneously reacted and responded to the last thing said and last idea held. Upholding that principle is what kept the scene together. But what got it off to a brisk start was adhering to the tenet of "Creating into Certainty." And with such a strong beginning, the actors would be on their way to creating a most interesting and comical scene.

To make another point about improv players and the way they approach their work: In that last exchange, they did a wonderful job of painting a very vivid picture. (We call it "Stage Picture" when the actors provide an environment without any props.) That's powerful creating imagery, whether you're doing improv or doing business. Here's an example: Say you're selling a new line of kitchen countertops. Before you show those samples, or pull out that brochure, you can lure the audience with a few short but descriptive remarks. For instance: "I've got the perfect gray-green countertop to match the tone of the tile."   The visuals you ultimately present will then bolster your opening. This is one more way "Creating Into Certainty" becomes useful.

In the end, we as business persons can't grope for answers. Nor can we ask others to grope. We must be focused on the mission of making ourselves easily understood. That way, "no audience" has to scramble to make sense of any "scene," nor will they get bored or frustrated.

Before you take on the practice assignments, here are a few general and preliminary questions I would like you to answer. How many sales calls or business meetings really provide you downtime at the outset to get your verbal act together? How many phone calls offer you the luxury of "getting around to it" on the other guy's time?   How many times are you suddenly surprised that the other person has misinterpreted what it is you've just said?

In business, we need to be as clear as the improv actor is during a show. The circumstances are the same. Both of us are performing. So, like the improv player, we must *clearly* set the scene and move it along at an engaging pace, with impeccable clarity all the way through. That's how we keep interest and ensure great communication.

Now the time has come to answer some questions that are a little more personalized. Record your answers on paper. Pardon the pun, but you'll get much clearer on what it is you need to work on.

1. Do you find yourself dancing around issues? Does it take time for you to finally get to the heart of the matter? Start tracking how much time you waste doing this.

2. Does it take a certain amount of start-up time to feel as though you're communicating with someone? If so, how much?

3. Do you tend to ramble or digress as you work your way to getting to any point?

4. Do you talk in partial phrases and implications? If so, what are your most common ones?

5. Do people frequently ask you to repeat what it is you're saying? If so, that's a wonderful clue that you're clear only to yourself.

6. Do you use specifics to describe ideas and things, or do you use vague or general terms?

7. Do people complain that you don't "understand" them? If this is the case, you know you're not communicating clearly to them. What they're feeding back tells you so in no uncertain terms!

8. Do people let you know you confuse them? If so, it could be that you're contradicting yourself. Don't say one thing, then

follow it up with something entirely different. Be specific and consistent.

9. Is your mind on more than one thing when you begin a conversation, or are you truly tuned in and "in the moment"? Get that discipline going to release anything but what is currently before you. This alone will help you think in specific terms.

10. In conversations, do you find the people you're talking with "beating a dead horse"? If so, you know then that none of you is "Creating into Certainty." It could be that you're rehashing things in an effort to get to the real thing, to strive for clarity.

11. Are you in and out of your head — distracted momentarily — as you talk to others? This will cause you to talk cryptically — in pieces.

12. Do you always speak in complete sentences or fragmented phrases? If you can begin to think in complete sentences, it's a wonderful way to present more precise ideas during your conversations.

Answers to all of the above should give you a pretty good idea of which of the following homework assignments will be helpful in terms of improving your ability to put ideas, feelings and thoughts across successfully.

1. Take at least one business conversation a day and listen to yourself and the other or others. Is the information you're sharing easy to understand and assimilate? If not, make a journal on who is falling down in the process. Reviewing your notes will be illuminating.

2. The day before an important meeting, grab pencil and paper (or computer) and script out how you think the conversation will go. Notice which dialogue is not clear and definitive, and which is. Now, rewrite that scene so every player's remarks are

easy to understand.

3. Make it a practice to kick off each piece of communication with the mindset that you are going to make your initial remarks specific and exact. Soon your subsequent remarks will simply follow suit.

4. Record some of your meetings if you can. As you play them back, pretend you're one of those fussy and manic Directors who scrutinizes each piece of dialogue. Write down what works and what doesn't. Now edit the scene, putting in changes, to make it work more effectively.

5. Take at least one piece of communication a day and assess how you feel about it. Does it feel like you're connecting well with the other person? Are you "Creating into Certainty," but they're not? Can you find ways to keep them on the right track, such as asking pointed questions that provide clarity? Stay conscious of when the communication begins to drift because of lack of "certainty" and take charge. Get things back on course; help the other person. If you're clear, others very often follow suit.

6. Read great copy. This could be a well written article in *Time*, *Vanity Fair* or your favorite trade publication. If you can read a piece that is designed to educate or instruct, all the better. Notice how the writer crafts his words and brings clarity to the subject. I really believe devoting several hours a week to reading helps us to become more articulate.

7. Think of exercises you can create that will help you approach your communication with more specifics and less generalities. Do at least one of these a day.

In time you will become very adept at "Creating Into Certainty." Just like the improv student, it first takes an awareness of when it is you talk "around" things. Next, you'll find yourself veering toward explicit verbiage rather than conversing in general terms.

Congratulate yourself when you see progress. It's through self-appreciation that we reinforce our new habits. Now, just for fun, let's go back to the warehouse and take another peek at those three; only this time, let's see what happens when they all play according to the "Creating Into Certainty" rule.

TAKE TWO: "These and Those"

(Int. This-N-That Cargo Company warehouse facility. A female supervisor is barking instructions at two guys — precise particulars on their next delivery. They stand by waiting for a directive as to what to load onto the truck)

CONNIE FUSING

(Clipboard in hand, she begins to gesture toward several identical cardboard cartons within view) 'Kay guys, let's move the three boxes in the center, the one to the right and the four directly to the left.

UNSER TIN

(Overall-clad, heavy-set longshoreman type nods. He understands as he assesses each assignment) Oh yeah. **(He walks toward the center stack, puts hand on the top carton)** You mean the three right here **(moves to the right, puts hand on large carton)**, this one and **(gestures directly to the left of the center stack)** those four there.

VAY GUH

(Hulk Hogan type, booming voice. Condescending) Yes, Unser. All those, like the lady said.

CONNIE FUSING

(Gesturing toward the three stacks, pointing at each, one at a time) Yep, one, two, three.

(They both step into position to do their job)

VAY GUH

(Approaching the stack to the left) She said this one first.

UNSER TIN

Yeah, she said this should be number one.

CONNIE FUSING

(Perusing her clipboard, then stopping to listen) That's right, I said that one is one, numero uno.

VAY GUH

(Nods in the proper direction) And after one will be two. (He bends to lift the first carton)

UNSER TIN

(He bends with him. Nods in the other direction) And after that, three.

CONNIE FUSING

(Gesturing again to be double sure) Yep, that's correct, then it's two, then it's three. It's as easy as one —

VAY GUY

… Two —

UNSER TIN

Three.

CONNIE FUSING

Gentlemen, I'll be back from the coffee station in three point two minutes. (**As she exits she points at additional stacks of cartons one at a time**) And put four, five and six back in the storage bin on row six, fourth slot, second drawer.

UNSER AND VAY

(**Together**) Certainly.

-Lights-

Chapter 17

Editing the Scene
Answering the Question

TAKE ONE: "The Pressure Conference"

(Int. large company amphitheater. Both the press and company stockholders are eager to find out why Big Blast Leaf Blowers, Inc. is losing money. On hand is the Chairman of the Board to welcome the group and to introduce the head of corporate communications)

M.C. HENTRO

(A bit nervous but keeping his cool) Welcome, ladies and gentlemen. I know you're here today for some straight answers as to why our third-quarter earnings have declined dramatically over our second-quarter earnings. So, without further ado, I would like to present our head of corporate communications who will be happy to answer all your pertinent questions.

MISS LEADING

(Stepping forward to the lectern with a big smile and lots of confidence. Oblivious to the angry faces staring in her direction) Hello, everyone. I wanted to tell you that our new blowers are a real blast and —

MR. KUEHENAY

(**Raising his hand to interrupt**) For the record, you're Miss Leading, is that correct?

MISS LEADING

(**Patronizing**) I was once married to a wonderful man by the name of Hugh Hahnperppus. But when I dropped him, I also dropped his name. Did I mention he was a gardener, which is unusual for a man of Greek descent. I think they're usually restaurant owners or shipping magnates, aren't they, but my ex had a green thumb, he loved a good shrub —

MR. KUEHENAY

(**Getting perturbed**) That's not what I asked, Miss Leading. I asked about your name so I could get it in my story. Now what about these third-quarter losses? Are they the fault of management or an inability to build the blowers?

MISS LEADING

Our third quarter showed significant growth when you consider that, until a year ago, the leaf blower was a preferred product of only male consumers ages 25 through 50. But just this quarter we've had a 30 percent increase in women purchasing the product line. Interestingly, these women are also owners of jackhammers and chain saws so I think we're seeing a real trend here —

(**There's a disgruntled din coming from the audience. People are beginning to echo Keuhenay's concerns. Soon there's a near riot. We hear various voices**) What about earnings losses? (**Another**) You're skirting the issue! Give us some straight answers! How many blowers are on back order? **(Still another voice)** Why hasn't the new Blowfish Blowhard Blower been released — it's two years overdue. **(A shriek)** Yeah, and where's the Baby Blabber Blower — still on the drawing boards?

MR. KUEHENAY

Let me be more specific, Miss Leading. We were told three quarters ago that the Bifurcate Blower — the one that could handle the back and front yard simultaneously — would be released last Christmas. What's the status of *that* product?

MISS LEADING

Our products are all revolutionary, as you know. Why, if J.D. Powers was issuing awards for ingenuity, we'd blow Black and Decker right off the lawn.

(More disgruntled noises from the room)

MR. KUEHENAY

(Out of patience) I think you're blowing us off, Miss Leading. You're not about to answer these tough questions, are you?

MISS LEADING

(Sympathetic smile. Big pause) Gentlemen, tough questions are the backdrop of Corporate America. We all know you can't take a private company public without tough questions. I have tough questions, too. For example: Does anyone else smell the smoke? **(Loudly into the microphone)** This room is on fire.

(Everyone makes a beeline for the exits. Miss Leading cocks her head and smiles as she watches them cram through the doorways)

-Fade to Black-

Chapter 17

Editing the Scene
Answering the Question

You don't have to be a politician to come off like Miss Leading. I know hundreds of people who never answer the question they were asked. I sit in meetings all day, sometimes flabbergasted at what I hear. People are responding, all right, but much of the time their answers are only remotely related to the questions put to them. Through my observations over the past ten years, I've taken copious notes during client meetings.

Rummaging through these notes one day, I began to notice some recurring themes. I deduced that people don't actually answer the questions put to them for one of the following four reasons: They're avoiding the issue; They never really heard the question, or tuned in for only part of it; They've been intent on wanting to spin their answer a particular way for some personal benefit; (by far the most common reason) — or they very innocently interpreted the question through their own filter in terms of their own agenda; this often happens as a result of people being so anxious to "sell" their point of view that their responses are ultimately "self" centered. None of these four situations makes for good communication. In fact, what we get is quite the opposite — really bad communication or worse yet, no communication at all! I've watched answers zoom past questions like ships that aren't even passing in the same night!

My friend Michael Gellman, the Second City Director to whom I referred earlier, suggests that people listen to only the first 10 percent of the other person's dialogue, whether it's a question or a statement, and then give no more than a 10 percent response. With these kind of odds, no wonder people have difficulty coming together! And the hardcore reality is: If you can't "get together," it's hard to sell or to solve. Whatever the reason people are not answering the question is irrelevant, what matters is that, clearly, then, we all need to be direct in our answers. So, as we have done through lessons in earlier chapters, we need to be considering behavior modification geared toward making ourselves more cognizant of the questions people ask and more attuned to serving up answers that fit.

I've coached my PR clients for years: "If you're a great communicator, it's because you're adept at answering another person's question, frankly and openly." While some would disagree with that assertion, I believe people should not skirt issues but hit the questions head on. Any audience will have great respect for those who are forthright. That doesn't mean my public relations clients can't "sell" in the process of telling the truth; it's just that they're very careful to give back what the question-asker wants and needs before dressing up the answer to include their own point of view or personal message.

Unfortunately, as I mentioned earlier, most people bypass the answer altogether and go for the "I-need-to-get-what-I-need" approach. Here's a quick example:

Questioner: Does your air carrier company deliver to all the western states?

Answerer: Our company flies to 32 cities nationwide, including San Juan and Honolulu. We have tremendous capability.

As you can see, the "Answerer" did not in fact give an answer. If he had, it might have gone something like this:

Questioner: Does your air carrier company deliver to all the western United States?

Answerer: Yes, we do. And to every major city within each of the western United States, as well. Now, in addition to those destinations — just to point out the scope of our service — we also deliver to other cities nationwide, 32 in all, including San Juan and Honolulu.

In the second scenario, the answer didn't really change all that much; it's just that the information was fed in a more appropriate and responsive fashion. In other words, the answerer showed courtesy by answering first what was asked of him, then going on to provide the message he wanted to get across. As subtle as some of the changes in the second version may have been, believe me, they make all the difference in the world in reaching the questioner. The second approach is what seals rapport. It lets the "Asker" know he was being heard — a far cry from the impression the first time around.

We should all aim at providing answers according to the questions that are posed to us. We should avoid the tendency to tweak our answers to fit our own subjective agendas. Such tweaking indicates that we're totally into ourselves. Or that we're hiding something. In either case, how can we possibly have cohesive communication? And, as I've mentioned a number of times already, sloppy communication breeds misunderstandings, which in turn, immediately or eventually, foster broken relationships. That's the last thing any of us wants; we're trying to build our client base or circle of contacts and business associates — not lose them. But it's hard to trust anyone who doesn't really answer our questions; it can't create an atmosphere that cultivates good vibes. Trust, as you learned early on in the book, is at the core of all relationships, and it hinges on the quality of communication that takes place. Without trust, we're always teetering on separation. If we can't build rapport, we can't bond; and if we can't bond, we can't sell. And, as I continue to point out, we're all selling something. When you violate the "Answer the Question" principle, one more thing happens: you come off as rude. Nothing ticks me off more than when I ask someone something they don't answer. I take that as a real put down. Subtextually, the person is telling me that what I had to ask wasn't important. Over time, you can build up a great deal of resentment toward people who continually do this to you. On the other hand, you may finally decide that they're just foolish — too inane to even understand what you're saying. Rude or foolish; not very appealing choices, are they? Why not just answer the question?

By now, you've no doubt become an ardent improv-comedy

student and can probably guess which of the rules we've already covered can be easily applied to assist in "Answering the Question." In addition to the bylaws on listening, you're probably also remembering "React and Respond" and "Serve and Support." They're key to what could have made our press-conference scene work. I always tell my clients and my actors that if their focus is on the other person — with the intent of doing whatever it takes to make the scene work — they will always "Answer the Question." If you step outside yourself and really listen to what the other person is asking, you can't possibly misinterpret their question. I also instruct that reacting and responding to the last thing said or last idea held will also keep you on track. If your responses are in direct response to what is asked, you cannot fail to answer the question. Again, you must listen, react and respond, serve and support. And the rules regarding "Refusal and Denial" and "Be Here Now" also apply. You must be in the moment to hear the question; then you must address it accordingly.

In the improv arena, "Answer the Question" means a couple of things. First of all, it primarily applies to the actors and their relationship with the audience. If they try to forgo a set-up from the audience in exchange for their own ideas, they have violated the "Answer the Question" premise. Example: If the audience gives three actors a set-up that calls for two people to be bus passengers, and the other, the driver, they must follow those guidelines. If two of the actors buy into the idea that they are passengers, but the third actor suddenly decides to be a mugger, they will have completely dismantled the integrity of the piece. When the audience requests two passengers and a driver, that's what you give them, because the audience is an integral part of the show. You do as they ask! If not, improv actors lose credibility.

Now, audience requests can be very demanding; the combination of set-up ideas can come from several audience members and be completely incongruent. But that's where the talent (and most often the humor) comes in: If you're a good improv player, you make it work! I remember one run when my troupe was doing a take-off on the "Sally Jesse Raphael" show. Each show, the audience would call out the problem to be discussed during the segment. The actors then had only two or three minutes to get their heads into pretend characters and the premise of the talk show segment. One night, I recall, the audience asked for skateboarding nuns, with Tourette's syndrome, who had secretly given birth to drug-afflicted babies. It was tricky, but the actors held tight to the audience's suggestion and made the scene work. They stayed true to every facet of the request, incorporating each idea into the overall scheme of the scene. "By "Answering the Question," they kept their credibility. In the business setting, our goal should be the same. When we don't answer questions — the way they're put to us — we lose face, whether we consciously realize it or not. Some may disagree with me on this, countering that not answering the question is often very powerful, but I still assert that if you want honest and worthwhile relationships with the people you do business with, your best bet is to give answers to the questions that are asked.

I'd like to share with you a few examples I personally witnessed of not answering the question: As I present the first two, I have to chuckle because I know they weren't even aware of what they were doing! In the last example, however, the answer was carefully manipulated to serve the needs of the person in the "answer" seat. Example One:

MARTHA

So, I see you're back from Europe. How did you like Paris?

BELINDA

Oh, you're not going to believe this! We rented this car in Rome, and all of a sudden, here we are in Milan when we can't get reverse to work. We drive all over Northern Italy until we reach some small mechanic shop. Of course, none of them can speak English, so here we are doing this sign-language thing. Oh, you would have laughed so hard. I'm telling you, next time, I'm taking every Berlitz course on tape. It's funny now, but it wasn't at the time. We wasted so much time getting that car fixed, it kept us from keeping to our sightseeing schedule. We only had ten days, you know.

As you can see, Belinda never got close to answering the question, "How did you like Paris?" Instead she was "Going Into Story," a term we improv people use when someone digresses. I was having lunch with these two women, so I interjected the following:

CHERIE

Belinda, I know that car fiasco left quite an impression but Martha asked how you liked Paris. You didn't tell her one way or another. Well, did you or did you not like Paris?

BELINDA

Oh, we loved Paris when we finally got there. It was charming and romantic and so much to see! It was probably my favorite destination.

Had Belinda focused on what Martha had asked in the first place, this second answer would have been her first. Instead, she let the question about Paris trigger the memory of the car problem; evidently, the delay had caused them to reach Paris later than expected. When she was asked the question, rather than answer it first, then digress with "We got there late," she simply blew Martha off and answered according to where she herself was in her head. She had the focus on herself. So even if she was listening (and I think she was) she chose not to actually answer.

The second example happened to me when I ran my car into a pole and had it in the body shop (one of the more stupid things I've ever done!). Naturally, when I called to see how long the car would take for repair, I was already in an irritable frame of mind.

ME

This is Cherie Kerr, and I was wondering how long it's going to take to fix my car?

RACHEL

He's coming in the morning.

ME

What? I took it to the Jaguar dealer night before last, and they said they'd deliver it yesterday. Is it not there?

RACHEL

I think he's coming around noon.

ME

Why wasn't it delivered yesterday? I don't understand.

RACHEL

What?

ME

(**Completely exasperated**) My car! How come it wasn't delivered yesterday? Where the hell is my car?

RACHEL

Oh, it's here.

ME

Then what do you mean, "He's coming around noon"?

RACHEL

I was talking about the insurance adjuster. He's
coming around noon.

I suppose it goes without saying, I wanted to kill Rachel.
I initially asked how long it would take to fix my car. I didn't
ask where it was. But Rachel tuned me out and provided an answer
to a question that was never even asked. This is a perfect example
of how easily information can become misconstrued. I don't know
about you, but I'm not perfect and I certainly have played the part
of "Rachel."
The next example features the Manipulator.

BRAD

Nice to have you on KRON. So then, Sal's a lawyer and
agreed to come on the show today to talk about lawyers and
the bad rap they continually get. What about all the negative press and ill feelings people in general harbor toward
lawyers?

SAL

Our work is never easy. We're constantly embroiled in conflict. But that's why our profession is so important. Think
about it; just about everyone needs a lawyer at one time or
another.

BRAD

But not everyone has a conflict; sometimes a regular Joe
just needs a will drawn up. But that person can be unhappy
with the service, the bill ... what about those people and
their bad feelings? Don't you find it strange that so many
people dislike lawyers, Sal?

SAL

> You know our local bar association does more for the community than most other non-profit organizations put together. Why, my office recently donated one hundred hours to the homeless to secure their right to camp out on the steps of city buildings. I guess the public should be made aware of all the wonderful things we do for the community. I, myself, have taken a great interest in helping the Native American Indian.

What a butt! Not only did Sal completely ignore the question, he had the nerve to use this talk show to commend himself for himself. This is not uncommon; I see this kind of verbal dynamic going on in sales calls, in board rooms, in planning meetings, ... oh, well, the list goes on! Rather than answer the question, head on, people like Sal pounce on the opportunity to talk about how great they are! When I hear stuff like this, it makes me want to riot. I get the urge to turn over cars!

You can probably think of many other examples of people not answering the question. Now it's time to look within, though, and do your own personal assessment, take a look at how often you are guilty of not "Answering the Question." Take the following pop quiz, then follow up with the homework tasks — all of which you can add to your valuable improv-training arsenal.

1. Do you listen to the whole question or only part of it? Most of us listen "partially." Take in the entire question, then answer it.

2. Are you direct with your answers, or do you build up to them with several paragraphs of expositional dialogue? Building up to the real answer often causes confusion and irritation. Answer first, then tag on or expound upon.

3. Do people have to repeat the question a second time, sometimes rephrasing it? If this is the case, you know you didn't provide an appropriate answer. Take note of how often this happens.

4. When you hear a question, does the answer you're about to giv-
    tend to be directly aligned with your own agenda? If your agen-
    da seems to keep popping up as a preamble to your answer,
    chances are your stuff is taking priority. Remember the "Serve
    and Support" and "React and Respond" rules. They'll keep you
    from tumbling into this trap.

5. Do you answer only part of a question — the part you want?
    Some questions need more than one answer. Try and answer
    them in the order in which they were asked. This provides
    tighter communication all around.

    Now for the homework — some ideas that will help you
increase your ability to "Answer The Question."

1. As you did in the last chapter, write down questions. Next,
    write your answers to them. If your answers are not specific, or
    in direct response to the question asked, keep rewriting those
    answers until you do the job. Doing this homework assignment
    each week is a great way to correct "poor-answering." As I said
    before, when you write things out, you tend to learn the lesson
    better. Remember your old spelling tests? Same idea.

2. Take a rehearsal time each day to just listen to others "Answer
    the Question." Notice how often they meander or digress.
    Now, take just a couple of those questions, jot them down, and
    later, when you have a few minutes, write out what would have
    made for better, more sensible answers.

3. When someone seems vague about what they're attempting to
    ask, use your instincts and be perceptive. Listen to the entire
    question and the subtext, then attempt to assess what the heart
    of the question is. If you're not clear, repeat to them, in ques-
    tion form, what you gleaned to be the heart of what they asked.
    If you're on track, answer. If not, ask them to repeat their
    question, letting them know that you need more simplicity and
    clarity.

4. Be agile and creative enough to be ready to answer questions you did not expect. If your listening is focused, your responses will be quick and appropriate. Have a friend or colleague write out a bunch of non-related questions and put them in an envelope. Take them home and pull them out one at a time (like flash cards) and answer them as succinctly as you can. This is a great drill, and one I highly recommend. When someone at work assists you with this exercise, they can include questions you *might* have to answer. Co-workers make for great homework partners for many ExecuProv homework assignments because they know your job and what you're likely to come up against on a regular basis. So, my request is that you solicit a partner from work, one whom you can also help, and who wants to improve their communication skills.

5. Don't ever avoid an answer. This gives negative signals. Answer a question in a straightforward way, even if the answer is "I don't know, but I'll find out and get back to you." If you do find yourself avoiding a question (and it's not one that invades your personal privacy), make a note of it and try to understand why. Certain questions might push buttons in terms of fears and obstacles that you need to overcome to become a better communicator. In the realm of communication, none of us should ever have to fear anything. Avoidance always has some special meaning behind it. So, if you're part of this culture, get to the bottom of it.

6. When you find yourself not "Answering the Question," write down the question you're actually answering. Now compare the two questions. This exercise is very enlightening!

Now let's go back to that stockholders meeting and listen in while Miss Leading handles the questions from the improv player's handbook.

TAKE TWO: "The Pressure Conference"

(**Int. large company amphitheater. Both the press and company stockholders are eager to find out why Big Blast Leaf Blowers, Inc. is losing money. On hand is the Chairman of the Board to welcome the group and to introduce the head of corporate communications**)

M.C. HENTRO

(**A bit nervous but keeping his cool**) Welcome, ladies and gentlemen. I know you're here today for some straight answers as to why our third-quarter earnings have declined dramatically over second-quarter earnings. So without further ado, I would like to present our head of corporate communications who will be happy to answer all your pertinent questions. Miss Leading ... .

MISS LEADING

(**Stepping forward to the lectern with a big smile and lots of confidence. She takes note of the angry faces staring in her direction**) Hello, everyone. I wanted to tell you that our new blowers are a real blast, and —

MR. KUEHENAY

(**Raising his hand to interrupt**) For the record, you're Miss Leading, is that correct?

MISS LEADING

(**Straightening her blazer and standing taller**) Yes, I most certainly am. And, I will continue to be. You see, I dropped my former married name, Hahnperppus, when I dropped that husband. So, yes, just refer to me as Miss Leading.

MR. KUEHENAY

(**Writing all that down**) Okay, now, Miss Leading, what about these third-quarter losses? Are they the fault of management or an inability to build the blowers?

MISS LEADING

(**Looking him in the eye**) Both. You see, our management team blew it. They keep hiring people with carpal tunnel syndrome. These workers have to be trained to use their feet to assemble the parts, so naturally it takes a little longer to build the blowers. But, hey, we here at Big Blast give new meaning to the term "toe jam"! (**Everyone laughs reluctantly**) Let me mention, though, that third-quarter did show significant growth when you consider that women are now using our product line. We expect those new sales to reflect a 30 percent increase in revenue in terms of fourth-quarter earnings.

(**There's a disgruntled din coming from the audience. People are beginning to get agitated. Soon there's a near riot. We hear various voices**) Why only 30 percent? (**Another**) How many blowers are on back order? (**Still another voice**) Why hasn't the new Blowhard Blower been released — it's two years overdue. (**A shriek**) Yeah, and where's the Baby Blabber Blower — still on the drawing boards?

MISS LEADING

(**Motioning for them to be seated**) Let me address each of those questions. We estimate 30 percent increase in revenue, fourth-quarter, but the board anticipates it could be as high as a 50 percent increase. We have 3,424 blowers on back order, but management is cutting a deal with Eddie Van Halen, who's agreed to come in and assemble our back-ordered product. That means we'll be on track in six weeks. Now for the Blowhard Blower, we've finally worked out the kinks. We hired a team of lawyers to complete its design. The Baby Blabber Blower is no longer on the drawing boards; it's currently in production; its due date is October.

MR. KUEHENAY

That's all well and fine, Miss Leading, but what about the Bifurcate Blower — the one that's alleged to be able to handle the back and front yards simultaneously? That was supposed to be delivered last Christmas. What's the status of *that* product?

MISS LEADING

We dumped it. During our testing phase, it kept flattening houses. Our liability insurance doesn't cover dwellings, only large trees.

MR. KUEHENAY

So, now what?

MISS LEADING

(Wanting to hedge that question. Instead) We, uh, go back to the kitchen and stand the heat. Speaking of which, is anyone else on fire? **(On cue, her trick shoulder pads begin to smolder)**

(Everyone makes a beeline for the exits. Miss Leading cocks her head and smiles as she watches them cram through the doorways)

-Fade to Black-

Chapter 18

Scenes Like Forever
Economy of Dialogue

TAKE ONE: "Yakkety Yak"

(Int. small office. Gary Luss, energetic young man, is shuffling his leads, getting ready to pick a card, any card. He flips one, catches it between his teeth, sets the others down and reads the sales lead of the day. He eagerly prepares to dial. But suddenly the phone rings)

GARY LUSS

Hi, hello and hola and greetings and good morning and top of the day to you and buenos tardes!

WARD N. EDGEWEISS

(Startled at such a telephonic welcome) Hello. Name is Edgeweiss and I'm inquiring about your hotel for an upcoming convention. I just need to know if you're a full-service facility.

GARY LUSS

(Thrilled he asked) Well, Mr. Edgewise, so glad you inquired and asked and queried and solicited that information. I'm Gary Luss by the way, before I forget, incidentally,

257

by the by and just thought I'd mention it. I work in the catering and sales department here at SleepLate Hotels —

WARD N. EDGEWISE

That's nice, but all I wanted to know is whether you are or are *not* a full-service facility.

GARY LUSS

Full service, completely outfitted, totally equipped, perfectly appointed, state of the art and we also have amenities galore —

WARD N. EDGEWISE

Oh that's nice, well that's all I wan —

GARY LUSS

Did I mention that breakfast in bed is served 24 hours a day, and our Can't Get Up Buffet is wheeled down every corridor around the clock and if you holler out we just slide things under the door. **(Big breath)** And did I mention that caffeinated toothpaste is used as a garnish on everything, even our snacks — our nuts, our chips, our pretzels? And did I mention our Gurney Golf Course? See, it's where every player is wheeled from hole to hole by his caddy, and hey, par counts if you can lift your head to tee off but we consider that everyone is wakeup-challenged so everyone gets a 300 handicap and, oh, did I mention our Supine Spa, where we feature the Snoring Sauna, the Slumber Steambath, and Face-down facial? Oh, and hey: let me tell you about our Snooze you Lose Happy Hour — it's free and if you nod out our servers will hook you up to your IV beverage of choice, hell, you can consume one cocktail for two weeks in which case we'll hold all your calls. But if it's just a matter of passing out for a short period of time, we can always roll you and members of your party out to the LayDown tennis lawn where, if you sleep fetal, hell, you might get a big rush as you're whacked over the net by your sleep walking opponent … and did I mention the Comatose Café?

WARD N. EDGEWISE

Mr. Luss, I just wanted to know if you were full-service. You've more than answered my question. I'll call back if we decide to book a block of rooms.

GARY LUSS

(**Disappointed. He was just warming up**) Oh. Well. In that case. Goodbye, Sayonora, See Ya, Ciao, Adios, Later, So long now, Bye Bye and Arrivederci.

-Lights-

Chapter 18

Scenes Like Forever
Economy of Dialogue

Don't you just want to scream: "Hey, Gary, put a muzzle on it!"? Well, the Gary Luss disease is all too common. Some have it real bad, others just a tad — just on certain occasions. But we all have it to varying degrees. It just depends on who we're talking to and what the circumstances are.

Okay, count them. How many people in your work environment over-explain everything? Granted, sitting in on the discussion between Gary Luss and Ward N. Edgeweiss was somewhat exaggerated, but it happens; you and I both know it does. Sometimes we're the victim and sometimes we're the perpetrator. Whether it's done to us or we're doing it to someone else, it's got to go. No one has that much time to listen to extra dialogue. We both know too much talk is boring. "Less is more" is not really the case here — instead, it's more like "less is better."

My friend Dr. Alex Kappas, one of the great "behaviorists" in the country, claims that people who go into too much detail to make what should be a simple point do so because they are afraid they will be misunderstood. I tend to agree with that, but I also think the origin of this problem spills over into other categories, too — just as there are several reasons why people have trouble "Answering the Question."

There's not one singular reason why people have difficulty saying only what is necessary or appropriate. Some people "need" to think aloud on our time before they can actually get to what it is

261

they really want to say. They are what I term "scattered communicators." They're all over the place — their dialogues are like wayward tops spinning uncontrollably until they wind down. Other people blabber because they are screwing up the courage to say what it is they're reluctant to say. I see this over and over when a subordinate is trying to communicate something of a touchy nature with a superior. In their struggle to say just the right thing, they keep repeating the same idea in only slightly different ways, adding a little extra go-around in the hope of getting closer to the point they were too intimidated to make right out of the shoot.

Then there are people who can't help but dominate the conversation. They love to hear themselves talk. I remember handling the details of a press conference for a guy — a judge — who was running for office. He held a press conference to announce his candidacy. What should have taken five minutes, took 45. I was furious, and so were his campaign manager and the small amount of press who turned out. At the conclusion of one of the longest and most boring press conferences I'd ever helped to arrange, I asked the guy why he did it — why he stood there talking non-stop for 45 minutes. He smiled and said, "Oh, I was having such a good time." "Well, we weren't," I wanted to blurt. I decided not to waste my breath, though; he was so in love with hearing himself, I knew that any constructive criticism would be left at the side of the road. I figured he'd talk himself right out of the race. He did. He lost miserably. The real obvious self-centered types are not tolerated very well. And sadly, sometimes they never get the message. Those are the ones I have the least patience with.

Finally, I believe some people are too chatty just because they are; maybe it's something in the brain. I believe in that kind of stuff. One of my children is ADHD (Attention Deficit Hyperkentic Disorder), and his hyperkineticism causes him to talk a blue streak. It's just the way he's wired up. (He's a creative genius, by the way.) It's not his fault, but we continually work with him to tone down and shorten up his communication.

Whatever it is that causes us to be even a little like Gary Luss, we need to take a close look at it. In business professionals, too much talk is annoying — a real turnoff. So we need to modify such behavior as we go about our communication tasks.

In the case of Luss versus Edgeweiss, the conversation could have been completed in just a few short sentences. If you paid close attention, Edgeweiss simply wanted to know if the hotel was full-service. Period. A simple "yes" or "no" on Luss' part would have sufficed as an opener. He then could have gone on to ask Edgeweiss if he wanted to know about any of the hotel's various amenities. If so, he could have gone on to elaborate, albeit not to the extent he actually did.

People like Edgeweiss get antsy or angry or irritated or all of the above when they run into someone like Luss. You probably know the feeling. After one encounter, you're overcome with dread whenever you know it's time to meet up with the person. And God help you if it's a one-on-one situation. I once had a panic attack when I was interviewed for an ExecuProv workshop and the company president proceeded to tell me not only the company's history but his personal one as well. I prayed for an earthquake — the 6.0 variety.

In this last chapter of Part One (yes, we're almost done covering the basic rules of improvisational comedy scene study), the lesson here is what we call "Economy of Dialogue." What this means is the improv player can say only what is absolutely necessary during any scene in any show. We implement the rule for a few reasons. First, we have only so much time to do a scene — usually one to two minutes. As I pointed out earlier, a great deal has to be covered in that short period of time, e.g., the who, what, why, when and where, not to mention a beginning, middle and an end.

Beyond helping us to be more efficient, shorter responses translate to quicker repartee, and it is through brisk, fast-paced conversation that we truly entertain the audience. Also, when our responses are to the point, it is easier to communicate more clearly with our fellow actors. When we say too much, the other performer can become confused. "Economy of Dialogue" promotes simplicity. We need to keep our improv work simple, concise and buoyant to assure consistent success during any scene on stage.

Michael Gellman, to whom you've heard me refer repeatedly, says that the improv actor should say only what is essential and pertinent. No more. What I've noticed, both with a slick improv player and a seasoned business professional, is that those who need few words to express their thoughts, ideas and feelings are far more impressive and powerful communicators. When they speak, we always listen. These are the people who effortlessly command our immediate respect. We call them "articulate," and their knack for "Economy of Dialogue" is one important reason why.

I always tell my students to remember the "need to know" rule. Tell them only what they really need to know, not everything. Most presentations last perhaps 10 minutes to an hour. Most speeches usually go no longer than 45 minutes to an hour. During that time, you're either informing, educating or persuading. Realize something: You can't possibly tell your audience every single thing about your subject matter in that short period of time. So then, it's incumbent upon each of us to carefully select the highlights and the salient points only, and to stick to them. If people want or need more explanation, they'll ask for it whether they do so openly or subtextually. If they do, you can provide it. If they don't, move on. In short order, that is! "Economy of Dialogue" applies equally to phone calls, meetings and one-on-one conversations. The rule isn't reserved solely for monologues.

Another thing I always pass on to my students is this: If you subscribe to the "Economy of Dialogue" rule, you will have more productive time to do other job-related tasks. The old adage, "time is money," still fits. For those of you who are self-employed or work on commission, this is critical. And, off the job, just think how much more free time you'll have to do other things — like go to the gym or spend time with family and friends — when you save time not talking. I'd be willing to bet that each of us wastes at least one hour a day just saying too much.

But before you get carried away at chopping down all those long sentences, let me caution that when I talk about "Economy of Dialogue," I'm not suggesting that you become rude and abrupt. Not at all. There's a big difference between being curt and being frugal with your dialogue. So don't go overboard. Just begin to think about how you might chisel down some of your verbiage — how you might get more thrifty word-wise — whatever the business circumstance.

For those of you who've enjoyed attending an improv show and seen the actors in action, you may already have a grasp of what I'm talking about in terms of "Economy of Dialogue." You've gotten a good picture of how they toss their banter back and forth with the speed and accuracy of well-thrown frisbees. For those of you who've never seen improv performed by professional actors, I ask you to find a well-trained troupe in your community and watch them perform. It's not only a real treat, but a great way to see these lessons demonstrated.

At the Orange County Crazies Theater, the actors perform a piece wherein, after taking in all the set-up particulars, they are asked to execute the scene in one-word sentences. It's one of the hardest improv pieces there is because, even though there is freedom to be spontaneously creative, there are tremendous restrictions imposed, as well. That's the kick of it. Both the audience and the actors love it when the set-up elements given to create and complete the piece don't make for an easy fit. And trying to put an entire scene across speaking one-word sentences is a pretty tall order. But it can be done, and it's wonderful to watch. In improv shows, the quicker the verbal volley, the greater the thrill.

I thought it might be fun to give you just a taste of a one-word-sentence scene. Don't forget: The scene has to move forward in the midst of all this restriction. So, let's say our set-up is two guys sitting in a restaurant, and they can't get served.

HARRY

(Reading the menu) Starv-ing!

BILL

(Reading his) Famished!

HARRY

(Motioning to the server) Waiter?

BILL

(Noticing that Harry didn't get the waiter's attention)
Hey!

HARRY

(Chiming in) You!

BILL

Shoot.

HARRY

Damn!

BILL

(Offering Harry the basket on the table) Crackers?

HARRY

Okay.

BILL

(Holding a pitcher over Harry's glass) Water?

HARRY

(Holding his glass under it) Thanks.

BILL

Harry?

HARRY

What?

BILL

Nothing.

HARRY

Speak.

BILL

Sushi?

HARRY

Hokonoko's?

BILL

(**Smugly**) Yeah.

HARRY

Let's.

(They get up from the table and exit)

You would be surprised at how many times a day we actually talk in little bites like this. Whenever you speak with a close associate, a significant other, your child or best friend, you very often talk in one-word sentences. You probably hadn't noticed. Naturally, I'm not asking that you speak in only one-word sentences; I'm simply asking you to notice how much can be communicated in just a few words. Harry and Bill's scene proved that. This being the case, it's not hard to imagine how we can easily cut down our word count in our day-to-day conversations. From now on, I'm asking you to think about it first, then give it a whirl a little at a time.

We live in an age where things move very rapidly. Technology is outgrowing itself every day. Those who communicate via the media do it quickly and succinctly. Everything is in soundbites. If you use the Internet, you see how few words are used in a web page to describe a consulting firm, for instance, compared to the same information as it used to be presented in a brochure. With technology, brevity is a necessity. So much information is thrown at each of us every day, we barely have time to grasp it all. And, if you're long-winded, beware: You may be sabotaging your professional self.

I've mentioned many times that a good actor is a good observer. The way in which to overcome your habit of talking too much is to first become aware that you're doing it. Next you can begin to edit out what isn't necessary. Remember, many of us have a tendency to want to provide a Movie-Of-The-Week version of something, when in most instances all that is needed is a short news segment. So become a good editor. Try not to get so attached to your content that when you go to edit a speech or presentation, you feel personally hurt. Know that it's better to delete superfluous information than to weigh people down with it. Approach the material as though someone else prepared it. Now, pare it down as though you're doing that person a favor. I'm of the belief that most people have excess in their presentations because they're just too attached to the content — there's too much of themselves invested. Then there are those who just don't know when enough is enough; they're simply oblivious to how the overall product will come across. They're the ones who become deeply immersed in the "what" of it all and can't stand back objectively to see what should be sacrificed for the sake of a better show.

I once worked with a guy to help him rehearse a speech. He brought in 32 overheads when he actually needed only 10 to make his presentation work. Each time I suggested deleting one of them, he got a pained look on his face. It was as though we were playing checkers and I kept scooping up his chips. But after he made his presentation, he confided that he definitely saw the value in the editing we had done. Most writers, likewise, will tell you that writing is re-writing. We're always editing. So try and ask yourself: if you were the audience, would you enjoy the speech or the conversation in its present form, or would you want it shortened and tightened? Therein lie your editing guidelines.

The following suggestions are just some of the ways you can get behind the idea of "Economy of Dialogue." Try them out, then see what other creative methods you can devise on your own so you don't end up coming across even remotely like poor old motormouth Gary!

1. Go into your rehearsal mode and take a small chunk of time just to listen to yourself providing someone information. As you do this, you'll be well into the improv actor's "mind," because obviously you'll be doing more than one thing at a time, i.e., speaking to someone while monitoring the conciseness of your dialogue. At first, don't do this exercise during super-important "scenes," like the one with your boss who wants a complete report on how your current project is going. Instead, start out with a not-so-important conversation, like the one when you order your airline tickets.

2. Begin to listen to others when they talk to co-workers and business associates. Do they say too much? What could they delete? Be a silent editor, perhaps taking notes on the pad in front of you, and determine what was expositional and what was essential. This is when you get to play "Director," and it's really fun. Be fair. And note what they said that really honored the "Economy of Dialogue" principle. You'll learn a great deal.

3. Do what you've done before in writing out your potential dialogue, only this time focus on editing. Just like a newspaper editor, get picky with what stays and what goes. As you enter into conversations with others, soon you'll find yourself editing

the proposed dialogue in your head just before you speak. When you get really proficient at this, and you will, you'll notice this edit-before-you-speak process happening at a very rapid speed. For example, you might say: "We need milk and bread and, I know, you said bananas, and I think I'll get some pretzels like you've asked three times already this morning. Do you want anything else?" That's pretty wordy. Try this instead: "I'm going to the store now to get a few things and your pretzels. Anything else?" This is where the "need to know" rule applies.

4. As a writer, I've spent numerous hours editing my own copy. One of the ways in which I learned to get better at it was to study newspaper articles and magazine feature stories. First I looked at headlines, noting how few words could tell it all, e.g., "Dog Bites Man." Next, I began to read these pieces sentence by sentence. I could easily see how the authors either monitored themselves or how they must have had a damn good editor. Writers, in general, learn early on that every word must count. So then, I want you to put on your writer's cap as often as you can. This discipline will automatically help you tighten your commentary.

5. "Economy of Dialogue" isn't only valuable when you're talking to others. It's also very helpful on the job at it relates to your written assignments. Go back through some of your files — reports, correspondence, inner office memos, training manuals (can you think of others?) — and give them an editing runthrough. This exercise has great impact in getting the lesson across, because you've been away from the material long enough to be more objective and less attached to it. Whacking away at some of the debris is then much easier.

6. After you've rehearsed "Economy of Dialogue" for short intervals, begin to expand your effort into longer stretches and during more important conversations, like the ones with your boss. As with many of the other homework assignments from previ-

ous chapters, you'll find this easier and easier as you go along.

7. We do this in our advanced ExecuProv weekly class: Just for fun (or it could be for profit, too) declare "D" day — "D" standing for dialogue. Everything you say has to be said in as few words as possible. Other people don't have to know what you're doing — most won't even catch on. But in addition to this task being a challenge, it's a real blast.

Remember what I said earlier about those who are articulate. We tend to have great respect for them as business professionals. Remember also what I pointed out in the beginning of this part of the book: People buy people; then they buy things. Speaking concisely is a wonderful way to make a positive impression.

Before we move on to Part Two of the book, which provides some improv comedy "tools" — some clever techniques to use in conjunction with the "rules" — let's take another listen at that conversation between Gary and Ward.

TAKE TWO: "Yakkety Yak"

(Int. small office. Gary Luss, an energetic young man, is shuffling his leads, getting ready to pick a card, any card. He flips one, catches it between his teeth, sets the others down and reads the sales lead of the day. He eagerly prepares to dial. But suddenly the phone rings)

GARY LUSS

Hi, Sales and Catering. Gary Luss here. How can I help you?

WARD N. EDGEWEISS

(Feeling welcome and comfortable) Hello, Gary. I'm Mr. Edgeweiss and I'm inquiring about your hotel for an upcoming convention. I just need to know if you're a full-service hotel.

GARY LUSS

Why, The SleepLate Hotel is indeed a full-service facility. We have every amenity you can think of — all of which have been specifically designed for the convention-goer who just doesn't like to get up.

WARD N. EDGEWEISS

Hey, that's great. Well, if we decide to book a block of rooms, I'll get back to you.

GARY LUSS

Please do. At that time I would be happy to tell you all about us — all the amenities we offer — and answer any other questions you might have.

WARD N. EDGEWEISS

Okay, then. Goodbye.

GARY LUSS

Bye bye, now.

-Lights-

PART TWO

THE TOOLS

Chapter 19

The Tools of The Trade

The first part of this book was designed to give you a complete overview of the most commonly used and, in my opinion, most important rules needed in order to become a great communicator. This is so whether you're an improv actor or a business professional.

I trust you've done a wonderful job practicing and completing all the assignments laid out at the end of each chapter. If so, you're now ready to move on to the next plateau. It's time to take a look at some of the tools we improv-comedy actors use to enhance our scenes or get more out of our co-actors. Tools are defined in this book as special methods of communication or positive "tricks" you can use to enhance and maximize relationships among the participants in any given "scene." The concept behind the use of these tools is the same as that behind the use of any tools. Sometimes one is more appropriate to the job than another. If you were building a house, for instance, a hammer might be more suitable than a screwdriver. With improv tools, it's the same thing. Sometimes "mirroring" might be a way to create a stronger bond, another time "humor" might be more appropriate. Which particular tool you pull from your tool belt can be a very subjective and personal pick. (I used to opt for the heel of my shoe to pound a nail in the wall rather than a hammer, for instance. It was less painful when I hit my thumb.)

In my mind, when it comes to using improv tools, there is no right or wrong. There are no absolutes. You simply use the tool or tools necessary to make your communications (scenes) work. And there are plenty to choose from! But the ones put forth in this part of the book are the ones I feel you most need. Each is geared to make your communications more meaningful and productive.

Before I get started, I should mention that the tools available to the improv player are all considered to be power tools. So use them with care! I certainly wouldn't want you to hurt yourself in the process. Metaphorically speaking, I wouldn't want you to cut off your tongue to spite your mouth!

Also, remember that the rules you just learned must be adhered to in order to make all your scenes work. So I'm counting on you to nail them! Otherwise, these tools won't make a whole lot of sense.

Now, the tools I introduce to my students include the following: Building Rapport, Mirroring, Listening Beneath the Surface, Playing To Their Agenda, Arming Yourself With Humor, and Making A Positive Out Of A Conflict.

As for which tool to use when: As you already know, spontaneity is the heartbeat of ExecuProv's work, and as such, I believe you need to wait until the scene begins to unfold before you can pull the right tool from your belt to get to work. In each of the subsequent chapters I will offer real conversations in a "before" and "after" format, much like our sketches in the first part of the book. These will serve to illustrate how each of the tools is actually used. It is through these examples that you'll come to understand both the point of the tool and how and when to effectively use it.

Chapter 20

====

No Rapport – No Nothing

Good business is not so much what you're selling as the people you're selling to — and your relationships with them.

In every speech, in every class and in every private coaching session, I tell my ExecuProv students that the only thing that ever matters in all their communication is to develop relationships. The way to do this is through establishing, building and maintaining rapport. If they forgo or forget all else, I tell my students, they must nevertheless remember that rapport is at the core of everything in terms of harmony with people in the business world. Without rapport, you can't sell. Without rapport, you cannot make meaningful human connections with the people you come in contact with because in the end, human connections are the ties that hold our business world together.

Fine, you may be thinking right about now. But what exactly is rapport? Well, Webster defines it as a "relation marked by harmony, conformity, accord or affinity." My friend Dr. Kappas says this about it: "When you break it all down, rapport is really made up of three elements: trust, like and respect." I think he's absolutely right. When those three things are present, you have rapport. If you're trying to make the sale (and don't forget, we're all selling something: a service, a product, a philosophy, an idea — or, if you're an actor — a part), you need, first off, to garner the other person's trust. Next, you want them to find you likable. And naturally they have to respect you in order to choose to do business with you rather than with your competitor. Unfortunately, when I conduct my evaluations with students prior to class, I notice that, more often than not, they tend to be fixated on the sale rather than on creating a meaningful relationship. Most of us are so results-oriented, so bottom-line-driven that we skim right over the relationship-making and go for the kill. It's the American way! I know people who barely say "hello"; instead, they launch right into *their* need, like bargain hunters at door-opening time at a Macy's half-off sale.

I believe the relationship comes first. Some of you are probably saying, "Yeah, okay, of course," but I'm not so sure you behave like you fully mean it. It's one thing to nod when I ask you to stop and think about it, but in the real world, we all know it's typical, (especially if you're a salesperson), to hammer away at attacking as many leads in one day as you can. I maintain that you should solicit fewer leads and instead focus on creating more relationships. Imagine, for instance, that you went about your business day tomorrow forgetting about the revenue-producing part of building new business, forgetting about trying to accomplish some work-related goal. What if you stopped obsessing about these things and just pretended that the only thing that mattered was making "friends"? That creating good vibes and getting the other person to like, trust and respect you was the most important thing? What if that was all you focused on? I'm convinced that your initial approaches to people would be totally different from how you usually come at them. And the outcome would be very different, as well. Much better — I guarantee it!

Rapport in improv is a very interesting thing. The way we go about teaching it is this: We tell our students not to get so hung up on the "what" in a scene but rather to focus on the "who" and the "why." The latter always brings the communication back to the human level, we constantly remind them. Since scenes are communication and communication is all about relationships, the "who" and the "why" always take center stage.

John Michalski, a former Second City Director I greatly respect, teaches his improv actors nothing more than the intricacies of relationships. He asserts that what all improv scenes are *ever* about is relationships — how people feel about one another and the mechanics of how they interrelate. "How do you feel?" he posts on large cards around the stage.

To get a better idea of how rapport works in the context of an improv scene, let's say the audience puts a golf instructor together with two female golf students. First-timers. If they focused their dialogue on "what" they were doing — trying to hit the ball, working on their swings, choosing the right club, etc. — it would not be nearly as interesting as if we were to hear about "why" they were there taking the lesson in the first place, and "who" they were. When we're privy to that, we hear about relationships. We see more develop — positively or negatively — between the golf instructor and the students. We witness something far more interesting. What if we found out, for instance, that the two taking the lessons had been threatened with divorce unless they learned the game? What if we also learned that the golf instructor hated the game and wanted to be a ballet teacher? What if we further learned that the women had each dated the golf instructor at different times? That would be far more compelling to the audience than just watching them hit the ball or get instruction on how to.

Staying on the "what" narrows the playing field in improv. I think the same holds true in business, especially when what we really want is to get rapport going. Remember, the "what" is more "thing"-oriented. It's impossible to make connections through things.

In business, just like in improv comedy scenes, we always have to situate our audiences with a "who," "what," "why," "where," and "when." You've heard me talk about this before. But again, most of us tend to go right to the "what" and get entrenched there. A good telephone example: "Hi, I'm Bill Burns with ProTech, and we have a special offer for you today. If you hire one of our temps, you'll get a second one free." Where's the rapport? Where's the attention on first creating a bond, a relationship? Now, consider what it would be like if Bill had spoken with the mindset of the full-pro improv player — thinking about "who" and "why" first. In so doing, he would instantly have established a relationship. Example: "Hi, I'm Bill Burns with ProTech, and I know your company is often in need of temps because I'm fully aware of how busy you guys always are. If you need additional staff right now, who would you be looking for? I'd like to help." This approach provides the other person an entry into the conversation, at which time he most often will make his needs known. In turn, the door will open for Bill to satisfy his need.

Let's say, though, that the person Bill called didn't need any help. Example: "Thanks for the call, but we don't need any extra staff today. We're all set." This doesn't mean end of conversation. Nor does it mean end of relationship. No. The idea is to not let go until rapport has been generated. If Bill Burns was using the "Yes, and ... " and "Adding Information" rules, he could continue the conversation and get to know the person a little better. For example, Bill: "Glad to hear you're set, and I know how it goes when suddenly, out of nowhere, you're not. So by all means give me a holler — and I mean that in the literal sense — if you're frustrated and need to vent next time you're up against it." The other person might then say, "Boy, I could have screamed last week when both word processors didn't show." Bill: "Yeah, how did you handle it?" And so on, and so on. As a result of Bill Burns' effort to create a relationship, he would have established some measure of rapport. The next time he called this prospective client, he'd be ahead of the game — because he would already have set up a relationship. Chances are, the other person would remember him with positive feelings. And that's all any of us ever want from those around us in the business arena.

The Bill Burns example is only one way to go about building rapport; what might prove even more effective in any situation is a short hello, then a kind of stepping-back to let the other person begin to talk. This way, you can get a handle on "who" they are and "why" they might need your services. As I mentioned earlier, there are no absolutes; you really have to follow your instincts and go with what feels appropriate to the situation and the given circumstances. All too often, we cut the other person off to get our point across, when in fact we could have learned a great deal about what they needed and wanted in just their few opening remarks. Once we know where someone is coming from, we have an excellent opportunity to go for the ideal rapport-building choice. But we must listen!

As a journalist, when I was first writing personality profiles, the number-one piece of advice my editor gave me was to suggest that I do little talking and mostly listen. Rather than have a battery of questions to reel off, one right after the other, he suggested that I would probably find out everything I wanted to know about my subjects by letting them dominate the dialogue. He was absolutely right. If people talk long enough, they reveal a great deal about themselves. Again, when they do, you have the upper hand in sliding in remarks that get them to open up more and create a bond. The ability to take the back seat and simply listen can be a great way to come upon rapport without really trying.

If we use this improv tool — creating rapport — at the top of any conversation, and then follow the prescribed set of improv rules as we continue on, our communication can't fail. When the rules and the tools are in force, good communication is infinite. (I've seen two-minute scenes that could easily have continued with food and bathroom breaks only, for two whole weeks!) This holds true even if we're enjoined in some kind of conflict, as we often are in business situations. Something will eventually get resolved if you do it the improv way. When you go for rapport, the rest will take care of itself.

In my communication travels, here's another thing I've noticed about rapport-building: When you call or meet with someone who immediately lets you know they don't have time to spend with you, you can cleverly maneuver them into talking about themselves. Oddly enough, people will find the time to chat away about their own needs or interests. We all love attention. We all love to have other people listen to us. Someone may not give you 45 minutes, but they will give you more time than they first wanted to. So, again, get smart. What can you do to get them to talk about themselves — to establish rapport? Every performance is different, so be creative. Be agile! Be improvisational! And above all else: Hold true to "Be Here Now."

The following is a "before" and "after" example of a conversation that colorfully pinpoints the rapport lesson.

TAKE ONE

(**Int. new car showroom featuring the Mantra, the car of the 21st century. A sales person is standing nearby as a young lady — thirty something — enters**)

SEAN

(**Overzealous**) Hello. Why, you look like a Mantra driver. I can tell by just looking at you. I bet you chant when you drive. (**He laughs. She doesn't**) This little baby right here gets 16 to the gallon, drives like a dream and comes in 32 colors. Or, hey, this one over here is a sporty unit. You look like the convertible type, hair all tousled and such, you'd like this one, it's a beauty. Want to go for a test drive?

MARY

No thanks. I just stopped in to get a brochure.

SEAN

Well, we also have the family SUV; it's called the Unit. (**She seems disinterested and he notices**) Well, how about a pre-owned model? Heck, we've got certified Mantra Minivans on special for today only.

MARY

Can I get a brochure, please?

SEAN

(**Sees another prospect enter. Begins to head that way**) Yeah, sure, they're right over there on that rack. Help yourself.

-Lights-

No offense to the automobile industry, but these kinds of first meetings unfold every day. Not just in car showrooms, but all over America. The players and the locale may differ, but the point is it's just too easy for some people to dive into the "what" from the outset. To hell with the people thing!

What I would much prefer to see, and what I would highly recommend, is that this salesman establish a friendly relationship with the potential customer. Take his time. Not overwhelm her. Not be overly friendly. Just take a few moments to get to know her ("who") and her reason for being there ("why").

Let's run this one more time, only with the priority being rapport-building and nothing else.

TAKE TWO

(Same set-up — interior of a car showroom)

SEAN

Hello. How are you today? **(Walks toward her and extends his hand to shake hers)** My name is Sean. **(Good eye contact)**

MARY

Hi, Sean, I'm Mary, and I'm fine. Thanks.

SEAN

(Upbeat but not overbearing) Is there something in particular you're looking for?

MARY

Well, I don't know. I actually just came by for a brochure.

SEAN

Sure. Let me get you one right away. Say, can I get you a
cup of coffee or something while I head that way. I was
just going to get a cup for myself.

MARY

(Uncertain) Uh, I —

SEAN

Ah, let me just get you one quick cup.

MARY

(Reluctant but accommodating) Well, just a quick cup.

SEAN

Sure thing. If you have time, I'd be happy to walk you
through the brochure. I'd also be glad to show you some
of our Mantra models, or better yet, let you take one for a
test drive if you like.

MARY

Well, I don't know … .

SEAN

(He hands her a brochure) Just let me know. Have a
seat, I'll be right back. (He returns with two coffees.
She's reading the brochure) Any idea what you're looking for in a car, Mary?

MARY

Well, yes and no.

SEAN

Tell me the "yes" part and maybe I can help you identify
the rest.

MARY

Well, I want something my kids can mess up and won't
ruin. And, I want something that has a little zing to
it ... **(She goes on in great detail. He listens intently)**

**(Another prospect enters. He motions to another salesperson
who quickly greets the person)**

SEAN

Oh, I know all about the kids and how they can make
messes in the car. I have two boys, and ... how old are
your kids?

MARY

**(She goes on to tell Sean all about her family. They continue
to create rapport as they banter back and forth about their
families)**

Maybe Mary didn't buy a car that day, but you can be sure Sean
made some inroads into getting her back in the showroom and
eventually selling her a car. This time around, his focus was simply
on establishing a relationship with his potential customer — not on
making the sale. If each of us could pretend that the sale didn't
matter and that we were getting paid big bucks for just making a

strong connection, we'd probably get both!   Capitalism is a great idea; I think it keeps all of us motivated. But how about Capitalizing on relationships first?

I realize that car dealerships have a special way of training their sales personnel and that the example I've provided may not be their style. What I wanted to illustrate was the contrast between the first approach, where rapport was hardly a consideration, and the second, where it was obviously the only thing that mattered. My underlying point is this: This conversation could have taken place anywhere between any two people in the American business world where a sale was at stake. Take a day off and watch people. If you hadn't noticed, you soon will!

As you go about rapport building, I'm sure you'll begin to see the value of some of the improv rules like "Be Here Now," "React and Respond," "Serve and Support," for starters. With those rules in mind, can you see how easy it is to create the atmosphere for a strong rapport? Following just those three principles will get you off to a terrific start. Now, add the concepts of "Give and Take," "Adding Information," and so forth. As you go about playing with each of the tools that create better relationships, I want you to be able to pick and choose which rules you think apply and integrate them in your communications.

Here's something worth considering: Don't underestimate your competition. If you want to stand out from them, rapport is the only way to do it. People will often spend a little more money with someone they like, rather than pay a little less using the service or products of someone they have no "connection" with. Look around you and the people you buy from. I'm willing to bet, if the rapport isn't there, you don't keep that person and the services they sell for very long. I once fired my pool guy just because there was no vibe. Not because there was a bad vibe. Just no vibe. I knew when it came to needing to really be able to communicate a need or a problem to him, it would be like trying to swim in that pool with no water.

Something else: No one can build rapport quite the way you can. There is only one of you, and so your style in approaching people and bonding with them is unique. Enjoy that about yourself.

Strive to make yourself memorable (likable) to all your business contacts. You don't want your competition to beat you because they have a better relationship with, or are more likable to, the would-be client. We remember the people who we take an instant liking to. When we're ready to do business, they're the ones we usually call.

One last note about the work of improv comedy players and how rapport affects them: Because they fly by the seat of their pants, it's really important that they have good vibes — good chemistry — with one another (and with anyone from the audience who may join them on stage). Without it, the scene might crash or not get very far. So, "rapport first" is key. For improv players, it's top priority. All of us business professionals should follow suit.

The following are a few suggestions on how you can use rapport to bolster your existing relationships and nurture new ones.

1. Always think "human connection" as you come in contact with others. Are you just going through the motions or are you truly bonding with people? We can all detect pretense and feigned interest. Stay "in the moment" and enjoy the rapport-building process. People are fascinating. Enjoy getting to know them.

2. Call people by name early on in your conversations, but never "over-use" anyone's name. It's a dead giveaway that you're desperately trying to bond.

3. Provide a nice intro at the outset of the conversation, but let the other person do most of the talking if possible. This gives you great signals on how to steer the communication, which will deepen the rapport. It also makes people feel that you're sincerely interested in them. Whenever people show an honest interest in us, we like them. (Remember, "like" is a strong component of rapport.)

4. Learn as much about the person or persons you're about to meet before the meeting. Whatever information you can use during your initial contact with them shows genuine interest on your part. This could be finding out about their products, their com-

pany background, their main reason for meeting with you. If it's a new sales call, bone up on the prospect; it will be apparent during that first meeting.

5. If people seem to want to brush you off because they're too busy to talk to you (and this happens frequently in the workplace), see if you can get them to start talking about why they don't have the time. I once got someone to tell me all about his accounting debacle simply by saying: "Sounds like you're having the same kind of day I am." It was a great opening.

6. Keep a log of how many new people you came in contact with on any given day. Now record how many relationships you established with each of these contacts. Did you build a rapport with 50 percent; 60 percent? The goal is to get to 100 percent. But give yourself time. And give yourself credit for taking the time required to change the way in which you usually treat people in new situations.

7. See what else you can do to build rapport in the relationships you've already established. It doesn't mean much to create relationships if we don't work at maintaining them and helping them grow. In business, it's all about networking and, in the end, who you know. You want to make certain you're building a strong base of business contacts, all of whom feel a strong bond with you. You want that base to multiply so that whatever you need, whenever you need it, you have people to turn to. Be careful with all your contacts. Don't forget the "what goes around comes around" principle. Don't take advantage of those you've worked so hard to build rapport with — always give back as much as you take. I try to give more (I think it's the Catholic guilt thing).

8. Make a list of what else you can do to create rapport and to practice it. For instance, can you take more time to strengthen the ties with your children on a daily basis? Can you slow down a bit to get to know someone you've only met in passing? Can

you finally get to know the person behind the counter at the cleaners — the one you've been saying "hello" to for the past several years? These people make for great rehearsal-scene partners! And, daily, these drills will help change the way you behave when you come upon others as you move about the workplace. It's new habits we're after in order to maximize our communication all the way around. So, again, make your own list of what you can do to improve in this area — to use this very valuable tool.

9. Think about your sense of "PR." Do you send personal follow-up notes? Clip an article you know would be of interest to someone? Do you remember birthdays? Good public relations is one more way to go about doing the rapport thing. I suggest taking a few minutes out of every day to put into play your own PR campaign. It doesn't take long, but doing it sure goes a long way.

10. Last, but not at all least, begin observing the people around you. Keep a tally of who you "like, trust and respect." Next, see if you can pinpoint why. This last assignment is a real mind-blower!

Chapter 21

Mirror, Mirror That's Your Call

I'm sure we've all sung that song I mentioned earlier at one time or another; the lyric goes: *All out or all in/through thick and through thin/We're gonna go through it together ...* . The chorus goes: *Wherever you go, you know I go/Whatever you do, you know I do ... Together/Together.*

Well, that's the concept behind our next improv tool. Being in the same place at the same time is a phenomenal way to bring people together. I'm not referring to a specific locale when I say this, I mean joining the other person wherever they happen to be mentally and emotionally. In improv parlance, we call it "Mirroring." What that means is what it says: we reflect the other actor. We become a mirror of the other person — what they're doing and what they're saying. Our behaviors are practically synonymous. And that which is compatible and combined is fused. It's astonishing to watch. Mirroring then, whether it is used on stage or at the office, is the art of matching another person's energy and mood to create a strong interpersonal bond.

Although mirroring is not a tool to be used in every single communication situation, it is a wonderful one to put into play. It also happens to be one of my favorites.

Now, as we use the mirroring technique in the business arena — we end up with what the improv actor ends up with: tight communication. But mirroring is a very subtle tool; it's a delicate way of attaching on a very subconscious level. Most often the other per-

291

son doesn't even know we're doing it. And that's where the art of it all comes in — to get in the same "space" as the person you're communicating with, without their even realizing what's taking place. It takes a real pro to do this perfectly, but anyone can learn how.

If you're not exactly catching on to what I mean by mirroring, let me explain it in the context of a work-related situation. Let's say you're about to enter someone's office (most of us do this many times a day, with different people in different settings). Well, most often when you walk through the door, you tend to ignore that person's state of mind. Instead, you launch into one of several behaviors, such as trying to get them out of their bad mood, overpowering them with your enthusiasm, flustering them with your urgency, or jumping head first into your business agenda. Though there are many other behaviors that fit this scene set-up, these are, I believe, the most common. Yet none of them does much to create or build rapport.

I used to know a guy who entered any and every room with the same cheery greeting.: "Hey, isn't *that* great!" he would say. Most often, someone would query, "What's great? What are you talking about, Stan?" People thought they'd missed something. Stan's standard reply was, "Life and all the many surprises it brings." And then he'd continue, "So, what do you have that's great today?" He was always over the top in the way of enthusiasm. I suppose he was just trying to pump everybody up. Or, perhaps he was claiming his territory. But in any case, sometimes when Stan would make one of his "Broadway" entrances, we'd be in intense discussions about a crisis. It was an ad agency. Crises happened. And one particular crisis finally taught Stan a lesson. Five of us were in a brainstorming session for a new ad campaign for a homebuilder, when suddenly one of my account executives, Bonnie, burst into a nervous fit. She confided that she'd just poured coffee all over the client's final artwork. She was nearly hysterical. Just then, with split second timing, Stan arrived in his usual demeanor with his usual burlesque opener. "Hey, isn't *that* great! Life and all its many surprises. So what do you have that's great today?" That's when Bonnie finally said what we all had wanted to say for months.

"Nothing. I don't have jack! Life is *not* always great." And right after she said the B.S. word in its entirety, she screamed, "Go to hell, Stan!" There was silence. After a four-count, we collectively burst out laughing. The good news was: Stan finally got the message. He learned that you just can't pop through the door without taking note of the climate. But what about you? What about all those times you walk into a colleague's office? What do you do? Try to appease them? Patronize them? Blow off their state of mind with a "forget it" hand gesture? Ignore them? How about the times you encountered so and so, and he was nervous and agitated — totally rushed — and you slid down on his sofa, stretched out and slowly said: "Hey, relax." It probably wasn't said, but that person likely (and possibly unknowingly) hated you, if only for a quick moment.

Yes, this is how resentment is born and fed. It would be far more harmonious to mirror the colleague's unsettled energy. And, interestingly, when you mirror someone's behavior, you can *say* things that don't mirror at all. You can *say*, "Relax," for instance, because your *behavior* is saying, "Hey, I'm with you." It's fascinating to watch someone mirror another's exact behavior and tone, all the while, speaking dialogue that is quite the opposite. In comedy, it's very funny stuff when two things are incongruent. In the real life business-world, it's just one more way of establishing rapport.

Stepping into someone else's space and displaying a mood or energy opposite or antithetical to theirs is a sure way to create a sense of separation. On a very subconscious level, the other person is told that his or her emotional state is neither valid, nor important, nor worthy of notice. If, on the other hand, you were to enter a person's office and, upon immediate contact, mirror where they're at, you would have them — you have would bonded. If, for instance, Stan had entered the room and immediately begun to mirror Bonnie's energy — pacing and moving with her, all the while asking pertinent questions — there would have been a sense of instant unity. When you mirror, the other person feels good about you, usually without even knowing why.

When my ExecuProv students master the fine art of mirroring, they love it. It makes them feel extremely powerful. Me? I think it's synergy in its purest form.

Mirroring can happen in an assortment of ways — through body language, tone of voice, overall attitude, the pace and volume of your voice. The various elements can be used simultaneously or singularly — whatever seems to fit with that certain person at that particular place and time. If you notice, all five mirroring components are subtleties; you're not verbally and openly stating that you're in the same frame of mind. You are simply and implicitly showing that you are by the use of one or more of the mirroring tools.

One of the greatest improv comedy actors of our time is Robin Williams. If you watch him enough — study him — you will note how often he mirrors those he's with, whether it's an interview or he's just cutting up on stage. He's instant in his ability to do this. Most really good improv players are.

In beginning training classes with all improv comedy students, we teach them: If you don't know what to do or say in a scene, just mirror the other actors. If there are three players, and all of them mirror one another, it puts them in a real "React and Respond," "Be Here Now," "Serve and Support" and "Yes, and … " mentality. Quick and agile, they often take turns leading and following, (that's where the "Give and Take" comes in). Improv actors will often resort to mirroring in the beginning of a scene just to get their bearings.

As business people, we can easily do the same. We can jump right into someone else's "space" until we have a grasp, then move the scene somewhere else.

Now here's the big trick: You never want to mirror someone indefinitely. Usually you want to mirror for only a short time. Because once you've fused — more or less become one in the moment — you can lead them to a better "place" mentally. That's right. When you and someone else are together, and you gracefully flip to another mood (usually a more positive one), the other person almost always follows suit without any conscious consideration. A good example is Bonnie. She was freaking out. And we went with her. Then Tom, one of the funniest guys I know, suddenly burst out laughing. He has a very maniacal and contagious laugh. Caught off guard, Bonnie and the rest of us instantly responded. We had all gotten into the same "playpen" with her — we were wallowing in the tension — so there we were, ready to switch when the time was right.

I always tell my students to mirror just at first — during the initial few moments — then "switch" the person, especially if they're in a negative mood.

Now, I don't know about you, but very often when I enter someone's office, they are not kicking back smoking a cigar, or laughing out loud. They're immersed in something and nine times out of ten, the person I come upon is in a stressed or distracted mood. They aren't exactly just sitting there twiddling and whistling as they wait for me to enter. If we're on the other end of this — someone enters our office and we're behind the desk — we're not always ready to welcome them either; to the contrary, many times people's arrival feels like an intrusion. It's very Corporate America to be doing some *thing* till some *one* gets there.

Of course, in the beginning my students resist the whole idea of mirroring. They think that their colleagues will feel they're mimicking or mocking them. And I admit, it's strange to imagine walking into a room where someone is obviously jangled or stressed and immediately begin to mirror their behavior. Our impulse is to be soothing, or concerned. To ask what's wrong. And it's a useful impulse. But mirroring is useful, too. And it can be amazingly powerful.

I have to laugh when I ask my ExecuProv students to take to the stage and do a scene using the mirroring principle first time out. They stand there looking at me with a great deal of trepidation. Using the tool, to them, is like picking up a chainsaw; they're afraid. But once they get the hang of it, they enjoy the results.

Now, mirroring doesn't mean you parrot the other person's words; nor does it mean you completely mimic their body language. The process is more subtle, as I said. We use it through energy — by mirroring the mental state the other person is in. If some of the process spills over into body language (e.g., both people slouching in their chairs), that's okay, but again, we mostly mirror the other person's mood and energy. It's more an attitude thing. Now that you understand the process, I'm going to assign some "Mirroring" tasks.

1. Start to be a bit more aware and alert when you first come upon others. Notice what mood they're in. You don't have to throw yourself into a mirroring posture when first learning this tool; just observe. That's a wonderful start, and it's how many improv actors hone their skills. They just sit back and take it all in.

2. For your first practice, I suggest that you mirror someone you're close to, like a family member or good friend, someone you know well — because you know their moods and how they react to most things. This way, as you first grasp the tool, you can anticipate a bit. After you've practiced successfully and gotten the hang of it, try it on one person per day at the office. Soon your mirroring reactions will become automatic.

3. Before you walk into anyone's office, or encounter them in the work environment, wipe the slate clean. Don't project what their mood might be, and don't plan ahead. This is where all your wonderful improv savvy will come in. Just be spontaneous and let their mood and energy lead you.

4. After you've gotten really good at mirroring, take the next step and see how adroitly you catch your partner off guard. Now, switch their mood to a more positive one and see how wonderful your communication becomes. Remember, your job is to maximize every piece of communication. Mirroring is a more terrific way to make that happen.

5. If you're not sure you should use the mirroring tool, don't. Better not to take chances with this one until you build some expertise with it. Take your time mastering it; you don't have to use it every day in every situation. Again, you'll become an accomplished improv player soon enough, and all this mirror-

ing will happen without any planning or much effort on your part.

6. Learn to trust your instincts. Remember that mirroring relies heavily on the "feeling" function within us all — not the "thinking" function.

7. You'll need to let go of that constant urge to control everything, and let your intuition lead you. Mirroring is not one of those situations when you can filter, analyze, manage, modulate and think through what is appropriate. Just go with the flow. Try to feel what the other person is feeling. Get absorbed into their energy.

8. Lastly, notice how you feel when you suddenly become one with someone else's energy. It's a real high when you fuse, for it is there that the communication between you and another person sets the foundation for a deep-rooted rapport — one that only grows stronger over time.

Chapter 22

─────────

Digging Deep
The Single Most Important Thing Said

Don't you love it when you meet someone who seems to completely understand you, without your having to explain everything to them? I do, but it doesn't happen very often, I'm afraid. That goes for all of us, I suppose. In my life, my mother and daughter are the only two people who seem to fall into this category. Unfortunately, my mother is now with the Great Communicator. Thank God I still have my daughter!

Maybe for you, the person who doesn't need to hear everything to know what you're thinking and feeling is a husband or wife, a best friend or someone at work. I would estimate that each of us has at least one person in our lives we wish we could Xerox because they seem so in tune with where we're "at." It would be wonderful to clone such individuals. They seem to read our concerns and wishes almost before we become aware of them ourselves; or they're immediate in their ability to read between the lines of what we're saying and respond to us in comforting and helpful ways. I think there are two basic reasons why this is so: One, this special person (or hopefully persons) knows you well and can easily anti-cipate your moods, can interpret your nuances and knows what you're really trying to communicate even when you don't say it outright. And, two, they genuinely care about you.

Some people are blessed with a handful of these people in their lives, while others feel a hopeless sense of isolation because they don't have such close connections. But in any case, each of us certainly has times when we feel completely understood. After all, each of us comes in contact with so many people throughout any given workday. Few of those we encounter take the time to consider where we're coming from. (And we do it to them, too!)

Over time, lack of understanding takes a toll. Some people just give up and shut down with a "whatever ... " mindset. If you're one of those, you should reconsider. There are ways to turn that sense of defeat around. For openers, you can begin to put into play some of the rules I've discussed with you to strengthen ties and get more out of your everyday communications with others. You can also put to good use the new tools I'm exposing you to — they, too, will add to your communication reservoir.

When it comes to being understood, we can't expect everyone in the workplace to be able to read between the lines of what we're attempting to say; each of us needs to take full responsibility for transferring our thoughts and feelings directly. For most of us, though, this is easier said than done. Occasionally, with that "special person," we'll risk it all and tell it like it is, but rarely will we do this at the office. The truth is, none of us wants to be vulnerable. Unfortunately, then we train ourselves to talk around things rather than express them openly. We're afraid. We're insecure. Some of us get tongue-tied or don't even know we're thinking certain things on a deeper level. In turn, we take what other people say at face value, hardly ever considering that what they're really doing is hiding behind words and phrases and moods. So many people send us distinct messages only to have us respond merely to what they say, not necessarily to what they really mean. We're too preoccupied with ourselves to focus in on the subtleties; we run around in an "uh-huh" mentality.

After watching people in offices across America trying but failing to get through to one another, I agree wholeheartedly with Dr. Kappas' belief that the "most important thing to all of us, is to be understood." Lack of understanding is, in fact, my students' biggest complaint. When I do my pre-class interviews and ask them about their relationships with others in their work environs. They continually confide that their boss or co-workers don't seem to understand them at all. Moreover, they claim they are often misread —

accused of communicating one thing when they sincerely meant something else. No wonder we have wars!

There are many aspects to my training and many areas within the scope of it that intrigue me, but the one area that really compels me to find new ways to help is in the area of understanding. So here I go again, pulling out the improv comedy handbook to share with you what improv players know and do to effect a better and clearer understanding of one another.

Interestingly, the improv comedy player's on-stage communication focuses more on what is unsaid, than what is actually said. Players monitor subtext, which we covered in Chapter 15. They attend to what is being expressed subtly or round about with words that say one thing, but, may be hiding something else. Emphasis is always on relationships between people and how they feel toward one another.

Those who study improv comedy learn to relate to others in very profound ways. For instance, if one actor says "How are you?" in a tone that sounds like he couldn't care less, and the other actor says "Fine" in a whimper, both performers instantly know a lot is going on. They react and respond to the undercurrent, not to the spoken word. If one goes on to say, "I'm sorry you're feeling bad; I can hear it in your voice, but I still need to go to the opera because my parents are there and if I don't show up, they'll think I gave their ticket away," that person is really saying, "I can't disappoint my parents; they will think I don't appreciate them and I can't take it when they make me feel guilty. It's horrid." But see how that true inner thought was never actually expressed.

Now, the corresponding actor — if she was reading between the lines, if she went beyond what was actually expressed and gleaned the hidden messages — might say, "Oh, I know how fearful you are about your parents' laying guilt on you. Why don't you just admit it and confront them once and for all?" With this response, we have a real, genuine understanding — we also have a much more interesting scene than the one that could have been played out at a much more shallow level. And shallow is a key word here, because that's how many of us play "Life In The Office" day in and day out. We skim the surface like superstar skaters, barely touching down, hurrying around our busy rink.

In your life, especially at work, how often do you "listen" by going beneath the surface to absorb someone's real meaning, whether you pick up on it through attitude or astute word interpretation? Probably not very often, for as I have mentioned repeatedly, we tend to be into ourselves and skip over people's meanings. How often do people pass you by, chatting away with superficial talk according to what you said but didn't really feel or mean at the time?

If I had my way, each of us would take a class in elementary school called "Tell It Like It Is." The curriculum would include lessons such as "How To Learn To Say What You Really Mean," "How To Overcome The Fear Of Being Straightforward," "How To Read Between The Lines Of What People Are Saying," and "How To Interpret The Foreignness Of The English Language." These would be taught in first or second grade; later, students would learn more complex dynamics, like "How To Communicate Totally With Everyone, Every Time." Given my way, I would instill a whole new meaning in the term "Reading Comprehension."

Of course, if you're like most people, you never got these lessons in school. But don't worry; it's never too late to learn.

My first request on the way to better understanding is to ask that you become more direct, honest, forthright, and articulate when you talk to others. Being specific (creating into certainty) and being more exact with what you want and need will only help you get it. If you're the type that doesn't want to be at communication-risk, get over it! You only cheat yourself in the end. Take chances. Don't offend people by getting too bold, and don't be self-centered. I'm simply suggesting that you present what you have to present with authenticity.

Similarly, when you listen to others, I'm going to ask you to start listening differently. That's the emphasis here: tuning into others. In Chapter 15 you got a taste of what I'm talking about; now I want you to go a step further: I want you to find **the single most important thing someone is really saying when they come to you with a need or want.** Let me explain. People come into our work environment daily by phone or in person and we listen to them explain something. Usually they're trying to get us to give them something. It can be material or abstract. Nonetheless, it's usually something specific. And I want you to listen to *everything* they say, because nearly 100 percent of the time, there is one central theme, one important point hidden deep within their words. Your job is to find out what it is and to respond to *it.* If you listen long enough, they'll repeat it over and over in a variety of different ways.

I want to illustrate how someone can deliver a couple of paragraphs saying one thing but meaning something else — something additional or something entirely different from what their actual words suggest. If you listen to the dialogue in its entirety, you will find there is an overall essence — a theme, a point, a message — that they're really trying to convey but don't say. See if you can pick it out.

(Int. office. Justin has agreed to meet with Tony on the upcoming Baltic Ball, Baltic Insurance Company's big yearly fund-raising bash. Justin and Tony are both handling the many details to put the event together)

JUSTIN

Hey, Tony. Come on in. What's going on, man?

TONY

I just wanted to go over the table decorations with you.

JUSTIN

Yeah, okay. Not my department ... yours, but okay.
Shoot.

TONY

I was thinking, instead of the black and white theme, we

should break it up with another accent color. Yellow.
Fuschia or teal. Some zippy color. I mean, if we go
black and white it looks like last year — well, except for
the fact that you're doing white orchids on the table rather
than daisies, and I know that gives it a more elegant look,
but Samson knows I did the table decor last year and I will
be in that debriefing meeting with him the next day and
if — he wasn't happy with the Tellis Cookoff because of
the color scheme. Oh, I know — what about a burgundy
touch — you know, napkins, place cards in burgundy ink
— oh, I got it — raspberry baby's breath intertwined in
the flowers so that when you first walk in the room you
get this flash of color — you know, the burgundy against
the black and white. It would pop, right?

JUSTIN

Burgundy? I don't know. That seems so late-'80s, you
know, art deco, retro or something.

Now, at face value, we have Tony asking Justin's opinion on
burgundy as an accent color for the table decorations. However,
having read Tony's remarks, you're probably thinking that what he
was really getting to was obvious. Unfortunately, when those
words fall upon the human ear, it isn't always so apparent.

The crux of what was important to Tony was evident to me after
I took in his whole monologue. Was it to you? It's quite possible
that you and I may have slightly different takes on what he was
expressing — what we picked up between his words — but I'll bet
we're not far off from one another in our assessment of what lay
beneath the surface.

In unearthing the real message, I first listened to Tony's tone to
grab onto his state of mind. His sentences were run-on and he
talked non-stop. He appeared nervous and unsure of himself, to say
the least. If I'm both a good communicator and a good listener, I'm
going to find genuine ways to make Tony feel good about his work

and himself when I respond. But that will come later. The first thing out of my mouth should address his innermost, deepest concern.

At first glance you may have thought that Tony wanted to do something unique, something different from last year. You would be right; we did hear that. And, if you dug a little deeper, you may have sensed that Tony wanted to stand out for doing something more creative this year. This, too, would be an accurate calculation. Probing further, you probably guessed that Tony was worried about Mr. Samson and what he would think about his creative abilities. This summation also has merit. But digging deeper, to what — to me — is the heart of the matter, we hear anxiety not about how Tony might be criticized at the debriefing meeting, but about whether or not he will keep his job.

Tony's appeal to Justin was: "Help me find ways to look good; I don't want to lose my job over this." Now, Tony never said any such thing, but if you read between the lines, you can detect his worst fear. And, that's the first thing Justin should respond to — Tony's deepest concern — if he wants to truly bond with him. Justin should say first-off after Tony's rambling words, "Hey, relax, man. Samson loves your work. He can't do without you and you know it." Then he could go on to talk about accent color choices, about impressing people with an exciting visual. That would have solidified their relationship — provided a strong bond — because Tony would have known that Justin was understanding the unspoken.

Here's what typically happens, though. Someone like Justin starts talking about the color burgundy and why he thinks it's a bad choice. Bad move. Sure, burgundy was at issue, but it wasn't the real issue, and zeroing in on it isn't going to establish a strong connection with the other person. Responding first to the single most important overall message someone is sending is one more sturdy tool you can use to assemble and build stronger communication. When I use this tool, most people don't have any idea what I'm doing. I can just tell that they trust me and harbor good feelings toward me because I've demonstrated understanding beyond the obvious. There is nothing more impressive to another person than

when you verbalize something they won't — when you feed back
to them in words what they've only expressed in a clandestine way.

As you work with this tool, as you go beneath the surface —
burrow to find the real meaning of what someone is trying to convey — there may be more than one answer. In Tony's case I spelled
out several unspoken messages, none of which was wrong. They
all had credence. What I did, however, was to keep digging, to
unearth each hidden message until I got to the bottom of it all.
Sometimes you have to keep excavating until you hit the key mis-
sive.

I truly enjoy using this tool because I like to watch the relief on
the faces of those with whom I am communicating. Sometimes
they'll actually sigh with relief. Sometimes they'll say, "Did I say
that"? and occasionally they may even get defensive, trying to con-
vince me that they're not worried about losing a job, etc. In my
experience, however, most people are quite receptive and apprecia-
tive. And using the tool provides an opening for me and the other
(or others) to come to on-target, viable solutions — not just gloss
over something with a quick fix, or miss the mark altogether. I've
heard people talk for hours, spinning in circles, never really hom-
ing in on what is at issue or what someone is concerned about.

Has this ever happened to you? Are you one of those people
who tries to convey something and always feels the other person
just isn't getting "it"? Or are you one of those people who is so literal, you simply listen to what someone is saying and respond only
and exactly to that?

Whichever side of the fence you're on — and I believe we all
spend time on both sides every day — it's time to master the use of
this new communication tool. It's one more terrific way to connect
to people.

Responding to the single most important thing said is particularly important in our work environment because we spend more
time with business colleagues than with most other people in our
lives. If we make the use of this tool a habit, people will always
feel comfortable and at ease with us. We will build trust. We will
gain a reputation for being someone everyone likes to work with.

Life is flying by us at asteroid speed in this fast-paced, highly technological world. It's just so easy to overlook people's real messages because we're all so damn busy! But it's those who take the time to tune into others who build strong relationships. And don't forget: Success in business is all about people and your relationships with them. Without good relationships you don't have a whole heck of a lot!

Here's something else: The company heads who hire me constantly moan about lack of productivity and wasted time. I assert that a great deal of the problem comes from simple misunderstandings, which come from people not taking the time to pluck out the real messages. When you take the time to respond to the single most important thing said, you start your communication with a distinct direction. And, you can continue to steer the dialogue on a straight line all the way to the finish — the resolution. I don't know about you, but I have sat through meetings where people have actually asked, "What are you getting at?" and the other person tries again but can't seem to get his point across. This can go on for hours. You may have a meeting agenda with eight items on it and never even finish the first one. That's why it's so important to get off to a meaningful start by reading between the lines and feeding back to the speaker an understanding of where he is at. This will allow you to follow up with subsequent communication that gets results and makes the other person feel understood.

Here's one more reason the use of this tool is so valuable. Chemistry happens. And it multiplies as one person plays off another person's unspoken communication. Any good team of improv players will tell you they love working with their fellow performers because they can count on them to grab on to their nuances and make good use of them. They use perception and insight along with all that quick wit to enrich a piece of work. So, improv impresario that you now are, it's time for you to be operating along those lines. Slide one more tool into your belt. This one you can also use at your discretion.

Here are some tips on how and when you can put this new technique to work:

1. Start listening to everything someone has to say to you before

you respond. Sometimes we cut people off in the middle of their dialogue and begin addressing the first few things they've conveyed. Better to let someone speak, let them finish all their thoughts before we verbally give something back. If you allow the other person this communication opportunity, you will learn much more about what they really want and need. It's all in there somewhere!

2. Try to recap conversations with those you come in contact with each day, keeping in mind how often you responded to what was spoken on the surface, and what you responded to that was more hidden or covert. If you went beyond the obvious and gleaned very important messages as a result of reading between the lines, give yourself a big thumbs up. If you were also able to feed back a response that catered to a person's underlying need or want, give yourself another accolade. If you wish to practice on those close to you — family members or good friends — do so. Next, take one person at work and practice on him or her. Note the positive results. Keep a diary of these; they'll be fun to go back over and read a few months down the line. The record of such instances will help you develop a better understanding of what people mean, as opposed to what they say. I always think seeing things on paper in black and white has more impact in terms of getting the lesson. After you've conquered one co-worker, try this tool out on another. Over time, you will find yourself listening to both: what is really said and what is unsaid but meant. Like a veteran improv player, you'll get really good at this eventually. Watch your relationships grow!

3. Work at communicating your real feelings and thoughts — not in a huff or in a sarcastic manner, but with a sincere kindness. You'll find yourself feeling better for taking more responsibility, and you'll like the control you feel when you can predict the outcome in certain conversations. If you are direct and forthright, instead of stepping around issues, you may just get what you want and need. Those around you — the ones you spend a

good deal of time working with — may begin to follow suit. We tend to model those people we admire.

4. Be a good observer of at least one conversation a day that you're privy to but not an actual part of. Watch the dynamic between those talking. The people letting their wants or needs known will be fascinating to watch. You'll be able to see whether they are taking responsibility for good, sound communication, or whether they are sabotaging themselves. Conversely, listen to the listeners: Are they sensitive? Do they hear the real message? If so, do they respond appropriately and effectively? Like a good Director, you'll now get the chance to critique others. No better way to learn than to observe.

5. As you mine for the hidden meanings in things people say, don't just stop at the first layer. Dig deep until you truly feel you have your finger on the pulse. We're all motivated by some need or want, and it will become apparent to those who care enough to see beyond the first dimension.

6. Don't forget that one of the best ways to come upon the single most important thing said is to listen for the theme that seems to be recurring.

7. Chart your own conversations — your part of them — to see how many thoughts, feelings and moods you hide. Is it serving any viable purpose to do so? Is there really much risk in being straightforward? Just how hard do others have to work to get to the bottom of your dialogue?

8. Though this tool — feeding back or acknowledging the single most important thing said — can be used at all times, don't use it when it doesn't feel comfortable. Save it for those really important times; use it when you think it matters most.

Chapter 23

Whose Agenda Is It, Anyway?

Okay, here's the scene: A handful of people are planning to meet in the conference room. They're asked to arrive at 3 p.m. They do. The meeting starts, and boom! Everyone starts peddling their own highly important, impeccably prepared, big-deal priority agenda. Why? It's very simple: Everybody tends to think their "stuff" is the most important. After all, it's their stuff. Come on, 'fess up! You've done it, right? Gone to the meeting, plopped yourself into your chair with an extra bounce, jockeyed for verbal position, and blurted out an "item" or two before anyone else could introduce theirs. Most of us can hardly wait to make our points, to spill our business guts. It's really important: our stuff.

I don't want to dampen your enthusiasm or stifle your eager energy by suggesting that you shouldn't enter that 3 o'clock meeting with a certain intensity. It's that single-minded focus that often gets the job done. So please, don't consider any of what I've said thus far as a reprimand. It's just that I'm trying to get you to see that there is always more than one agenda when you go to a meeting. The other guys have agendas, too — whether there's one other guy or a dozen. Often, in our quest to get the job done, we overlook this.

I'm not saying you shouldn't have an agenda, or that you should give parts of it up. What I'm trying to say is that we all should do the following when we walk into a meeting: assess the climate, feel out the other person or persons, and go with the flow. This is not to say you can't get your points across in time; you can. Just don't stay focused exclusively on your stuff, at the expense of everyone else's.

Through my work in the business community, I have come to tag one of the biggest problems in overall communication: Agendamongering. It's a communication malady that afflicts thousands. An Agendamonger is someone who thinks his or her agenda is the one that takes precedence. Their agenda is the most important one. These people enter into conversations fixed on their "stuff," but it's like falling through a trap door: Right away, they get sucked into some dark hole — the inside of their own head. Climbing out of that hole can take forever. Sometimes people don't even know they're in there; they just wander around a conversation like a drunk in a dark room, continually groping for the light, carelessly knocking things over as they go. They don't stop to realize that people's egos and feelings are getting toppled — they don't realize that real communication requires a sensitivity to more than just getting their program across.

Here's what I recommend to avoid these pitfalls when you take your next meeting: Prepare like crazy, get all your stuff together — but when you arrive and settle in, wait to see how the meeting unfolds. Then play your agenda accordingly. By ear. Item number seven for example, may need to become item number one. Item number nine may not be appropriate after all. And item number one may not even be discussed until the very end of the meeting.

It may be that you deviate from your prepared agenda altogether. That's happened to me a number of times. I once thought I was going to talk about a "Humor in the Workplace" class with an airplane manufacturing client. But listening to his intro, I could see my agenda fly right out the window. It was "People Skills" the potential client really wanted. So I made a quick and smooth search through my mental repertoire and pulled up the appropriate agenda. Now, if I had plowed ahead with my initial agenda without waiting for the meeting to unfold, I could have been giving this potential client information that missed the mark completely. I may have lost the sale. Instead, I went with the layout of the scene and made my way to a very happy and conclusive ending.

Always remember: The other person's agenda will steer you in the right direction, so listening may be the first tool of choice. Remember the old improv adage, Be Here Now? Nowhere is it more fitting than at the top of any meeting. My advice is: Go with what fits where, and do it spontaneously — in the moment. This is the way you always want to play the agenda game.

Speaking of improv techniques, no place will the skillfulness of yours be more evident or more crucial than in the meeting. It takes great agility to maneuver in and around all the agendas, but like a great Indy 500 race car driver, you can do it if you hang onto the wheel and keep your eye on the road. Keep your hands poised on your improv tool belt, reach for the appropriate one as you zig and zag around other people's agendas. You've now got a good handle on the basic improv rules, so rely on feeling out the other guy before deciding whose agenda goes first and how much time is spent on yours versus theirs. This savvy is the most important tool, by the way. It's all you really need to make that meeting — that piece of communication — meaningful and productive. Those who can go with the flow — slipping their agenda in here and there — are usually far more successful than those who bulldoze their ideas across even before taking their seat. Agendamongers slam people's attention spans against the wall. They overtake or go against the flow. They force-feed everyone in the room item after item after item from their own highly piled agenda plate.

Not long ago I went to a meeting with three other people. We were there to discuss a direct-mail campaign. I was helping pinpoint a target audience, another person was handling the design of the collateral piece, someone else was there to talk printing, and then, of course, also in attendance was the client, a woman selling image consulting. As we took our seats, everyone but me began to talk. Soon the printer took over, his eyes pinned to his steno pad. It wasn't so much that he was arrogantly dominating the conversation — in fact, he began softly with this question: "Would you all like to know what I've chosen for card stock and ink colors?" When everyone said "yes," however, he began to zip down his list of agenda items like a high speed dragster leaving the rest of us at the pole. Sure, everything on his list had to be addressed at some point during that meeting, but he just kept right on going, leaving the rest of us virtually no room to cut in. Cutting him off was all but impossible. He just continued to tick off each item as though the printing was the heart of the job. We hadn't even started to provide the information we were asked to gather and report on in the meeting when he wrapped. He barely took a breath as he finally said: "So, I guess that's everything." "But what about us?" I wanted to shout; we had "things," too.

The picture I'm trying to illustrate here is that, many times, people aren't deliberately being rude, or self-centered, or coming from ego. They just get so wound up in their responsibilities, they forget that other people have them as well and that other people need to share their agenda items as the meeting progresses. Of course, we all know there are individuals who *do* try to steal the show, who have to be the center of attention — but that's not who I'm referring to at this juncture. I'm talking about the average professional nice guy who just seems to get immersed, forgetting the others.

I want you to recognize how easy it is to open up your agenda bag and dump all its contents on the table. Easy — but very counterproductive. Because as kind and professional as we might be, Agendamongering can really hurt us. There are many dangers. By not waiting to see what other people have in their bags, you may miss an important opportunity to modify your agenda — to your benefit, by the way. By not waiting to see what other people have in their bags, you may also miss out on making a solid connection with the others in the meeting. But here's the biggest drawback: You communicate from a singular point of view — your own. And right away, the communication becomes lopsided. When that happens, it's hard to really come together (a '60s expression) — with anyone at any meeting. The end result? Often, no sale (not just of a product, but of a persuasive idea) because you have no solid grasp on who has what on their agendas. It's bad enough to lose a sale "in-house," but what if you hoard the meeting and the meeting happens to be with an existing or would-be client? Uh, oh! Now you've really got a potential problem.

As you know, I'm often asked to sit in on meetings to observe and assess business professionals' behaviors. A prime example of

what I'm referring to took place one day when a rookie salesperson was assigned the task of pitching a potential new client. The
rookie worked for a client, a major accounting firm that had invit-
ed the would-be account to its headquarters. Now, I swear to you,
the following took place. (I have, however, changed the names.)
Here's what the salesperson, entering the room, had to say — much
of it before he even reached the sofa where the two would-be
clients were seated: "I'm so glad to meet you, Ms. Smith, my name
is Allan Thorgood with Johnson and Peters, and I just want you to
know that our firm is the right accounting firm for you. First, we
have several other companies in your field on our roster; we know
exactly what your spreadsheets need to look like, your quarterly
reports, year-end reports, stockholder notices, dividend checks,
graphs, schematics, financial statements and prospectuses." One
of the potential clients opened her mouth to say something, but
Thorgood cut her off: "Oh, and did I mention that we always serve
good coffee, our offices look like something out of *Architectural
Digest* and Friday is Corporate-Casual Day?" He laughed as he
added, "And we not only validate your parking, we validate *you*
every chance we get." We all gasped. He kept right on going. "Ah,
well, since there seem to be no questions, I'd better be going. Have
another meeting in 20 minutes." Someone raised a hand to get a
last word in, but instead, Thorgood, in his exit, threw a parting shot
over his shoulder, never skipping a beat: "And, of course we bring
in lunch and dinner during those long meetings. Hope you like liv-
erwurst on peanut butter and jelly."

Oh boy, I thought. This is not good.

As you probably noticed, Thorgood had no sense of breaking up
his agenda to accommodate anyone else in the room. He had been
instructed to make a short sales pitch and that's the way he handled
it. He'd been given a briefing with a list of selling points the client
would be most impressed by, and in his over-zealousness he disre-
garded anything and everything those two women may have had on
their agendas. His focus was on the laundry list of selling points —
not on the client's needs. Thorgood, like so many of us, was in such
a hurry to run from one appointment or task to another, he just
grabbed his "stuff," threw it up like confetti, and then moved on to

the next party.

If you put your newly acquired improv techniques to use, and if you whip out your agenda-maneuvering tool, you'll have a much greater success rate when it comes to landing the sale or pleasing the client, co-worker or boss. The key is to what we call "smell the audience" — to first get a feel for the vibe in the room. Next, you want to listen to the first few things said and play off of them. After that, you want to make your agenda flexible enough to introduce or incorporate the items on it when and where they're appropriate.

Don't forget that when people come together to communicate, most of the time it's not for a one-sided purpose. Each party in attendance wants or needs something. So, in all your eagerness to be a good worker bee — from CEO to mailroom clerk — don't forget to do the agenda dance with poise and grace; don't step on toes. If you pause to listen and feel the goings-on in the room before you start to present your agenda, you'll always be ahead in the good-business game. When in doubt, let the other guy's agenda take precedence. You can't lose. The main goal is to make every meeting and every piece of communication work. If you're tuned into agenda etiquette, it always will.

Here are a handful of reminders and tips on how to handle your agenda versus theirs:

1. Start with the awareness that there will always be more than one agenda.

2. Know that your agenda may not always go first, nor will it necessarily prevail.

3. Assess what's appropriate: Did they call the meeting? In that case, perhaps their agenda takes precedence. Were you the one who asked to get together? Then maybe you should take the lead. But always — and I mean, always — make sure you have a good grasp on the other person's agenda. In any meeting, you learn a lot from just listening to the first few things someone says. It tells you what you need to do to meet their needs. Wait until the meeting is underway before you set sail on your

agenda items. At that juncture, you can decide how to present them and whose agenda is in the driver's seat. This is particularly true when you're trying to sell someone something. I've seen hyper-kinetic salespeople pop right through a door and race to extend their hand for a good hearty shake, all the while pitching their product. They take very little time to warm to the other person. Then, there are those who are gentle in the initial exchanging of pleasantries, only to abruptly change the subject and begin talking about their "agenda"!

4. Know that what you don't cover verbally, you can always forward in a memo or a report or by e-mail. We don't have to feel compelled to cover every single item in person. Present the most salient items; save the rest for later.

5. Try not to be one of those people who tend to rebut every remark made by the other person — the tit for tat mentality. And, for goodness sake, stay clear of the verbal dance floor with that oh-so-familiar rumba: "My item is more important than your item."

6. Until you really get them down, run through your list of improv rules before each meeting. As you already know, if you follow them you can't go wrong; your communication cannot flounder. But do a quick review. It's easy to forget some of the most important principles.

7. Focus diligently on your listening skills: both surface and subtext. They will serve wonderfully in guiding the presentation of each of your agenda items. Stay in the moment at all times; it will keep you agile and sagacious.

8. Shortly after the meeting, make a written report in your diary of how you handled your agenda items. Did you defer to the other guy? Were you able to spontaneously re-arrange the order of your agenda? Did you mix and match your items in response to theirs? How adroit were you at improvising a new and added

agenda item? The answers to all these questions will help you examine the proficiency and effectiveness of your participation in meetings. Ultimately, the only goal is to become a stellar communicator. As you review the entries in your diary, keep that in mind. And always give yourself positive strokes for overcoming hurdles, noticing positive changes in your business behavior and new ways of playing the agenda game. Next, record the compliments you received from the others who were in the meetings with you. We tend to forget these all too soon, yet they are so important to savor later. Too, they serve as inspiration and motivation to do well — something we all need. Adding these notes to your entries will also be valuable during your periodic review.

Chapter 24

Conflict and Opposition
Oh, Boy!

Almost every workday we encounter people who are difficult to deal with or people who are just plain oppositional. You know the type: If you say "blue," they say "green." The good news is, there are various ways to deal with these people. Though I'm no psychologist, I have learned that the tools we use on the improv comedy stage to handle these folks — whether they come from the audience or from the troupe itself — can also be aptly applied to any business situation.

One of my business students, a man who holds a degree in clinical psychology, and who works as a Human Resource Director for a large food manufacturing company, whispered to me as we watched a scene unfold on stage one day, "I love this stuff. It's like applied psychology." I nodded a silent affirmation. After class, he went on to say, "What I've learned over the past couple of years in class is that these improv rules and tools are great techniques to employ anytime you're caught in a tough bind trying to communicate with another person who's driving you nuts." I agreed wholeheartedly, for, having used these rules and tools with the toughest of clients (and ex-husbands), I knew first-hand that his belief was dead on. He remarked that certain rules such as the "Yes, and ..." theory and "Refusal and Denial" were just two of the rules he himself had used with manipulative and obdurate types — employees with the non-improv spirit.

You, too, can arm yourself with the improv comedy player's

arsenal when it comes to finding reasonable solutions to dealing with the naysayers, the not-gonna-do-it-your-way types. This is not to say that conflict is a bad thing, or that we should try to avoid or prevent it. Conflict will always exist. And indeed, conflict sometimes brings us to great answers. If you get a bunch of people in one room and everyone is throwing a different opinion on the table, it can create a great energy, a kind of brain trust out of which wonderful things can happen. That's why we call meetings. That's why we get together.

Conflict is then, and should be, part of our everyday lives. But healthy conflict isn't the kind of conflict I'm talking about. This chapter is devoted to dealing with the troublesome handful of people who tend to get in our way — the individuals who just wear you down — that choice few everyone dreads whenever they walk into the room. You know who they are!

With these people, naturally, you can use all the improv rules outlined in Part One of the book; I consider those tenets to be the most positive choices when you're trying to handle someone who is making the rest of the group miserable. In fact, if you do a quick inventory, you can see that implementing any or all of these fundamental principles is a great strategy for getting through any tough "scene." However, sometimes you need a little something extra. You need a few additional key improv tools.

I cannot think of one workday when there hasn't been at least one testy or obstinate person mucking up the good energy. Granted, these people may have been only slightly tough, or may have started out tough but then backed off, but the reality is, they still stopped the momentum of the "scene." Yep, conflict in the workplace is clearly all around us. And if your work-life is like mine, you probably have at least one person who tends to create strife for you and everyone else on the rest of your team.

That's when you have to find alternate solutions.

And just as there are different bits to insert in those interchangeable screwdrivers, there are mix-and-match tools for the courageous communicator. In dealing with the tough types, you have to vary your approach, because no matter how hard you work at integrating the improv rules in conversation, there are those who just won't go with the flow. Communicating with these people is like trying to hold a melting Jell-O mold together: it's hard to contain the situation as it slides. Like dissolving Jell-O, the communication gets liquid, it lacks real substance; it can also get slippery and sticky. That's when we're forced to revert to other options — more specifically, razor-sharp improv tools.

There are three major tools I put to use when any communication conflict is getting out of hand: winning the person; ignoring or isolating the person; or, finally, asking them to leave — cutting them from the scene.

To better explain the tricks in my toolbox, let me revert back for a moment to what happens during an improvisation comedy show — conflict being the focal point now.

I've mentioned throughout the book that the audience is asked to provide a set-up prior to the commencement of most any improv scene. In addition to a who, what and where, we improv Directors also ask the audience for a conflict — a difficulty, an issue, a problem — to center the scene around. Conflict gives more interest to the piece and gives the actors a "hook" on which to hang the scene. In addition, it creates an instant atmosphere — a setting of sorts — some "thing" the actors can strive toward finding a meaningful resolution for. They need this fodder in order to effect a total piece of work in a very short period of time.

Conflict in an improv scene usually comes in one of three forms: man against nature, man against himself, and man against man. Obviously, it is the latter type of conflict that I'm talking about here and the heart of what this chapter addresses: man against man.

Now, in the life of the improv player, I talked about getting a conflict from the audience — a suggestion to beef up the scene. But the improv player can experience a different kind of conflict, too, the kind that comes from a dissident member of the audience (a heckler, for instance) or from another actor on stage. This kind of conflict is distracting and maddening, and it's the type of conflict we, as business professionals, find ourselves up against constantly. So, if you're presenting to a hard-headed person, or trying to maintain decorum with someone who is allegedly on your team but doesn't act like it, the following strategies are for you.

The first tactic is an obvious one. It's the optimal choice of "winning the dissenter." You do it by simply utilizing the basic improv rules. But there's an added twist. In addition to employing all the improv rules, you also want to be constantly thinking: What can I do to win this person? What little wrenches and ratchets can I pull from my tool-belt to diffuse the tension and get them to go my way? Well, for openers, you'll want to bone up on the critical improv rules of "Go With," "Yes, and ... " and "Adding Information." The use of these alone can help restore balance to a push-pull situation. And the great thing is, the other person doesn't have to have a clue about what the rules are for you to make the tension subside.

Let's look at a snippet of conversation that makes good use of some of our basic improv rules. And let's incorporate a few tools to illustrate how, in tandem, they can be used to win over the other person.

Let's say there is a conversation between Harry and Mary — Harry being the person you fantasize about pushing out the seventh story window:

HARRY

I hear that, Mary, but it just won't work. Who ever heard of writing children's books with some of the characters having foreign accents!

MARY

Yes, and I can understand that you think it would not be politically correct, and I am addressing that issue by making all the characters diverse enough to cover a broad cross-section of cultures. Everyone has an accent.

HARRY

That's nuts! We'll have every racial activist in the country boycotting the entire series.

MARY

Yes, and that's how it looks at first glance, Harry; I understand your concern. Yet I'm asking you to consider that when you position the content of the books around our overall purpose, I think you'll get the opposite result from such groups.

HARRY

Oh, you mean hitting hard the heart of the series: the idea that we want children to embrace all cultures?

MARY

Precisely. Yes, and not only embracing them but understanding many cultures at a very root level. Providing dialects creates a true-to-life identification. The "Understanding and Loving Your Neighbor" series can be fun without being disrespectful. Besides, done cleverly, it gives us a hook. And that's what you're all about, Harry: ingenuity. It's my sole purpose to make you look good.

HARRY

Oh, Mary, Mary. You're always so out there.

MARY

And speaking of looking good, Harry, where did you get that tie? I want to get Ralph one.

HARRY

Oh, you like that? Thelma gave it to me right before our divorce. But Mary, you're getting off the subject. In terms of your idea: you're a little too over the edge.

MARY

Yes, and so was the originator of the television series "The Simpsons" but look at how they made some very important contemporary sociological statements in a fun way. Oh Harry, you might win a Pulitzer for this.

HARRY

Well, well … a Pulitzer? Ah, okay, you sold me. But let me make a final decision after you bring me the first draft.

MARY

You got it!

As you can see, Mary didn't get defensive or hostile with Harry. She simply used the basic improv rules in a most effective way. Sure, they could have kept going at it — argued for a long period of time — but Mary could have hung in there with the "Yes, and …" theory alone, giving credence to Harry's point of view every step of the way. All the while, of course, she could have been bringing her points home and selling them. The added element — the tool to accompany the rules — was assuaging Harry's ego and charming him.

Though this example was an exaggerated one, a pinch of compliment and a kind word went a long way. These are only two tools that fall comfortably into the "win someone" category. Can you think of others? Here's the key: When you demonstrate personal attention to someone's person — e.g., "Great tie!" — it's hard to resist "Going With." Most people find it difficult to shut us down when we show genuine personal interest in them and take the time and effort to say so. So, for starters, try this first choice, steering clear of being patronizing or phony. Just look for some interesting and honest ways to pay tribute to the person — to get them on your side. It all comes back to the rapport thing, doesn't it? The rules plus some personal and specific attention unique to the individual — that's tool number one.

The second tool you can readily utilize is to ignore the person who is being the pain in the neck. I want to mention here that this is one of the only times I advocate breaking a sacred improv rule. In this case, you can "refuse" or ignore a person until he or she displays some form of positive behavior, then build on that behavior to get the rapport back on line. I've seen many people get the hint a short time after being ostracized. Alienating someone can be a wonderfully powerful way to subtextually say: "Your behavior is unacceptable to the rest of us." No one likes isolation. So, ignore a difficult person, just like ignoring a defiant child, and sooner or later they'll get the message. If they really want to be part of the goings-on, they'll stop the antagonism and present their points of view in a more positive fashion.

What I try to get across to people when they complain to me about being left out of the discussions at meetings is that it's probably because they irritate others with their attitude and approach. No one likes to be around people who make a habit of finding fault with other people's ideas, or who seem to go out of their way to sabotage communication. Some people I've worked with in my one-on-one classes didn't even realize they were being difficult until it was plainly illustrated to them via video playback. Many of them said that was just their "way." Sometimes bad habits are hard to break, but we must break them if we want to get along with others. And get along we must if we want to be successful in the workplace. If we're left out of important conversations, we won't get very far. So remember, alienation is communication's number one enemy.

Let's put tool number two into play by running a second scene with Harry and Mary. This time let's assume Mary's back with the first draft Harry asked for, but let's add another player to the mix: Barry. And let's see what happens with the "I'll just ignore you" approach.

HARRY

This draft, Mary. It's a little bold. I'm sure we may offend somebody.

MARY

Well, Harry, what is it specifically that you think may be offensive?

BARRY

The whole book is offensive, Mary. It screams of bigotry.

MARY

But the whole point is to instruct youngsters about how needless bigotry is.

BARRY

It's stupid, it's inane and nobody's going to buy it. Besides, we'll probably get sued.

HARRY

That's going a bit too far, isn't it Barry?

BARRY

Not only will we get sued, we'll probably get death threats … letter bombs … .

MARY

I think you're overreacting, Barry.

BARRY

Don't tell me I'm overreacting. I know I'm right. I'm always right. And what's with the little Hindu kid selling Big Gulp slurpies at an outdoor — what used to be — lemonade stand? Or, hey, I really like the little black-belt-kid whose mother keeps side-swiping her car ... real funny!

HARRY

We're dealing with politically-charged times, Barry. I don't think —

BARRY

That's the problem, no one here is thinking. "Understanding and Loving Your Neighbor" — yeah, right, what a crock! The book series was a bad idea from the get-go, I told you both that.

MARY

Harry, we need to change the world. That's what World-Change Publications is all about, you said it yourself.

HARRY

Yes, I did. That was in the mission statement. We had to point out cultural differences, understand them, mix them all together to get people —

BARRY

Oh, big whoopee — that mission statement is about as current as the Magna Carta. Okay, who here remembers the message of the Magna Carta?

MARY

Yes, Harry, that's it. Get people to come together without any biases, like the first line states in the mission statement. And that has to start with the youngsters — with the —

HARRY

Yes, Mary, you're right. With the people in this world who haven't been tainted yet with all kinds of negative messages — who know they may be different from their friends in certain cultural ways but, so what — that's heritage. We need to celebrate that. Let's end this racial hatred.

BARRY

Oh, you want to talk hatred … this book —

MARY

That's the whole point, Harry. Teach them from first grade on that we're all in this world together to do great things — like conquer space.

BARRY

Oh, so that's supposed to justify the astronaut dog with the Russian accent?

HARRY

Mary, we're going to go for it. Finish this draft with those few changes and let's take it to the censors.

MARY

I'm on it, chief.

BARRY

Well, um, well, I guess you can add my name to the draft. Maybe I'm just being too narrow-minded ... .

As you could see, part way through the dialogue, Mary and Harry skipped over Barry and just continued the conversation with each other. Barry finally jumped on board at the end. There are times when someone like Barry will continue to dig in his heels and resist, but so be it; that may feel appropriate to that individual. But more often than not, what I've noticed in a business group dynamic is that the odd man out will finally join in with something positive, like Barry did at the very end. Again, no one likes to be left out or discounted. It usually makes them feel ridiculous. Maybe you've walked around in Barry's shoes a few times. I know I have. When I get too one-way about something, or am just in one of those testy moods, the people around me are most effective at snapping me out of my obdurate posture by disenfranchising me for the time being. I don't like being ostracized. When I am, it forces me to become more amenable to other people's ideas — to at least give them credit for what they're thinking, even if I don't agree. The effective tool here, then, is to opt to ignore someone, to leave them on the sidelines until they can become a more productive player. However, I want to reiterate: This doesn't mean we can't have differing opinions; what counts is how we present them. Barry was sarcastic and caustic and denigrating. He could have held true to what he believed but been far more diplomatic in the process. He could have offered some alternative suggestions in a kind and respectful way. Unfortunately, some people are callous and insensitive to how others react to their harsh criticisms. But if they persist, eventually people will choose to ignore them.

Now let's talk about tool number three, the most drastic method for handling the stubborn and combative types — *those* people —

you know who they are. This tool is easy enough to use: You simply leave the room or ask the hell-raiser to do so.

Whether it's a business-knucklehead or another actor on stage, I instruct the good guy — the willing trouper — to find his or her own ending. One option is inviting the difficult actor to make an exit; the other is making an exit yourself.

Gary Austin, founder of the L.A Groundlings and one of the greatest improv teachers to hit the planet, cracked me up one day when I was on stage butting up against an obstinate, no-give actor. "If the other actor isn't going to cooperate with you," Gary said, "leave. Find an ending. Exiting the stage will always provide an ending." He was absolutely right. Since that day, I have seen many actors use the exit tool. Often they'll make a dramatic and hysterically funny one-line statement as they head for the stage exit and leave.

I remember one scene in particular when two actors were doing a piece about their Aunt Mildred. The scene began with both of them pacing, waiting for her to arrive for Sunday brunch. Another actor on the sidelines, who the audience suggested should play Aunt Mildred, was waiting to make an appropriate entrance. But one of the two actors — the one who was not "Going With" at all — kept insisting that Aunt Mildred wasn't coming that day because she was dead. (Big-time denial, by the way!) Finally, the other on-stage actor got so fed up with trying to set up an interesting entrance for "Aunt Mildred" that he simply headed for the door. His final remark: "Dead? Well, I'll take a look. If I don't see her coming, I see no reason to go on. I'm going to slit my wrists." With that, he slammed the thin stage door behind him. This left him the option of returning to the scene or making that his ending. He chose to make that the ending. It was just too burdensome and embarrassing to continue with the other actor. He later told those of us watching he'd wanted to punch the guy out.

Sometimes making an exit is the only way to resolve a situation. If the going gets tough, there is nothing wrong with excusing yourself from a meeting, or even taking a bathroom break, and starting the scene from scratch upon your return. Exits can be a reasonable means of intervention. I, myself, have occasionally wound up a telephone call or meeting by feigning a coughing fit when it seemed the opposition was just too overwhelming and non-productive. "Need some water," I've sputtered, when in truth I really needed my cell phone to call my therapist.

On the other hand, I have at times been very direct in similar situations by stating: "People, it doesn't look like we're getting anywhere. Let's take five and come back to the table with open minds and new ideas to resolve this issue." Sometimes you just have to accept that there *is* no way to come to a harmonious or productive conclusion with others. In that case, taking a short time out may be the answer needed to diffuse tension and provide a chance to start the scene from a brand new beginning. Then, too, there are times when a final ending may be the only appropriate choice because continuing to meet would be a waste of everyone's time. Finding your own ending, and deciding when to do so, will become more instinctive over time. The guideline for making such a decision? Has a reasonable amount of time passed with no movement in resolving the conflict? Then it's time to say "bye-bye."

Now let me talk about a second way to use tool number three — to find another abrupt ending to the discord that sometimes permeates a room. Think of this version as the heavy hammer approach: You halt the scene long enough to ask the "dissenter" in the group to leave. I recall one incident when I was teaching a workshop for a group of district attorneys. One of them was a real pill. He kept challenging every lesson and even had the gall to make fun of some of his colleagues. (Remember, when you take on an improv assignment and are committed to the process, you're risking it all, so you deserve as much support and encouragement as you can get.) I finally halted my dialogue mid-sentence — interrupting pointers I was giving to a group of three on the stage — and simply said: "You know, John, I need to ask you to leave. It seems to me that this isn't the class for you." He arrogantly strode out the door and threw a smirk over his shoulder as he left. There was dead silence (and a great deal of surprise from the rest of the class) for about five seconds. Then suddenly, everyone burst into applause. The rest of the workshop session was highly energized and productive.

I believe that there are times when you can't win someone, but neither can you really ignore them. They tend to contaminate the atmosphere. And, removing the pollutant may be the only solution. I always, however, make every effort to use the first two "conflict" tools, before resorting to the latter. But I have no compunctions whatsoever about asking someone to leave one of my classes. I figure I'm there to do the best job I can for those who want to be there to learn or work. If someone has to be difficult to the detriment of everyone else — that someone has to leave.

In my work, I need a positive energy. In your job, I'm guessing you do, too. I refuse to empower the openly rebellious, the passive-aggressive manipulators and the defiant personalities. They serve no constructive purpose, instead they bog down the momentum and leave everyone feeling badly. If that's the energy anyone is putting out in your next group meeting — or even a one-on-one situation — have them leave. They obviously don't belong. But again, if at all possible, opt for the first two approaches in dealing with difficult people initially. That is, try to win them or ignore them for an appropriate amount of time (or altogether). You always want to give the difficult ones every opportunity either to turn their behavior around or to hang themselves. Also, you want to be thought of as the type of person who takes the high road in your communication dealings. So use this last tool with care.

Rather than present a scene using the "you gotta go" tool (since I think you've gotten the picture), let's move on to some work tasks that will help you in using all three tools when the need arises.

1. When you come upon discord and opposition, take time to assess the situation and to decide how best to handle it. My recommendation is that you start with rule number one as a remedy, then proceed to the other two tools if you need them.

2. Try and learn from those who are difficult. Be honest: Are you sometimes guilty of behaving the same way? If so, make note of what you don't like in others and let those things serve as warning signs when you find yourself falling into the same negative traps.

3. When you come upon a difficult person, gather as much information from the scene (take notes if you can) and go back to your office and rewrite that person's dialogue from a more positive approach. Scribble down some ideas or phrases you would have used in lieu of their choices, to re-create a scene that worked even in the face of conflict.

4. Learn to distinguish what is necessary conflict and what is not. If the conflict you're embroiled in seems to have movement, i.e., you're making your way toward finding a resolution to the problem, stay with it. But if you're spinning in a circle, feeling frustrated or depressed, you know you've got to put your tools to use. Always remember, there is a way out of a difficult and oppositional situation. If the first two tools don't seem to get the job done, you can always find an ending by calling a time out or having the one causing the problem leave.

5. I am absolutely certain you have at least one person in your work environment who habitually creates strife. Rehearse the conflict tools on them until you perfect each one. Soon you'll be able to use them quickly and appropriately as the need arises. When you really become aware, you will see just how many people in your daily circle fit the description of the naysayers, the "no, buts ... " and "it's my way or no way" types. Believe me, they're everywhere! Make files on these people and jot down possible ways you can use all three tools on them.

6. Always be the better person in the face of conflict. You don't want to gain a reputation for getting into it — getting on the same level with the knuckleheads. There are times when you may be tempted, but don't resort to their antics; it will only make you feel worse.

7. Think and react like a seasoned improv player. They encounter a great deal of opposition (most often from the audience), but they always handle it with aplomb and finesse. You can, too, when you use these tools and practice them regularly.

8. If you're in conflict with a superior or client, which is often the case, keep your cool and work with rule number one as best you can. In conflict situations, there are those times when you just may have to ride them out. There are, however, many times when you can utilize the rules I've just covered.

9. Strive to make conflict a useful part of communication. Is it getting the meeting somewhere? Is it producing an end result? Is it creating a stimulus that can eventually get everyone going the same direction? Don't discount conflict. Learn to assess when you need to use any one of the three prescribed tools and when conflict is, ironically, providing better and progressive communication.

Chapter 25

Humor As A Power Tool

I always tell my students this: "Outside of love, there is nothing more bonding than humor. Nothing. You don't have to know someone's language to share humor with them; humor communicates all by itself. It's universal. It's powerful. It feels good. And it makes everything it touches work."

I teach classes on how to handle difficult situations with humor. In fact, in one class students are put on stage to re-create their difficult scenes. Their instruction: they can handle the tension or dissention only with humor — nothing else. At first they laugh at me, they think I'm kidding. After that, they get a little miffed. They are certain there are scenes in which they can't infuse humor. Too risky, they assert. Perhaps. That may be true of some scenes, but not many.

Without thinking much about it, most of us simply accept the idea that it's inappropriate to handle anger or tension or unreasonableness on the job with levity or humor. I beg to differ. I think you run a very small risk when you use humor as an alternative to a ho-hum response or a negative posture. It frustrates me that people don't use humor more often in work-related situations, especially the difficult ones.

Though I initially have to coax my students to give humor a try, eventually I am able to make my point in class. Once on stage, the students re-enact their scenes the way they first unfolded. Next, they re-do the scenes, taking the humor tack. Students get a blow-by-blow review of the "before." We stop and analyze it. A few minutes later, they experience the "after" — the new way — with humor. They always agree that the "after" does, in fact, work, and, indeed, work very well. Students observing from the audience are flabbergasted at how effective the humor comes across during the second take.

If it works so well, then, why don't we use it more often? For one thing, it's just not acceptable in the corporate culture in most companies. Though human resource directors spend hours training personnel in other areas, it wouldn't occur to many of them that a class or two on handling tense situations with humor might be requisite. Sure, I guess the idea of using humor is a vaguely or occasionally thought-of remedy by some, but really teaching people how to use their humor muscle to disarm, deflect and diffuse tough situations just isn't in the typical company training manual. And yet I believe that Corporate America would benefit greatly if people could develop and nurture their sense of humor so they would have it at the ready when they really needed it.

Another reason we don't use humor as a communication aid on the job is that we are afraid we will offend someone or make them angry — angrier, in some cases, than they already are. Personally, though, I don't know anyone who doesn't like to laugh, nor do I know too many people who can't be nudged off their negative position when humor is suddenly injected into the scene. You know how it is. You've been there. People are in a meeting; everyone is grumbling; someone gets ticked off. The energy is spiraling downward to a very dark place, tensions are running high, and suddenly someone makes a funny, spontaneous crack, and everyone in the room breaks up. The whole climate changes. So why be so afraid?

Here I want to talk about two of the reasons most of us shy away from using humor — why we as business professionals tend to play our communication straight and rigid. First, as I've learned through interviews and confidential chats with a good cross-section of clients, we avoid humor because we are inhibited. If you're too inhibited to use humor in your communication, you've probably fallen into the habit of running your business activities in a predictably contained, conservative fashion. Over time you've programmed yourself that way. Most people I know are not the same at work as they are in the kitchen with their best friend. Most of us have no qualms about being funny in the kitchen; we don't hesitate to throw out those spontaneous little amusing retorts and barbs that others find so pleasing. I find it exceptionally sad that we can't do the same at work, especially since all of us would much rather be in the company of the "kitchen" person than the inhibited, guarded one. In the kitchen persona, we're truly at our best as communicators. We are what I term "right down the center of ourselves." When we behave in the relaxed, genuine and sincere way we do around those we love, people not only enjoy us, they respect and admire us as well.

So, you may ask, if many of us are inhibited on the job, why is that? Normally it comes from some intimidating factor. It could be the worry about what our superiors will think of us or how our clients or customers might react. It could be that we might be criticized for it. It could be that the environment in which we work just doesn't lend itself to humor. Some of us are so incredibly stressed on the job, humor never even enters our minds. It never occurs to us. We're too busy being intense. In that mindset, most of us opt to play it safe — keep all our dialogue straight, serious and businesslike. Over time some people begin to shut down, or go within and withdraw, or get sick. None of us can handle lack of balance. If you have a great deal of stress — which is so Workplace-Americana — then you need something to come into harmony with your psyche — and that something should definitely be humor.

The second most common reason we scoff at the idea of using humor as we sit behind our desks and at the conference table? Sheer fear. Fear in the workplace is sometimes generated by the notion that we might be fired for our behavior. More often, it is triggered by the notion that we'll make fools of ourselves. Feeling foolish is the worst for most people; they would rather die on the spot. (Incidentally, that's the main reason people don't use humor in their speeches and presentations; they're deathly afraid of bombing and of the resultant ridicule.) I, myself, as I said earlier, hate public humiliation, so I can relate.

Yet, being in either state of mind — inhibited or fearful — and not breaking through those barriers precludes us from using our most magical asset: the gift of humor. Again, how very sad for us all.

I don't know about you, but I can't stay mad at anyone who is funny. I don't care how annoying the circumstances are or how frustrating the person is. I may want to stay irked and fixed, but when someone breaks the atmospheric ice with levity, I'm transformed. Completely. Most people who are emotionally well-put-together experience the same reaction to humor that I do. What a healthy way to go about dealing with stress! I've often noticed that those who refuse to be intimidated, or who won't give way to fear, are the most powerful people in the room. They exude a confidence that's incomparable! Everyone seems to gravitate toward them. When they want something, they usually get it. When times are tough, people seek them out for solace and relief. They're like magnets; we're literally drawn to them.

I mentioned that **humor disarms, deflects and diffuses tense situations**. It also does something else: **It puts things back into perspective**. What's more, and what I like best about humor when times are tough, is that it allows the communication to start from scratch in a new and positive way. And, don't forget we're talking about bettering our communication; that's our focus. People who were otherwise down one another's throats, or who could see only the downside to everything, get a lift from humor. That boost tends to re-arrange one's frame of mind. And there are so many times when we need that during the workday.

If we want to look at why humor is so positive scientifically, we need only read some of the ongoing findings on how the endorphins are stimulated in our heads; how, when we laugh or think humorous thoughts, our brain chemistry is re-organized to create a wonderful sense of well-being. If we feel better, we react better. Humor is the light switch that illuminates the room when it begins to get dank and dark. Here's a fascinating statistic for you and one that generates lively discussion during ExecuProv "Humor In The Workplace" classes: The average child laughs 200 times a day, the average adult, seven! That ought to throw you against the wall!

I suppose I'm one of those who takes risks with humor because

I'm at an age where I really don't care as much as I used to what people think, or whether I'm going to fail. I've lived long enough to know that most things work out for the best and that most things we're afraid of never happen. I'm also rather weary of being stressed and serious; I like to laugh, and I love to make others laugh. Because I'm self-employed, and am essentially a one-person operation, I suppose I have more liberty than most. I don't have a boss to report to or be intimidated by. And I use humor to keep myself inspired and on track outside of communicating with others. For example, I have fired myself, only to run to the chair on the other side of the desk to beg for my job back. I've negotiated raises, vacations and bonuses with myself, sometimes for hours. I have drawn names for the Christmas gift exchange, knowing in advance that I'm my only employee. I have given myself time off for good behavior and, when overworked, threatened to sue myself. I have sent myself flowers and once even threw a surprise birthday party for myself. I make humor part of my every day in some way. It's my answer to surviving in a world fraught with injustices and despair.

Though I use humor on myself, I most often use it in my dealings with others because I want my communication to work. I will always handle a situation with humor rather than anger because I have proven to myself that the former will usually get me what I want. Opting for humor gives me more control, and I love to be in control. If you really want to feel powerful, make someone laugh when they're tense, angry or really upset. I guarantee, it's a terrific high! And you're doing that person such a service.

If you're afraid to use the humor tool, just ask yourself: What would you prefer — someone to handle tension with you humorously or seriously? While some of you will say emphatically, "it depends on the situation," I'm of the belief that nine times out of ten, you'd vote for being on the side of humor.

I've had several situations when I could have responded with the same measure of nastiness I'm getting from the other person, or been completely intimidated by the aggressor and could have chosen to slump into my chair in silence. But I have too much Italian pride for that; and I'm a fighter, I don't give up easy.

I once had a client call and tell me off for a misprint I had made on their Rolodex card. That card was sitting in two dozen press kits. I let my client go off; he was in my face like a double-decker cream pie. I could have cried, reacted defensively, or made some humorous aside. I chose the latter. I waited until he was all done; then I said, "Well, Gary, may I ask you something?" He said, "Sure." I said, "How do you really feel?" He burst out laughing. After I apologized profusely, making a few more jokes (I ran my suicide options by him, asking him to choose one for me), we finally agreed that I would pay to have the cards reprinted and he would forgive me the oversight. I believe that because I initially took a humorous approach, he was more receptive to giving me another chance and to understanding that I, too, was human and could make mistakes. I could have been snippy, or sulked; I could have become distant and self-protective; perhaps argumentative and obstinate. I could have chosen self-pity and played the victim. But none of those choices would have gotten me very far. And not one of them could have come even close to topping the positive effects I got from taking the high road of humor. But the choices I first mentioned are usually the choices people opt to take when the going gets tough. Certainly they're natural and automatic responses, but ones that leave us powerless and, almost always, feeling bad. Who wants to feel bad? Isn't life hard enough?

I'm not suggesting that every difficult situation be handled with humor. That would be impossible. Each of us has to use our instincts and our good sense to pick and choose which scenes are appropriate for humor. But I maintain that the majority of the time, selecting humor as a communication tool is the right choice. So, as you rifle through your tool box to pick a tool, any tool, constantly reach for the big one — humor. I am asking that you be less conservative and to explore and exercise your humor muscle.

I'm going to let you in on one of the biggest secrets of the improv player — something I touched on earlier in Part One of the book. In their training, what they learn to do is just not care when they start each scene. If there is any hesitation whatsoever they become inhibited, frightened and lose all spontaneity and timing. Poof! There goes the humor. Humor happens when we get out of our own way and go with our initial instincts. Over time, like the free-minded improv player, you too can learn to lean toward the sunny side of yourself. **Humor is a muscle; it must be worked out and toned or it will atrophy.** So, let go, get committed and look to the whimsical side of things more often.

There is no substitute. When you use it appropriately, everybody likes you. It's virtually impossible to refute its positive energy. If you were to place all your newly acquired tools on the table, humor would stand out. Consider it the jackhammer. It is the biggest, the strongest and the most powerful of them all. Once you learn to use it properly, you can drill right through any hard-to-penetrate or antagonistic surface.

Now, there are certain rules about the use of this tool. Because like a jackhammer, you certainly can't turn it on and just wield it around the room. You've got to know what you're doing.

So, here are some guidelines for when and how to use humor as you move about and through your workday:

1. Make sure humor is never hostile, sarcastic or denigrating. In other words, don't make humorous asides at the other person's expense. Be sensitive to the vibes and the feelings of those you're playing with.

2. Directing the humor toward yourself always works. When we make fun of ourselves, people will always laugh. It's a safe way to use humor on the job.

3. Don't heckle people with humor; appease them with it. Humor is meant to create pleasure, not perpetuate more strife.

4. Try not to use profanity or any politically incorrect humorous remarks. They make people uncomfortable. We live in times when people are far more touchy than they once were. Leave satire for "Saturday Night Live."

5. Don't force humor; that never works. Instead, go with spontaneous thoughts and your sense of wit. These always work.

6. During those tough situations, ask yourself: What would make me laugh if I were on the other side of this conversation? Remember how universal humor is; we are all pretty receptive to tasteful humor, whatever it is.

7. If you attempt a humorous approach and it incites more anger or dissention, back off. Wait a short time. Try it again. If it doesn't work, it might be best to exit the scene. I for one won't stay in tense situations, or I'll call for a time out. If things are getting resolved without humor, fine; if they're not, it's time to find an ending. If you can find a humorous one, the other person or persons will not be quick to forget you. In fact, they may find themselves bursting into laughter later as they recall your final line. You may have gotten more mileage than you think.

8. Don't be afraid to use humor, ever. Keep reminding yourself: Nothing in life is so important that you can't laugh about it. Through his work, Woody Allen has taught us that.

Now for some fun homework assignments that will help you stretch, tone and strengthen your humor muscle:

1. Observe people who are funny in tense situations. Study them; they're great leaders and great teachers for the rest of us.

2. Take in at least one funny movie or play a week and keep track of how many times you laugh and how you felt after it was over. I, for one, sometimes go to one of my sketch group rehearsals feeling down. By the time I leave, I'm up and feeling buoyant.

3. Find something humorous to keep at your desk. Let it serve as a reminder that nothing is that important! Let it spark your humor muscle into action when you need it.

4. Take a memo or report and rewrite it, making it as humorous as you can. Don't worry about it being perfect; you're not trying to get a job from Leno on "The Tonight Show." You're just try-

ing to exercise that humor muscle. Many memos and reports are terse or simply factual. What can you add or insert to change the tone to a humorous one? Not only is this good exercise, you just may find you want to send it around the office!

5. Take a low-risk situation at work and decide you're going to handle it with as much humor as possible. This could be during a cold-call sales call, a meeting, a brainstorming session or giving an update. A real low-risk situation might be an exit interview. In that case, let it rip!

6. After you've practiced in the low-risk category, try taking one of those really troubling situations and infusing a little humor. Take it a bit at a time until you build some strength and stamina. Soon you'll find yourself leaning on your humor muscle to hold you up when times are tough. It's easy to be humorous when there's no stress or tension. The real skill comes in your ability to shoot back with humor when you're being fired at.

7. Make notes during one of those tense meetings. When you have some quiet time, write a script for that scene, naming all the players and re-creating their dialogue. This time, however, you must pretend this script is a comedy, not a drama. Keep it light and make whoever reads it laugh. This particular assignment is the best one of all for working out your humor muscle. It is also very therapeutic. If you work in America, you need therapy! This is a task you can do continually. In fact, I would suggest you rewrite the script for any scene that didn't go well. Soon you'll see in black and white how effectively humor works (here and there), because you can keep going back and re-reading it.

Part Three of this book, which presents "before" and "after" scenes based on the use of our rules and the tools, will also include scenes substituting humor for strained dialogue. Let's move on to that section now and have some insight — as well as a few laughs — along the way!

PART THREE

THE SHOW

Chapter 26

It's Show Time!

In the first two sections of the book, I gave you most of the rules and a handful of tools used in improv comedy training. I also gave you a real behind-the-scenes look at how improv techniques are so interestingly put to use in the big leagues of live stage comedy. I'm hopeful that this in-depth look has offered new insights and a whole slew of options in terms of how to better communicate with those around you as you go about your daily business interactions.

I trust that you've done all your assignments thus far and that you've been putting your skills to work on a regular basis. To help you even further, in this section, I've put together some authentic true-to-life workplace situations — scenes as they actually occurred — to show you communication that works and communication that doesn't. By now, of course, I'm willing to wager that a good deal of the communication in these scenes — good or bad — will be obvious to you. I'm counting on the probability that, like a great actor, you've been observing a great deal of other people's conversations and behavior — not to mention your own.

One of the things I want to impress upon you before you look at the scenes and as you take your new skills into the workplace, is the idea that in the bigger picture, work is simply a show. That's not to belittle the importance of your job or how you communicate in it. It's just to say that I don't want you getting so worried about breaking any of the improv rules or forgetting any of the improv tools that you end up agonizing over what you could or should have done or said. What is important is that you try to learn from each performance — each experience, each piece of communication. Steady improvement in anything we do simply makes us better.

I also want to remind you to take stock of what is really important in life, such as health, family and friends. I think that very often, many of us are so driven to succeed or to make the sale we allow the "what" to overtake us. We don't stop long enough to say, "Hey, work's a series of performances; some shows run better than others. If this show (job) doesn't work out, or if I don't get this part (this sale), I'll get another one." It's really people and our relationships with them that should take precedence in our day-to-day lives. Like a gambler plunking down all he has on one blackjack hand, far too often business professionals put everything they have into that job! Keep a healthy perspective then. Think like an actor. If you can always keep a little professional distance from the "job," you'll probably find yourself more balanced.

If you perform your very best throughout each business day, that's all you can really ask of yourself. And therein lies the key: just doing your very best with any given set of circumstances, right there, right then. That's how seasoned improv players always function. They stay in the moment. When the scene is over, it's over. They tend to remember only what they've learned from it (though, naturally, they savor the great moments). They give it their all in every piece in every show, but they don't live and die according to the outcome. Improv, to them, is a series of shows within a bigger show, and they commit to play each one well; they let the rest go. Since you're trained like an improv performer; think like one. It will definitely help you keep your priorities straight.

As I've mentioned, I private-coach many business professionals. Nothing makes me sadder (I even take it home with me) than when people come to me depressed and downhearted because they feel they've blown an important scene. "What did you learn?" I always ask them. "What can you take from that situation and use the next time around?" We talk about this for a good while until they feel better. ExecuProv even has a class called "Making a Scene" where students get to rewind their faulty moments. The audience of students then helps those on stage rewrite that scene until it finally works. It's always a real eye-opener.

But here, again, we keep it positive and open-ended. By this I mean we try more than one ending to a scene, or we handle it from the beginning in an assortment of ways — just to illustrate that often there is no right or wrong — just optional ways of being communicatively effective. We stress taking the emphasis off regret and cutting ourselves a little slack for being human. The main point we try to make is that the outcome of no one scene can ruin anyone's life (their overall show). The secondary point we attempt to get across is that we need to focus on letting go of any feelings of self-recrimination and instead embrace the idea that every time we take to the stage of communication, we get a little better at it.

Dr. Kappas once told me that the reason people feel like failures when their scenes don't work is because they have too much of their own identity tied up in their jobs. "You are not your occupation," he has said. "Your occupation is something you do." And I guess that's the danger in being the star of your "Big Show." Sometimes you get so invested in it that when it seems not to get applause, so to speak, you fall apart.

Not every show can get you a standing ovation. And in the end, what counts is knowing that you performed your role better each time you played it; that's what the seasoned acting pros will tell you. I remember returning to the L.A. Groundlings one night to perform as an alumni along with some other former players. Boy, was I ready. I jumped up on that stage and couldn't wait for the audience's assignments. But, by night's end, I didn't feel as though any of the scenes in which I had performed had showcased my talent; in fact, overall I thought I did a crummy job. I could have blamed it on the fact that we had no rehearsal, or that I hadn't worked with any of the people before except one. I could have blamed it on the fact that I hadn't performed for nearly a year. And indeed, as I cried (really loud) all the next day, I found a million rationalizations for why I had "failed." (Only my perception, incidentally, not the others.) But I wasted so much time doing all this. When I finally regrouped, I realized that getting on that stage had been just one show and certainly did not disparage the sum total of my life's work as a performer.

Whatever the scene, remember: Tomorrow is another show. So,

focus on "the moment," and when it's over, let it go. In the process of putting your best foot forward and trying to excel, don't lose sight of what really matters in the "Big Show." Guard against losing your Self in the day-to-day scramble to make a living. And every time you criticize yourself for some communication faux pas, I want you to give yourself two positives. This little exercise helps you keep perspective and balance. Here's something I once did when I was feeling bad about a meeting I'd been in. I'd been pitching a new client. This guy either had a bad disposition or a bad hair day. By the scowl and the cowlick, I'd say both. In any event, he wasn't very nice to me. Although I kept trying to win him throughout our conversation, he was staunchly cemented in a "denial" mode. I left with my briefcase dragging between my legs (try to walk to your car in that position) and felt dejected the rest of the day. But when I returned home, I forced myself to make a list of the really important things in my life that I could be grateful for. I listed the typical — my three wonderful children, terrific father, close relationships with a dozen of my high school buddies, spaghetti and chocolate. The last item I jotted down was my gratitude for being lucky enough to have had that guy for a potential client and not a husband. Whew, was I relieved. This is a little game you can always play with yourself when anything in Act I or II seems to get you down. Start rattling off your blessings as you drive away. In fact, scream them loudly; it really relieves a lot of tension.

In addressing the danger of letting the Show get you down, I don't mean to minimize the importance of hanging tough with the rest of the business professionals on the playing field. We all need to compete, whether it's with others or ourselves. It's very American to compete. But when you do it, remember that it's a show, and if you don't break a leg each and every time, look ahead and begin to rehearse for the next performance. When you do: Play harder. Play smarter. But just remember, it's a play!

Also, when you perform, be a team player. Always be a good sport. Nothing like a co-worker with attitude — no one wants to be on their team. We need to be gracious and shake the hand of our opponent even when we don't feel like it. We need to "suit up" even on those days when we don't feel like getting in the game. We need to play with everything we've got, even when we feel we have little to pull from. That's the mark of a true professional, I think — giving it your all when you're not up to it physically or emotionally. I've seen improv players crying backstage, fighting with one another and openly declaring they wouldn't go on, but when the curtain rose, they straightened up and did their jobs beautifully.

Most of all, when it comes to the Show, we need to rehearse everything we know every day. You have a wonderful opportunity to perfect your performance skills because they're things you can practice during every piece of communication all day long. How many scenes are you in each day? Ten? Twenty? Thirty? Like any consummate concert pianist, you want to practice your new-found skills. Soon they will become habit. Soon you'll be bouncing off others with great agility and with responses that are quick and appropriate.

The last thing I want to mention about the Show is that, even though on your own marquee you are the headliner, you should always remember to respect the other "actors." Perform fairly. You never know who may be looking on without your knowledge (the big boss or the big client). You never know who may move on to a bigger position next week who could do you some good. If you're in show business and you're smart, you always treat everyone with equal respect and consideration. It's not unusual for someone who plays a bit part to become a major producer. In the business world, it's not unusual for the guy in the mail room to someday become the CEO. Don't ever think that clawing your way to the top is the way to impress. If you step on others, it may come back to haunt you. I've been in the workplace long enough to see that what goes around comes around. Show business, or just plain business, it's all the same.

As you go about presenting yourself "on stage," don't forget how important your sense of PR is. We all need a positive image, one that bespeaks credibility and integrity. As a performer, you want to remember the "consistency" rule — always communicate with your best PR demeanor intact. One crabby day can cost you a lot. That's a show-stopper that can follow you around for a long time. You can't afford bad press; it creates a stigma. The effort it takes to live down even one bad-mood day, isn't worth it. Save such energy for making the sale, whatever it may be.

Enough, then, on the "big picture"; now it's time to see how people are acting in the scenes I mentioned earlier. First we'll look at the non-improv players of the world—in other words, what to do if *they* don't know the rules.

Chapter 27

Oh, Great! What If They Don't Know The Rules?

It's been said: It's not whether the show's a hit, it's how well you performed your role. Well, I can get behind that. Sometimes we're a smash, and sometimes we get panned, but if we don't at least perform with integrity, we can't get a positive review. What I perceive to be most important to the show called "Job" is how we handle ourselves when we're in the throes of our performance. I know many a reviewer who hated the show but loved the actors, and vice versa. In your case, better your audience like you as a performer than buy in on just the show. Naturally, you'd like both, but I don't want you to lose sight of what's important: the way you "act." At the end of the day, you're the one you have to office with, so, as I mentioned in the last chapter, keeping your integrity intact is what really matters.

In business, just like in your personal relationships, you want to perform at a level that demonstrates your personal best. Always. **If you do it well — the Show — you build your portfolio. You are thought of as a solid performer.** Think of it this way: Even if you don't take top billing, you'll always be cast in parts. By the way, there is no such thing as an overnight sensation. Each of us performers needs to build on our body of work. We need to stay focused on refining our techniques and building our strength as solid performers — even if the others in our scenes (often our performance rivals) don't care or know what they're doing.

If someone is in your show and they're not following the wonderfully effective rules laid out in the improv comedy player's manual, it doesn't really matter. It doesn't have to affect your performance at all. You can perform around them. You will still shine even if the others who share your stage don't have the same training. All that really matters is that you do — and that you continue to follow the rules. If you were a legitimately trained actor and took to the stage with a novice, your performance wouldn't have to be diminished. The same philosophy applies in the workplace. Follow the rules you've just learned, and your communication will always work.

Your "motivation" as an ardent communicator — now that you've mastered the rules and know some of the tools of the improv comedy player — is to bring resolution and/or harmony to all your work-related situations. Take the "Yes, and ... " theory and "Adding Information." Even if those were the only two rules you used in any conversation, your communication would not only improve, it would work and work well. You can only imagine how successful you'll be when you put all the rules into — pardon the pun — play.

When I first observed some improv-school beginners at The L.A. Groundlings work with a seasoned player, I was amazed at how the latter maneuvered his way in and out of the conversation that took place in the scene. He managed not only to hold the scene together, he also cleverly manipulated the other actors into going his way. He made the scene work. You, too, can do this with all your scenes when you're fully tuned into the other players and where they're coming from. We learn how to do this in improv school — we actually have lessons in how to deal with those who don't have the training. One such drill is an exercise we call "Bad Improv." One actor is asked to take to the stage; the others (there could be up to seven other players) are required to make separate entrances and exits, one after another. These latter players are asked to break all the rules — walk through "space" furniture, refuse and deny, talk in generalities — whatever they can do to test the mettle of the actor in the hot seat. It's up to that actor, then, to do what we call "justify," to make choices that justify the other's actions and dialogue. For instance, if an actor who makes an entrance stands with his back to the audience, the original actor might turn him around by saying, "Look, you can open your eyes now. See, I put that painting right where you wanted it." Or the original actor might walk downstage, manipulating the other actor into turning around so she is forced to face the audience. Another actor (listening backstage to the conversation) might say upon his entrance, "Spaghetti? I heard someone talking about spaghetti on the wall. I don't see it." The hot-seat actor will say, "Oh, yes, there it is, right next to the painting. See, it's sliding down the wall onto the baseboard." And this continues until each actor has had his chance to try to throw the guy on stage off his center. If that actor is well-trained, nothing will throw him; he will simply deal with all the rule-breakers on an as-needed basis.

You can do the same.

Let's say you called someone on the intercom and asked them to meet you in five minutes to discuss the company picnic. They enter. First words out of their mouth are: "Say, I was thinking that at the Christmas party we should all dress like Santas and give a prize to the best one." You notice this complete "denial" but, rather than say, "No, we're here to talk about the company picnic, you numbskull," you say, "Ah, what a great idea, and I'll bet you have an even better creative suggestion for the company picnic. Go ahead; tell me; what is it?" In maneuvering the conversation like this, you have not discredited the co-worker, but you have managed to get him back on track. Now if he continued to talk about the Christmas party, you would be wise to continue to acknowledge his ideas but keep bringing him back to the picnic and your need to plan for it.

The lesson here, then, is to learn to "justify" if the other person seems clueless about the rules. And, of course as you can well imagine, many people will be. When we find reasons to uphold the "bad" improv actor's dialogue and action, the scene can never fail. It may stray off course momentarily; it may not unfold the way you pictured it. But that's okay. It will still work, providing you "Go With" initially then find reasons to qualify what's been said or done. We tend to do this well with old people and small children so why can't we do it with everyone else? It just takes a little finesse, tuning in and staying there, going with the flow and always finding ways to justify the other person.

Justifying is somewhat different from the "Yes, and ... " theory. In "Yes, and ... "-ing, someone usually "Goes With" everything that is said, then (adds information) along the same lines. **Justifying means finding viable reasons for what the other person is saying, and incorporating those reasons into the scene, irrespective of whether or not the other person's comments are appropriate.** Sometimes you have to make sense of the senseless, but you'll get really good at it if you stick to the rules and introduce some of the tools.

I'm always a bit reluctant to tell my students that their job is to manipulate, because I don't want them to misuse their power once they've learned these valuable improv rules. The idea is to hold fast to them as communication aids but never to misuse them. So when I say manipulate, I don't mean "change by artful or unfair means so as to serve one's purpose." That's one definition according to Webster, but there is another one as well: "to manage ... in a skillful manner." This is what I mean when I say I want you to learn to be a good manipulator. Every improv actor learns to be one, but never in a controlling or self-serving way, because, don't forget, they are always coming from the premise of "Serve and Support." You want to manipulate conversations for the good of the communication — not for your own good.

If you work closely with a team of people on a regular basis, you just might want to introduce them to the basic improv fundamentals. I had a client who did this in weekly staff meetings. Each week she debuted another improv rule and asked her team to take part in a few fun exercises to demonstrate how they worked. Soon everyone on her team was exposed to these new ideas; many began to use them. Over time, my client told me, they began to communicate on a much more solid basis. In fact, she also confided, their team became so close-knit that they often busted one another when someone wasn't "Going With" or reacting to the "last thing said" or "last idea held." Some of her colleagues asked to go through the ExecuProv training, which helped them master the rules even further.

The point is, this client took the time to share her new-found communication techniques, and eventually, she said, it made a tremendous difference. "I think people have a much greater awareness of treating each other more respectfully," she told me one day. "I can see a greater sensitivity in general among the group." (Note: this client also used humor as a means to break up tension and discord. Don't forget what you've learned about that power tool!)

Using the improv rules and tools on the unsuspecting gives you a sense of accomplishment. But sharing them can also be rewarding. So you have two choices: Do what my client did, and teach others the rules, or simply use them yourself, even if this means you find yourself constantly having to "justify" others. The goal, always, is to strengthen and fortify communication. When you keep that finish line in mind, it's easy to stay on course.

One more thing about what to do if *they* don't know the rules: Do whatever you can to reinforce your positive sense of team play. Read self-help books on teamwork; join a team of some kind where everyone is working toward a common goal; take an improv or acting class. Most local colleges offer such classes as do theater companies and community theaters. Working on a production together — whether you sign on as an actor or a behind-the-scenes crew member — can bolster a sense of teamwork. The more you reinforce team spirit, the easier it will be to keep utilizing your new improv training, even if the people at work don't have a clue.

One last thing: You can always do improv games with family members to sharpen your skill level. In fact, they're a great way to create fun and synergy at home. My kids and I, for example, always play "Last letter, first word" at the dinner table on holidays. The game goes like this: Everything you say has to begin with the last letter of the last word spoken. For instance, if I say, "Shannon, you look like you've been working too many hours," Someone else may pipe in with, "So, do you, Mom." I might say, "Maybe." We just keep the conversation going in this manner. It sets a nice pace and tone and really causes us to listen — instead of babbling simultaneously about our own lives. If your home turf is where you want to practice your new techniques before you take them to work, go for it. Wherever there is conversation, there is a scene. Where else can you practice? At church? Scout meetings?

There is a wonderful book by Andy Goldberg, "Improv Comedy," that offers a whole bunch of different improv games for the beginner. Anyone can play them. And they're a great way to practice. Start out with some fun exercises, then move up to the more advanced assignments. Even if you're a bit shy or feel you need to get some experience under your belt, you'll soon see the results, which will give you courage to take what you know to work.

In the end, there is no excuse not to use the rules, even in the company of those who don't have an inkling of what you're up to. Using them provides more control over the direction of any scene and will certainly ensure more harmony in all your communications. The beauty of knowing all the rules in the improv comedy player's rulebook is that you never have to be in the midst of a scene and feel a terrible sense of discomfort. Using what you've learned will always get you through, no matter the situation or circumstances.

Chapter 28

=====

Scenes In A Play

As I've mentioned throughout this book, each of us is involved in numerous scenes every single day. Sometimes we are very aware of how we come across; other times we're not. Personally, I believe that in most of our conversations, we're oblivious as to whether or not our communication is effective — or, indeed is working at all. Instead, we're too caught up in something ... whatever it is!

Through your new understanding of how improv actors go about their communication, I'm truly hopeful that you will see and hear other people (and yourself) in a much different light. Always remember: People buy people, then they buy things. So whether you're peddling an idea or a product or a service, you want to first make sure your connecting. Next, you want to know that through that connection, you're able to fully communicate in a meaningful way.

Although I offered a number of sketches to make my points in Part One of the book, I think it will be helpful, now that you know the rules and tools, to look at some scenes from real life. I will present the scenes, then follow them with a critique of why they did or did not work. By the way, I actually recorded the first three as they happened. In the last scene, which demonstrates the effectiveness of using humor as a power tool, I will show you both the real "take" and an alternative.

The first scene took place between myself and an assistant at my travel agent's office (whose name I have deleted to spare her any embarrassment). You might think the exchange is pure fabrication on my part, but I assure you, it's not!

I dialed the phone … it rang six times

TELEPHONE RECEPTIONIST

Whirl Travel …

ME

Yes, hello. I'd like to speak to Marsha Tenny, please.

TELEPHONE RECEPTIONIST

(Says nothing. Puts me through)

SOME WOMAN

Marsha Tenny's office.

ME

Marsha? Is this Marsha?

SOME WOMAN

She's not here.

ME

Oh. Well … will she be back soon?

SOME WOMAN

Don't know.

ME

Well, this is Cherie Kerr and I need to book some airline flights for ... a ...

SOME WOMAN

Well, I can help you, I guess.

ME

Okay. I need to book a flight to Vegas for myself and two of my co-instructors.

SOME WOMAN

Yeah? When?

ME

We need to leave on March 26 and return April 2.

SOME WOMAN

March 27 and return when? I'm sorry, say again?

ME

No, March 26. And, we need to return April 2.

SOME WOMAN

(Seems even more annoyed than when she first took my call) Oh. Wait. I need to put you on hold. **(I'm hanging forever. Finally she punches back in)** Oh, sorry 'bout that. Now, let's see. Sherry?

ME

It's pronounced Sure-*ee*.

THAT WOMAN

Okay. You and two of your guys need non-stop to Vegas March 26 … .

ME

Right.

SAME WOMAN

And … **(punching into her computer)** returning April 3.

ME

No, I said the second.

HER

Oh, well, okay. I can do that. **(Futzing with her computer for what seems like eternity)**   Alright. I've got three roundtrip tickets from LAX to Vegas leaving on March 26 and returning April 2.

ME

No, we need to leave from Orange County.

HER

Geez, you didn't say that.

ME

Sorry, Marsha usually helps me and she knows —

HER AGAIN

Oh, brother. Okay ... okay ... look I'm really busy. I was
with a customer when you called. I'm trying to book a
cruise. I'll have to call you back. Okay?

ME

No, that's not okay. Just have Marsha call me
back ... pleeeeaze!

HER

(Chomping on something. Ice cubes, I think)

Sure, Sherry. I'll tell her.

**(We hang up. I start throwing things like Patty Duke playing
Helen Keller, then reach for the Yellow Pages to look under
"T" for travel agency)**

I swear, this scene as I've written it is not an exaggeration: it's
how the dialogue went down. I was frustrated, humiliated and
completely turned off from doing business at Whirl ever again. I
had always liked Marsha. But suddenly I found myself mad at her,
too. Though she had always been helpful and courteous, I doubted
she would ever even get my message. By the end of the conversation with the woman who never bothered to introduce herself, I
didn't really care about any relationship. I just wanted to order
some airline tickets without the brain damage.

After doing all the lessons in this book, you may read this scene
and immediately be able to spot every single thing that went wrong.

But for kicks, let's take the scene apart.

- For openers, the phone rang six times. That's not good for any business. No one should ever wait that long to have their call answered. Four rings is the maximum.
- If you noticed, the receptionist never said anything when I asked for Marsha; she simply put me through. That's "Refusal" at a premium! I hate when that happens. I find it extremely rude when the person answering the phone just puts you through without speaking one word. What happened to "I'm ringing now"? Or "Here you go"? Or "I'll try that extension"? I feel like someone flung me out into space with nothing to hang onto. I'd rather someone say anything (even "go to hell") than literally cut me off and disappear.
- Next, when I finally heard a voice come through the phone, "some woman" never even bothered to introduce herself. What lousy PR that was! How could we possibly make a connection?
- She certainly didn't listen to what I said on the surface, let alone listen to my subtext.
- There was hardly any "React and Respond" to the "last thing said" or "last idea held," because she couldn't get the information straight.
- She not only openly "refused" me, several times, she also denied me. The big undercut came when she found out I hadn't mentioned that I needed to leave from John Wayne Airport in Orange County.
- There was somewhat of a beginning and there was a reasonable middle (starting to get the ticket order filled) but the ending left me, the audience, most dissatisfied. I didn't get my tickets — I didn't get what I set out for. So, there was no resolution, no conclusion. When that happens to any of us, we are left feeling frustrated, disappointed and powerless.
- There wasn't much in the way of "Give and Take," she kept stepping on my lines.
- Forget the notion of "Answering the Question"; we seemed to spin in circles. It seemed to take forever to handle information that could have been traded in just two sentences.
- In terms of "Creating into Certainty": Well, there really wasn't

much ambiguity, but it was hard for me to get a handle on what specific information I needed to give because her questions weren't as leading as they could have been. For instance, she could have asked what airport I wished to leave from. And, granted, I could have stated the airport of my choice up front, too. But don't forget, I was the customer. She should have taken the initiative to ask.

- Even after I corrected her, she mispronounced my name. This is the worst — one of the greatest insults to anyone. If someone has an unusual name and they say it to you, it's your job to lock the pronunciation in. Nothing makes us feel more invalidated than when someone can't remember how to say our name. It says in bold, neon subtext, "Hey, you're really not very important!"

- Overall, then, so much for trust, the most important element needed to establish rapport. I certainly didn't feel any bond whatsoever with "Some Woman," nor did I trust her on any level. There was no sincerity in her voice or approach with me. I sensed she would not pass my message on to Marsha.

Thus we have two people who are thrown together to communicate, but what for? It all ends badly. I'm left feeling frustrated and helpless, while "Some Woman" just lost business for her company.

While the above scene was short, and to some may not seem to be a big deal, I think it's characteristic of what happens all day throughout Corporate America. Simply put: People have established bad habits. They're so caught up in the rapid pace, they forgo focusing on one person at a time and giving that person their all. No wonder we have hurt feelings, resentment, anger and misconstrued information. To take it one step further: No wonder we have so much strife and hostility!

I've talked about a sense of PR and how we all need one. In this last scene, public relations wasn't even a consideration. As a result, "That Woman" lost my business for Marsha's company. I wasn't going to wait for Marsha to return my call; I needed my tickets. In my fast moving world, I only have so much time to book airline travel. Most business professionals I know are the same — we're not good at waiting. Also, I didn't want to risk letting my trip get screwed up. I couldn't afford for that to happen. I was teaching a class in Las Vegas, and if my reservations were amiss, I would have lost money.

In *my* book, time is time; communication is money. Even brief conversations have something at stake. Just like this conversation, many of our conversations are brief. Yet in the business world, we tend to take really good care of only those who seem most important to us, like the boss, or the client who sends us a large chunk of our business. We need to reorient that thinking. We need to always think about being at parity. And about consistency. We should treat everyone and every piece of communication with equal respect and consideration. That's the mark of a real pro. If you fall into the gap on this one, snap out of it. Think what you might do to change your ways using your new communication stuff.

Now let's look at another scene. This one took place in a meeting between two men and a woman who got together to plan a training session. The company was a restaurant chain with locations throughout the West, heavy in the specialty of outside catering. It was up to these three to do all the training for the customer-service team — the team that was responsible for handling both special requests and complaints from the various companies for whom they provided lunches and dinners, most often at their locations for special occasions.

CHARLIE

Let's go over this again. I'm going to cover company policy. Trish, you're going to teach them about client relations. And, Glenn, you're on quality control this time.

GLENN

Yep, I'm teaching them how to manage consistency with our menu items no matter how many meals we serve.

CHARLIE

Good.

TRISH

Anything new I should know?

CHARLIE

Yes. We're implementing a new incentive program.

TRISH

Hey, great. How does it work?

CHARLIE

Well, every time we get a complimentary letter on one of our employees from a client, the employee gets $1,000. Now, we're not really telling our employees about it directly, because we don't want their friends and family writing in, and we don't want to tip them off so they over-service people just to get a letter. So, I'm not sure how to … well, I was just going to tell them … um … I was just going to tell them there was someone watching … or … .

GLENN

Yeah, like a secret Santa … .

CHARLIE

Yeah, a secret Santa. You know, just sort of give them a clue but not tell them outright. We let them know, if their service is outstanding, then they'll no doubt be one of the recipients of a $1,000 bonus at some point. That's all. Let them work hard at making every client-contact a great one. Oh, and we can give only one of these out a month, so first one in gets the monthly prize.

TRISH

Cool. I think the arcane element lends a kind of mystique. I like it.

GLENN

How are you going to pitch it during the training, Trish?

TRISH

Ooh, well, I think I'll tell them that if they really go out of their way to please our customers — if they follow our company policies and add that personal touch to everyone they come in contact with — it could add up to dollars. I think I'll leave it at that ... make them wonder ... .

CHARLIE

I think that'll work. And, if the program doesn't pan out, we'll try something else.

GLENN

Hell, I got three letters last week on Mary Forte. Printers, Inc. loves her. She seems like a likely candidate.

CHARLIE

Yeah, I wish we had more people like her. But see, if she wins, let's say a couple of times, pretty soon the others may follow suit.

TRISH

But what happens if the others get discouraged because the same person keeps winning? I'm thinking now it excludes people from cashing in because what if two people send letters with postmarks one day apart?

CHARLIE

Yeah, I see what you mean. Maybe it isn't fair.

GLENN

Why don't we do the program so that any letters we get each month, the $1,000 is divided — you know, like lottery winners who split the prize.

TRISH

That could work. I think we should at least try it that way. It gives more people a chance and creates a camaraderie — a healthy competition. I don't think it has to get cut throat.

CHARLIE

Yeah, I like it. Besides, if we don't tell them at least the first time out, it could create quite a buzz. But I see a hole here. I think we'll have to plan for something entirely different each month. If they catch on, they may schmooze with the clients who are likely to write — or worse yet, drop the hint.

GLENN

I got it. Whoever wins is also responsible for coming up with the next month's incentive program.

TRISH

Yeah, and it should always have some secret or highly creative element to it.

GLENN

Yeah. Charlie, how 'bout that?

CHARLIE

Love it!

TRISH

What a neat idea. They can just share the contest idea with us and keep that mystery thing going.

CHARLIE

(He stands to prepare to leave. They stand also)
Yep, terrific idea. Sold. Let's do it. So, let me recap: We'll tell them to go out of their way with the customer; that doing so may create some monetary gain — wait and see — and at the end of the first month, we'll have something else to announce about our new incentive program because it's a program that will change every month. So, stay-tuned kind of thing. It sure looks like we're ready for the session tomorrow. You guys got the rest of your notes and your lesson plans?

TRISH

I'm ready, Charlie.

GLENN

Me, too. I'm going to spice up my part of the presentation with a few recent anecdotes.

CHARLIE

Ah, can't wait. Don't tell me now. Surprise me.

TRISH

I love your fun stories, Glenn, and so do the trainees.

CHARLIE

(Facing them in the hallway as they prepare to go different directions) Yeah, they sure do. I like the one you tell about the guy who used the same techniques on his staff that he did to train his dog. See you guys bright and early.

TRISH

You will, chief.

GLENN

Later.

As you can see, for the most part, this scene worked. Here's why:

- There was a good deal of "Give and Take."
- There was a whole lot of "Yes, and … "and "Adding Information." Because of that, something meaningful was accomplished. Together they resolved how to handle the incentive program.

- Their teamwork seemed to set a nice tone for the threesome's training session the following day. The more they work well together, the stronger they are as a unit. The good chemistry keeps showing up in all their work.
- They had no need to upstage one another. "Division of Responsibility" seemed to be a given with them. No one chose to "lay out," leaving the incentive program dilemma up to the others to solve. They all became involved and seemed pretty equal in taking their share of the load.
- There was obviously a good deal of "Serve and Support" and "React and Respond." You could pick up on it every step of the way. Clearly, each was in a "Be Here Now" mode, too, which made the supportiveness and responsiveness so readily possible.
- What I noticed most about this meeting as I sat by was that there was a clear beginning, a substantial middle and a conclusive ending. Charlie took great care in "situating" his audience (the others in the meeting) by setting up the particulars in his opening remarks. This scene could have been left with no resolution to the incentive program. Or they could have quibbled over whose idea should prevail. Instead, they incorporated one another's suggestions to reach a final solution. My biggest complaint about company meetings is that they most often lack viable endings. That translates into wasted time, something most us can't afford.
- Though you couldn't see it, I noticed as I sat in that each of them "Attended To" the entire time. And looking at whomever was speaking precluded them from stepping on each other's lines or from falling out of the listening mode.
- Their sense of rapport was excellent. Even though Charlie seemed to be the boss, you never got the idea that he felt superior in any way; he didn't try to assert his "stardom." Their apparent consideration for one another highlighted their strong sense of trust, like and respect. It came through in almost every piece of dialogue. This is the dynamic you see among the strongest of improv players on stage, incidentally. (I once had occasion to work with a guy who was a regular on "Mad TV"

during an all-improv night at the L.A. Groundlings. The two of us, and another alumni, did a scene about a defunct circus. This "star" never gave the audience or either of us "mentally flabby" alumni the idea that he was a stronger communicator in any way. He worked with us as equals, we rose to the occasion, and everyone looked to be at parity. Our communication was a success. I love to see balance in any scene; I don't care if one of the players is the President of the United States!)

As a final note, the scene we just viewed is one I present to many classes as an example of how a scene should go. Charlie, Trish and Glenn did an excellent job the day I was with them. I sent them a letter telling them so!

Our third scene, on the other hand, is one of my favorite examples of what doesn't work. It was hauntingly reminiscent of a Three Stooges routine. I know the "players" intended to go about their communication in a productive way, but unfortunately, that's not what happened.

The conversation took place in a car among three high-level executives en route to a meeting with their company's biggest client. The company the three worked for was an interior design firm looking to outfit the sales office of a model home complex. As we tune in, John, the CEO, is driving; Elmer is riding shotgun; and Earl is backseat, right. (I was silently positioned backseat, left. As in the other scenes, I'd been asked to ride along in order to critique their meeting.)

JOHN

What's the fastest way to get there?

ELMER

Get where? You mean Munsor Development or the Sales Office at Granger Ridge?

EARL

Where we goin'?

JOHN

I thought you knew, Earl. Is the meeting at Bob's office or the sales office?

ELMER

Why are you asking me? I didn't set the meeting. I thought Shelly did.

JOHN

You know my secretary doesn't set all my meetings, especially the ones with Munsor, for God's sake!

EARL

Why don't we just call the office?

JOHN

Whose office? Mine ... or Munsor's?

ELMER

Don't call Munsor; Bob will flip. We did this a couple of meetings ago. He's gonna think we don't communicate very well.

EARL

Well, duh ... .

JOHN

That's not necessary. Let's not argue about it. We got a problem here.

ELMER

Maybe it's out of line, John, and forgive me for saying so, but weren't you supposed to set up the meeting?

JOHN

I did set up the meeting. We're on our way to a meeting, right?

EARL

Yeah, but where the hell is it?

JOHN

I DON'T KNOW! Let's just go to Bob's, and if it isn't there, we'll head over to Granger.

ELMER

Granger is 20 minutes the other way, isn't it?

JOHN

I don't know. Earl?

EARL

I haven't been there yet, boss, I'm not sure.

ELMER

I've got an idea. Why don't we just call Bob's office, and

if he isn't there, we'll head over to Granger.

JOHN

How much time we got?

EARL

What time's the meeting?

JOHN

Ten, I think.

ELMER

Yeah, ten I think.

JOHN

Earl, dial Bob's office.

(He does)

EARL

Hi, this is Earl from Dargard Design, and we have a meeting with Bob this morning. **(Nervous laugh)** We're not sure where that meeting is being held. Wonder if you could help us out. **(He's on hold and says to the guys)** She's gonna ask. **(Back on the phone)** Ah, yes. Oh, ten o'clock. Good, good. And where? What! Toommmmorrow? We thought it ... okay, at Granger. *Tomorrow*, ten o'clock. We'll be there. **(Hangs up)**

JOHN

Uh, sorry guys ... I feel like such a jerk!

EARL

You are!

ELMER

I'll second that.

JOHN

Tell you what, let's go for pancakes —

ELMER

— and Margaritas.

EARL

Make mine a double. No salt.

Well, what a mess! Sitting in the back seat, I tried not to laugh. Instead I powered down my window and made some comment about getting air. With the car going about 50 mph I knew that the sound of the wind would absorb any chortle in the back of my throat — and that any uncontrollable burst of laughter wouldn't get tape recorded. (I had promised to play my recording back for them.)

This example is what I call "trickle-down" communication: "down" having a double meaning. As you can see, these guys couldn't communicate very effectively amongst themselves, and there's no doubt they must have been having similar problems with everyone else in their work environment. Quite obviously, John was a bit sloppy in nailing down the particulars of his meeting, wasting everyone's time. That certainly didn't create synergy within his own troops; rapport among the ranks is just as important as rapport among the client base. So, so much for John's leadership skills. In addition to throwing his staff off, he set up a situation that caused confusion for the client and his office. Not too impressive! Hopefully, the receptionist didn't pass her communique with Earl on to her boss.

But let's get beyond the obvious disaster of wrong-day-and-where's-the-meeting, and talk about the chatter in the car. Here's what I noticed:

- Nowhere was the "Create Into Certainty" rule more absent than in that car. You can see now, I'm sure, how vital that rule is! Not only were they confused about the "where" of the meeting, they were constantly unclear as to what the others were even saying.
- You can see that when questions are answered with questions, it's really hard to get anywhere. People spin in circles. These three guys were taking a ride on the Teacups at Disneyland! That problem is usually a result of lack of certainty all the way around.
- Of course, there was an abundant supply of "Denial."
- "Answering the Question" came and went.
- I will give them credit for some measure of "Economy of Dialogue," but ... .
- Their listening — especially John's — rates an "F" on my grading scale. I've said it before and I'll say it again: Poor listening is Corporate America's biggest plague.
- Ultimately, we end up stripping down to the basic improv fundamental — that of trust. This whole "scene" was fertile ground for lack of trust. Poor John. It will take a great deal for him to recover with his colleagues in this area. If the client finds out about the oversight, he's got to work extra hard to gain the trust back there, too. I'm sure you can see by now how crucial that foundational layer — trust — truly is. Without it, communication will always be in a state of distress (at some point it's probably going to crash). You can't have positive, strong and meaningful communication without trust. Think about it! How many scenes end up "so-so" for you? Check out the trust

factor; it lies at the base of everything.

Maybe you noticed other things about this scene. If so, write them down; it's great practice for you. Put on your Director's hat (or beret, if you prefer!) and really examine what works and what doesn't.

Now, let's look at the last scene. It's just a snippet of a conversation I had with a client, Chris, who wondered why he had not received a copy of a proposal I'd air-expressed to him in Chicago. I was working at home the day he called; the call was forwarded there from my office. Chris was to present the proposal in an attempt to sell his sales manager on the idea that I should go to Chicago to train the Midwest sales team. He wanted to pass out original copies of the document (I'd mailed four), so faxing was not going to be an option. Chris was really annoyed with me.

I will first run the scene as I might have handled it but didn't. The second take represents how I actually handled the situation. See which you prefer.

(My phone rings)

ME

Kerr Companies and ExecuProv, may I help you?

CHRIS

(Breathless and irritated) You sure can, Cherie. This is Chris. I just landed. There is no package at the desk from you. What the hell is going on? I have that meeting in two hours.

ME

No package?

CHRIS

Read my lips. No package. We're screwed. I told you —

ME

Oh, Chris! I can't imagine what happened. I gave it to my secretary and she told me she dropped it off at the Fed Ex office. I ... I ...

CHRIS

Well, I guess that means I have to take in a faxed copy. That is going to look like hell. Nice presentation, Cherie. I don't think I should present today. Maybe I'll just mail it to them next week.

ME

Oh, I'm so sorry and so disappointed. I promise I took good care —

CHRIS

Let me think about it. I'll call you back.

ME

Okay. Bye.

Now, again, that's not how I actually handled the crisis. In reality, I reverted to humor — my instinct whenever there's pressure. Perhaps it is my life-long, ongoing training in the field of humor that prompts me to do so. In any event, here's what was really said:

(My phone rings)

ME

Kerr Companies and ExecuProv. May I help you?

CHRIS

(Breathless and irritated) You sure can, Cherie. This is Chris. I just landed.

ME

Was it on one of those yellow slide things that automatically inflate? 'Cause you sound really upset.

CHRIS

(Starts to laugh) No. Look, there is no package at the desk from you. What the hell is going on?

ME

No package?

CHRIS

I said, no package! I have that meeting in two hours.

ME

Uh-oh!

CHRIS

Read my lips. I have that meeting in two hours.

ME

Oh, boy, and I can't get originals to you because there is a three-hour time difference. I'm pacing, Chris. Can you see me pacing? I look like Richard Lewis after ten cups of Folgers.

CHRIS

(**Laughs again**) I can't see you but I can imagine … .

ME

I'm thinking. I'm thinking. Oh, I am *really* thinking. I am so sorry. My secretary … oh, she makes me SO MAD. She must not have taken it to Fed Ex in time.

CHRIS

Apparently not.

ME

Chris, can I ask you something?

CHRIS

What?

ME

(**Softly**) How much time do you do for involuntary manslaughter?

CHRIS

(**Bugged**) I don't know. Why?

ME

(Loudly) BECAUSE WHEN GRETA GETS BACK
FROM LUNCH, I'M GOING TO SMOTHER HER IN A
FILE CABINET.

CHRIS

Maybe I just won't present today.

ME

(**Practically whining**) Ohhhh ... I'm so disappointed!

CHRIS

Let me think about it. I'll call you back.

ME

(**Big pause. Resignation in my voice**) Okay, but when
you do — let the phone ring because I'll be in the garage
with the motor running.

(**Chris cracks up**)

I was really upset, but rather than handling my rage with rage,
I handled it with humor. By the way, when Chris called back, I
answered the phone with zero enthusiasm. I sounded like a surfer
dude on heavy drugs. He immediately told me the hotel desk clerk
had made a mistake — that they had brought my Fed Ex package to
his room instead of the front desk. I celebrated with Ghirardelli's
nonpareils.

Although I illustrated only a few examples of real-life work
scenes in this chapter, they represent some of the typical situations
we all come up against. You've probably witnessed similar situa-

tions or perhaps been involved in them yourself. The idea is to pay close attention and begin to understand what is effective communication, what is not and why.

Here's your only homework assignment for this chapter: Now that you've become the consummate Director, I ask that you spend time every workday taking notes on at least one scene. It can be two minutes or 20, it doesn't matter. Just keep in mind what qualifies as a scene — any conversation between two or more people. At first, it's best if you observe others: your co-workers and clients, your superiors and subordinates. Later, you can begin to take notes on your own communications with others, and to do so at least once a day. Over time you will have trained yourself like the fully-prepared improv player; you will react quickly and spontaneously, you will go forward into any conversation with confidence and commitment, and you'll have tools at the ready. Over time and overall, I'm willing to bet you will have a much more enlightened vantage point as to the mechanics of how people relate and interact. Essentially, you'll know what makes their communications succeed or fail — whether they're in the midst of a conflict or not. The end result for you: a new and different approach to handling *all* your communications.

To get you on the right track, the last chapter provides some guidelines and worksheets that will assist you in breaking scenes down and creating new ones. Keep in mind, so long as you follow the improv rules from Part One and use tools here and there from Part Two, all your communications can work. Remember: There is no right or wrong, only some wonderful choices — options — that fall within the boundaries and guidelines you've learned throughout *"When I Say This ... ," "Do You Mean That?"!*

Chapter 29

Playing With Scenes

Now that you've spent a reasonable amount of time observing scenes (those involving others and those involving yourself), and taking notes on what worked, what didn't, and why — it's time to put your inventive and creative skills to work.

Although you've already worked on a number of assignments, the tasks in this last part of the book offer a unique challenge: that of being a writer. I am going to ask you to author a variety of scenes, all of which will call upon your highly-personalized creative abilities. Each writing adventure will be totally improvisational and will call for you to implement the improv comedy player's rules and tools. You will be in control, and, while that might seem very appealing to you (I hope it does) — don't forget — with all that freedom comes the responsibility of making each scene work. In the end, effective communication is your goal. Your task will be to write the dialogue for each of the following scenes (that includes every character). You'll then go back and critique them, much the same way I did in the last chapter, to assess what did and what did not work. Don't be surprised if you find yourself editing and rewriting each scene several times. That's common when you first play with scenes.

In addition to re-writing the dialogue where necessary, I will also ask you to be a good Director, and go back over each scene to "give notes." This means writing down what each of the players could have done to bring in a stronger performance.

The beauty of the following assignments is that you can work on each one of them every day. You may, however, wish to finish each task then revisit this portion of the book six months from now, creating new and original scenes to fit the various criteria and/or your particular needs. For example, you may be flourishing with the "Yes, and…" theory but be having difficulty conquering the notion of "Give and Take." By authoring scenes, you can stretch your improvisational muscles as you write. The exercise will increase your ability as a consummate communicator.

I suggest that you make a file for these assignments. Keep them handy. As I've said many times, re-reading is a great learning experience. We all tend to forget good ideas in conversation, so an occasional review will serve as a good reminder.

One last note: It may appear, as you do each assignment, that you're doing much the same thing each time. Not true. Sure, you'll be writing more than a dozen scenes, but all of them will be different in one respect or another. Each will require you to concentrate solely on one of the rules or tools. Remember, as in real life, there is no shortage of scenes! With that in mind, it's time to get to the fun!

ASSIGNMENT #1: TRUST

This first assignment calls for you to focus on the most fundamental tenet of the improv comedy player: trust. Here are the parameters for your scene: You and one other person are on the telephone. It's the first time the two of you have spoken. If you are about to have such an encounter at work, tomorrow, or in the near future, role-play it out now, anticipating what might be said. Write to the following specifications:

1. Set the stage picture. Where are you? Where is the other person? What is the situation, e.g. cold call, first encounter, a referral from another client? Describe the setting and situation so that any audience could follow along as though they were watching a movie. Use the same format as the "before" and "after" scenes in Part One of the book. Here's an example: (Int. my office. Seated behind my desk. Headset on. The other per-

son is seated behind his desk. Receiver in hand. He's eager to get my call. I dial. It rings. He answers, etc.) This will help you get a "feel" for the scene before it goes down. (Incidentally, this is a great exercise to do prior to any real-life encounter. Visualize it. When you get there, it will be easier to improvise!) Like a good actor, you're "warming up" — "getting into character" for the show. Getting all the props and scenery in place before you say "Action!" is a great way to prepare.

2. Describe the other character. Even though you have never talked to this person before, imagine him or her as thoroughly as you can. Decide that you will feel positively toward this person no matter how the scene unfolds. Try to picture the person. Give yourself an imaginary glimpse of what you think he or she looks like.

3. Write the dialogue for this scene, bearing in mind that the focus is on the "Trust" factor. Your dialogue should reflect your total trust of the other person while demonstrating that you can be trusted, too. Example: "Hi, Brad. I'm calling to let you know that you can count on ExecuProv to handle all your speaker-coaching needs, no matter how involved or how minimal." Throughout this entire scene, your job is to emphasize trust. If you choose to have the other character negate or eliminate trust from their commentary, so be it. You'll no doubt come up against such situations in your real business life. The more you can keep your presence and composure and stay on the "trust" trail, the better, especially in the face of negativity or distraction. Do whatever you want as you write for your scene partner; just remember, I want you to focus on your dialogue, your delivery. That's the object of this part of the lesson.

4. Now, as I tell all my students in my sketch-writing class, after you've completed your draft, go back and rewrite it! When you are satisfied, critique the scene. Make a list of what you think worked and what didn't. Based on your observations, prepare your final draft. Here's the question which will tell you if the

scene works: Is there an overall sense of rapport? Describe the vibe!

5. The next step is to take on the responsibilities of a conscientious Director. Write out notes that you would like to give each character prior to their re-performing the scene. For example: "Brad, you didn't seem as committed to building rapport; you were too quick to get your needs met; you should have said such-and-such." This also helps you get in touch with how to change the dialogue before you write future drafts.

6. After completion of your final draft, enjoy the fruits of your labor before you file it away. You just finished your first improv performance. Congratulations!

ASSIGNMENT #2: SERVE AND SUPPORT

1. Follow the first two instructions from your last scene: Create the environment and stage directions, and the instructions for who the players are. This time, have no fewer than three characters, but no more than five.

2. Your job this time around is to write a scene with you as the central character. No matter what you have the other "actors" say, I want you to improvise your dialogue from a "Serve and Support" point of view. No matter what you have the others say, stay firmly focused on doing whatever you can, through your dialogue, to serve and support the others.

3. Now go back and re-improvise the scene in another draft or two. Was there something else you could have done? If so, write it in. To tell if this scene worked, ask yourself: "Did I give up my agenda and get into the swing of theirs?"

4. Go back now and critique the scene and the characters in it. Give notes as you did before.

5. Enjoy the final product; file it away and congratulate yourself once again!

ASSIGNMENT #3: BE HERE NOW

1. Write a scene with "Be Here Now" at the center of your improvised thinking. Again, first set the stage and create your characters (at least three, please). This time, see if you can write in some distractions. As you create the dialogue, make sure the character you play is always "current." No matter what the other participants say, it's your character's job to stay in the moment. Don't let your dialogue lag behind what was said a line or two ago; and don't jump ahead and project. Be Here Now!

2. Go back and re-write the scene until it adheres, as far as you're concerned, to the tenet of "Be Here Now."

3. Critique the scene. Write notes to the players, suggesting what they could have done to "Be Here Now" and bring in a stronger performance.

4. Before you tuck this one away, hold it for a few days, then go back and re-read it. For some reason, my students often tell me they come upon important needed changes when they put this one away for a while. If you're satisfied, give yourself a big "High Five!" If not, go back to the drawing boards until you are.

ASSIGNMENT #4: REACT AND RESPOND

1. Same drill as before: Set the stage; detail the characters. This time I would like your scene to call for two people, you and someone else.

2. Your job this time around is to "React and Respond" to the last thing said or last idea held. Think tennis. Naturally, since you

get to write the dialogue, getting the ball back and forth across the net may not seem like such a challenge. But if you first put yourself in the other person's shoes — someone who's trying to get their agenda handled — and imagine what they would say, then it will be more difficult to skate on the dialogue you write for yourself. Remember, in this scene, you're simply playing off the other character. Challenge yourself; therein lies the fun!

3. As you rewrite this scene, see if you can advance the drill by adding another character or two. Your job is to "React and Respond" off each of them. Keep the dialogue quickly paced. It makes the mental muscles work harder.

4. Rewrite until you're satisfied, as with the other scenes. But here's something else you can do to get the lesson across. We do this in improv shows: Take a published screenplay or stageplay that features only two characters. Pick one of the two to be "your" character. Choose a section of dialogue between the two; say eight to ten lines each. Read your character's written dialogue, then write it down. Now, read the other character's responses. Write them down. Now, create new lines for your character — substitutions (newly improvised lines) — in place of your existing dialogue. These responses to the other character should have nothing to do with your original scripted lines. You can have your character say anything as long as your newly improvised lines play off of the other character's lines, and as long as they follow the "React and Respond" rule. Make sure your new choices stay within the boundaries of last thing said; last idea held. When you choose your published work, make certain it's one that features only two characters. As you get really good at this assignment, you'll be able to rewrite the entire play scene by scene. This is a very fun homework assignment, and it really forces you to play off the other person's dialogue. You'll entertain the heck out of yourself!

5. Naturally, you're going to play Director again, giving pointers and critiquing the scenes you've written. Write as many drafts as you need to, making sure that every remark your character makes is in keeping with the rule you're covering: "React and Respond."

6. Again, kudos for a job well done. File these masterpieces away for later review.

ASSIGNMENT #5: "YES, AND ..." AND ADDING INFORMATION

1. For a little change of pace, create a different set-up. This time create two characters in addition to yourself, and have these people talking about unrelated things. Each time your character responds to the other two, begin with the phrase, "Yes, and ... ." Keep doing this until the scene is over. Don't take advantage of the fact that you're the writer of the scene; don't make it too easy. Make yourself stretch. If you have to write several drafts, do so. The idea is that you never stop saying "Yes, and ... ." Now, write it again, making all the characters start each of their statements with "Yes, and ... ." Watch how neatly the scene begins to fit together. Of course, in real life, most people won't come from the "Yes, and ... " mentality, but writing the scene both ways is just good practice. Don't forget what I said earlier in this book: Your audience will always mirror you. That being the case, it's not too far-fetched for you to consider that those with whom you converse might begin to get into the "Yes, and ... " groove.

2. After you are satisfied with the final drafts of this scene, take them one step further by "Adding Information" to the last thing said, or last idea held. Make sure you stay in the "Yes, and ... " mentality. Yet allow the scene to develop line by line. Don't future-think it, improvise and let it evolve. Each time you rewrite any of your scenes, keep improvising. Don't get rigid or stuck on one idea. Expand and expound. Heighten and explore. These are just exercises. Lessons. That's all. I want you to be as creative and experimental as you can.

3. Put on your Director hat and check your scene (or scenes) to make sure they fit all the requirements. As before, you want to make sure you've done a thorough and thoughtful critique of

each piece of dialogue.

4. Before you file this one away, stop to appreciate how hard an assignment it was. Savor the end result. This took a lot of work!

ASSIGNMENT #6: ATTENDING TO

1. This assignment is really an easy one. Just do your set-up as before, but focus this time on stage directions. Your only job is to make sure that all the characters are looking at one another throughout the course of their conversation. Write the stage directions by saying things like: (And Rhonda looked at Bill as she said ...) (And Bill smiled confidently as he scanned the eyes of each person in the room ... ,) etc. Remember, as you write this scene, your focus will be on making certain your characters are looking at one another, that they're paying attention to whomever is speaking. Have fun with some dramatic descriptions of their attitudes and "takes" as they look at one another.

2. As you go back to review this piece of work, double check to make sure all the players had their eyes on the person who was speaking. Remember, the dialogue in this scene is not terribly important. Your assignment is to concentrate on more descriptive stage directions as they detail how or when one person looked at another.

3. If you're up to it, write the scene from each actor's vantage point, changing the stage directions accordingly. For instance, you would initially detail the stage picture from your eyes: (When he looked at me, I looked straight into his big brown eyes and said ...). Now, though, you would re-write it from the other's point of view, literally: (I bore my big, bulging brown eyes into his as I enthused ...). You just have to put yourself in their shoes! It's fun.

4. Of course, in your review and when giving notes, you might have plenty of changes to implement. Do whatever it takes. Eye contact is really more important than you may at first think.

5. Before you file this one in the "big drawer," appreciate how creative you had to be. You had to improvise your drafts from a very different angle, and this took agility and focus.

ASSIGNMENT #7: DIVISION OF RESPONSIBILITY

1. Do your set-up but get in gear to think even-steven. You want to write dialogue that requires each player to have equal time and equal responsibility in making the scene work. Staying locked into "tit for tat" will make it easier.

2. As you go about writing this scene, get industrious; see if you can incorporate some of the lessons from your earlier scenes, such as "Yes, and ... ," "React and Respond," etc.

3. As you give your Director's notes, be impartial and objective. Ask yourself if each player took their fair share of dialogue, if each character took responsibility for making the scene work. That's the job in this exercise. Notice the pace and energy you've created. If the scene seems to move along, you know you've hit the mark. If it seems sluggish and too dialogue-heavy, it could be that one person isn't doing their job satisfactorily. Play with this piece until it feels right. Reading it aloud also helps get a feel for the pace. It also breaks up monotony. Make it fun. Change voice and attitude according to character.

4. File this one, unless you would like to use it as a base for the next homework assignment.

ASSIGNMENT #8: GIVE AND TAKE
1. You have two choices in this exercise. You can either work with a previous scene or create a new one. Think in terms of "advance and retreat," "lead and follow"; let your dialogue reflect the mood of each character taking turns being "dominant" and "submissive." The task here really lies in the back-and-forth dance of acquiescing and taking over. If you've opted

to use one of your prior scenes as a base for this exercise, you're going to be rewriting the words to fit the job description. But go ahead; you may have two versions of the same set-up, but that's a good thing; seeing scenes from different angles provides a fascinating look at how much the dynamics can change according to the applied rule.

2. I'd like you to have at least four people in this scene. Put them in teams of two if you like, giving and taking, two on two. Then, go a step further; incorporate some give-and-take effort within each team, having them do the dance between themselves.

3. Do the same superb job with your critique, making certain that everyone was both generous and accountable.

4. File this away with the others. Again, take some time to enjoy your hard work. All of it takes focus and diligence.

ASSIGNMENT #9: REFUSAL AND DENIAL

1. You've had the opportunity to practice the "Yes, and ... " theory and "Adding Information," so this scene should be easy to write. I'd like you to make it a bit more involved, so as you go about your set-up, include six characters. You can put them in a meeting, perhaps, or some company get-together where everyone is required to converse with one another. Your attention in this scene will be on making certain that none of the characters ignores or undercuts (puts down) another. With six players this will be tough, but I know that with all the improvised writing you've done thus far, you'll handle the assignment just fine.

2. I always tell my students to base this exercise on a real-life work situation. For instance, let's say everyone in your department convened recently for some purpose. A set-up with that in mind will really be helpful. My suggestion is to write it the way you remember it having happened, with all the "Refusal

and Denial" highlights you can recall. Next, write the version that would adhere to the improv player's rulebook. Comparing the two will be most enlightening. My charges tell me they get great insight into what motivates people and what makes them shut down or withdraw. Don't forget: In all our communications, we want to draw people out and make that human connection. "Refusal and Denial," if you remember, are the two "sins" we ask improv players not to commit because they create "anti-communication."

3. As a strong Director, write out notes that you would give the players in the first draft. These will help you write subsequent drafts that honor the principles of no "Refusal and Denial." Take each actor aside (in writing) and counsel them on how they could improve their negative or faulty dialogue. Now you're ready to re-do the scene, following all the pertinent rules. Don't forget, your only focus in this scene is to consider dialogue that has no "Refusal or Denial."

4. In your rewritten draft(s), include as much of the "Yes, and ... " approach as you can. Notice that when you "Add Information," you can still have differing points of view without sinking into a combative atmosphere.

5. File these scenes with the "Yes, and ... ." and "Adding Information," before and after scenes. These tenets go together. An intermittent review will reinforce what you have learned and keep you steadily on track.

6. Give yourself a hearty handshake for a job well done. Even though you prepared for these scenes via your earlier assignments — the scenes highlighting the "Yes, and ... " and "Adding Information" rules — the "Refusal and Denial" scenes were not easy ones to create. They involved at least six characters and required good follow-through. I believe you'll be especially tuned in and sensitive to anyone who "refuses and denies" after having spent time playing with these characters

and your dialogue choices.

ASSIGNMENT #10: LISTENING

1. This assignment will be a fun one because it requires a little
   something extra. Start with a set-up with no more than four
   characters and no fewer than three. What you're going to do is
   play with an exercise we call "word cue." I want you to pick a
   word for each player — it might be "person," "want," or "yes"
   — something commonly spoken in everyday dialogue. Each
   time one of your characters speaks their "secret" word, another
   actor is to interrupt them with a corresponding comment. Let's
   say, for example, that one of your players is assigned the word
   "become." You might write a line of dialogue that has the actor
   saying, "If I have to write this report one more time, I know I'm
   going to become ... ." One of the other characters must then
   jump in and make a statement — perhaps help finish the person's sentence with a comment like, "Yeah — become manic!"
   This may sound a bit easier than it really is, for it takes great
   concentration to write a sensible scene, while focusing on listening to common words — stopping the flow of dialogue as
   you go along, then writing a line that fits the assigned task.
   Though you're writing — putting all this down on paper — the
   exercise will trigger audible cues and cause your ears to perk
   up. It's fun, and it's different.

2. Get clever with your second and third drafts as you improvise
   your way along. Have your characters use their "cue" words
   often enough to create a verbal flurry that will challenge your
   listening skills.

3. After you've played with the surface-type listening — listening
   to what is actually being said — go on to play with each character's subtext. Write an additional draft using stage directions
   that deal with a player's attitude. For instance, before writing
   the line, "If I have to write that report one more time," preface
   it in parentheses with a direction such as: (She clenched her
   teeth subtly as she said ...). This will cause you to "listen" to

where your characters are coming from emotionally. Don't forget that each of us has an attitude or mood behind what we say. Assign your characters feelings and points of view. Your job is to identify how someone feels as they speak, even if their words don't match their subtext. Playing off subtext makes for much tighter communication.

4. In your Director notes, make sure you catch all the places where you failed to listen to a "cue," or didn't stop to pay homage to someone's subtext. You may have to read your final draft more than once to pinpoint all the missed listening. My students tell me this homework assignment takes impeccable concentration. But that's a good thing: It helps to strengthen your mental muscles in the most positive way.

5. You can file your drafts away for the days when you want to brush up on listening. For those of you who are really ambitious, I recommend writing a listening scene at least every couple of months.

6. Don't forget to compliment yourself on a job well done!

ASSIGNMENT #11: CREATING INTO CERTAINTY

1. I ask that this scene take place between two characters. Pick a subject that two people can talk about — customer-service policy, for instance. The first time around, make the dialogue as vague as possible. Let your people talk in generalities. The second draft should be a complete rewrite, with each line offering total clarity.

2. Don't hesitate to rewrite the second draft if any line is murky or muddled. The object in this assignment is to get in touch with conversing clearly and distinctly. I suggest that you put aside for a few days what you consider your final draft, then pull it out for a second look to see if, as you read along, it is indeed easy to assimilate.

3. Don't hold back on giving notes on this one once you put on your Director's hat. If your notes offer various suggestions for re-writing any one line, you know you're doing an excellent job. Sometimes we need to keep improvising until we hit on a combination of words that make ideas clear and exact.

4. Do as you have with the other scenes: Put this one away for another day to review when you're following up.

5. This time, maybe in addition to a mere congratulations, treat yourself to your favorite chocolate, a glass of wine, or a good movie. I'm big on the reward system. I think we all need to say "thanks" to ourselves when we've accomplished challenging tasks.

ASSIGNMENT #12: ANSWERING THE QUESTION

1. Here's a fun one: Write a scene between two people where one is asking all the questions; and the other providing answers. In your first draft, let the conversation flow. Don't give it a great deal of thought. In your next draft, make the "answerer" give pinpointed answers that directly answer the question — not answers that come from his or her own agenda or point of view. I think the difference between the two drafts will astound you. Don't forget, as with all the other scenes, this one will require a set-up. I recommend making yourself one of the characters (preferably the "answerer"), using a scene set-up that is familiar — one which has either happened at work or is going to happen soon. A good example might be an upcoming encounter with a client or co-worker who you know will be directing a number of questions at you.

2. As you re-write, don't lose sight of your goal, which is to answer the questions directly, in the spirit in which they are being asked — not simply from your vantage point. Do as many drafts as it takes to get it right.

3. Be fair, but critical, as you play Director with this scene. Giving yourself objective criticisms will only make you better at responding to the questions people ask you. The more you play with this homework assignment, the more spontaneously appropriate you will be when it comes to answering the question on the job. I always have great respect for people who really listen, then answer directly.

4. Put one or more of these scenes in the file drawer or on the shelf. Sometime later you may want to make further revisions. I would ask that you do this exercise at least once every few months. You can always take a real-life situation at work and write a scene that would have made that situation a stronger piece of communication.

5. Give yourself credit for all the time and effort you've put forth.

ASSIGNMENT #13: ECONOMY OF DIALOGUE

1. Again, you'll need a set-up. For starters, I would suggest that this scene take place between two people; once more, see yourself as a central character. First, write a draft that involves a conversation between two people, letting them just blab away. On your second draft, shorten each line of dialogue. Now, take a third pass; shorten and tighten dialogue even more. In this exercise, less *is* more! Don't compromise the messages or the communication for brevity, but do see if you can "Create into Certainty" with as few words as possible. I'll give you an example. First take: "I thought I saw you, or at least it looked like you — or from the back I could see something that looked like you — at the mixer last week." Second take: "I thought I saw you at the mixer last week." Many of us talk like Take One all the time. We bore and confuse people. Better to keep things short and to the point.

2. After you are satisfied with your drafts, take the "one word" challenge and write a scene with characters speaking one-word

sentences. This may not be appropriate in your real-life situations, but it is great exercise for disciplining yourself to be more succinct. In improv shows at my theater, the actors do complete scenes speaking one-word sentences at a rapid pace. For now, I'm only asking that you improvise in writing: a much less demanding task. It's fun, and you'll be amazed at how much you can actually communicate in one word. As I mentioned when we covered Economy of Dialogue in Part One, people who know one another really well often talk in one-word "bites"; start listening to people who fit this description. Notice how much is actually conveyed.

3. Do your Directorial duties with great objectivity to see what you can offer as you sit on the other side of the table. Suggest what could have been communicated more concisely and how.

4. Compare all your drafts, and don't forget to acknowledge yourself for a job well done. Like the other scenes, put these in a file for later review. Also, plan to take a scene from work and see if you can rewrite it so the conversation is shorter and more to the point.

ASSIGNMENT #14: BEGINNING, MIDDLE AND END

1. Take any one of the scenes you have already written and delineate the pivotal points that show where the beginning ends, where the middle starts and ends, and where the end begins and ends. If you're really ambitious, you can do this with all the scenes you've written. It would certainly be good mental exercise. Soon you will get a good feel for what constitutes a complete piece of communication.

2. Take at least one of the scenes and re-write the ending several different ways. This is a great trick for finding new options for bringing closure to situations. Again, there is no right or wrong in this — just further illustration that there are various ways to wind up our communications.

3. Be sure to critique your work. Your job as Director is to make certain you have a complete scene. Rewrite, if need be, until you do.

4. Thank yourself, once again, for mastering yet another improv basic.

ASSIGNMENT #15: COMMITMENT

1. I have saved this one for last because it is a little different in approach. I want you to take any upcoming situation in which you do not want to participate; you could also work with an actual scene from the past, as long as it was, again, one you'd rather have avoided. The reason for not wanting to partake in the scene is irrelevant.

2. Provide yourself a reasonable set-up, focusing on all the factors that make you dread the scene. Your stage directions should describe this in detail. But they should also acknowledge your total commitment to the scene — dreadful though the prospect might be. An example might be: (Monday morning staff meeting with my boss and the sales manager. Both are ready to jump all over me for not making the weekend numbers. Though I don't want to have to come up with creative solutions, I will. Though I don't want to answer to their criticisms, I shall), and so on. We all anticipate confrontations. And that's what I want you to focus on.

3. Now, write a scene, with yourself as the central character, using dialogue that illustrates your total commitment to making the communication work, no matter how difficult it is or how much the situation is one you want to run from. If need be, go back and rewrite this until you are completely satisfied with the results. This is a wonderful exercise to do every time you know you're going to encounter a scene that does not appeal to you. Script it out the night before, or right before, if you can, with statements and answers that show true commitment. This exercise takes a great deal of perseverance and determination; however, the more you do it, the easier it will be to stay in the loop when you really want to bail.

4. Give yourself a terrific pay-off each time you perform in a scene you don't particularly want to be in. The idea behind commitment with the improv comedy actor, remember, is that they will jump in head-first each and every time, with the same amount of enthusiasm no matter their degree of interest and desire in doing a particular scene. You do the same. Soon you will build the inner strength to quickly and easily rise to any occasion.

Throughout these challenging "scene" assignments, I hope that you've learned a great deal about yourself as a communicator and that you've come to better understand what others need and want from communication.

Each of the assignments can be taken on over and over again. There is never a shortage of scenes, as I mentioned earlier; every piece of communication we engage in is different in some way.

As you work on all your assignments, be as creative as you can. Don't get discouraged if it appears that some are tougher than others. There is no one looking over your shoulder grading these assignments, so don't feel pressured. Instead, make them as fun and interesting as you can. Remember, they are nothing more than the results of what you've learned by reading the lessons in this book. If you get stuck, go back and re-read the chapter the assignment represents. That will help tremendously. If you're stymied, put an assignment aside and go back to it later. My request is that you enjoy this process and that you work at it regularly.

Try not to analyze and control all the characters; let them take on a life and personality of their own. In addition to writing out the assignments, you also have the option of role-playing them, as well. Get a cooperative group of people together and tell them you're going to play with scenes. Explain the rules, then try out some scenes following the above instructions. Doing this live rather than on paper can be great fun. Either way, though, I believe that through such creativity comes incredible improv magic — much of which you probably didn't even know you had.

Chapter 30

Final Scene
Epilogue

Before you hit the "stage," I want to huddle with you for a few minutes — I want to address you the way I would my troupe of actors before a show. In other words, I want to leave you with a few Director's pre-show notes — reminders to take with you as you go about your professional life using the rules and tools of the improv comedy actor.

• First, never lose sight of the reason (your "motivation") for acquiring all these new skills. Simply put; this learning process has been designed to assist you in communicating a whole lot better.

• If you've done the assignments throughout the book, you know just about everything the fully-trained improv comedy actors knows. That means you've got an edge. It means you can improvise with the best of them! But don't forget to rehearse what you've learned. You have dozens of opportunities to do so on the job every single day. Take advantage of each opportunity. Great actors never stop rehearsing — especially the improv ones — they are always working out. Get in the habit of going to the mental gym. Stay in shape!

• Don't forget that every piece of communication is a scene unto itself. Go at each one with the intent of making it your very best performance and making it work. That's what the pros do. As you go about your business day, perform with the professional attitude of consistency. Remember, improv actors always give it their best, no matter how off they may be feeling, physically or emotionally.

All this translates to commitment, the ability to hang in there even if certain scenes are not your "favorites." Act as though they are — that's the mark of a real pro. (You can always throw a fit later in your "dressing room"!)

- The more you use the rules and tools, the more agile, quick tuned in, clear and interesting you'll become. In the end, you come across as more powerful and successful. Take command of every stage!
- Remember: In good improv there is never one star; instead, there is unity and harmony. Play at parity; include everyone who's in the scene, in the scene!
- "Smell" your audience. Assess what they need and want so you can get what *you* need and want.
- Listen.
- Go at every piece of communication using, at a minimum, the three basic improv rules: "Serve and Support," "React and Respond" and "Be Here Now." If you forget all else, those alone will make you a better communicator.
- Always keep your sense of humor.

One final note: Know, deep down, that there is no one else who can perform quite like you. You have certain gifts — talents — ways of communicating — that other people will benefit from and enjoy. Of the hundreds of improv comedy players I've seen, no two were ever the same. You're just as unique. Don't ever cheat your audience or yourself by holding back.

Take pride in the quest to improve your communication skills. It's a process that takes time, energy and a good deal of effort and discipline. And that's good, because, in the end, it makes you a great performer. I already know you're great! So, break a leg! Or, do what I once did when no one was around to pat me on the back for a job well done — give yourself a standing ovation!

It's a wrap!

ਣੂ

ABOUT THE AUTHOR

A founding member of the world-famous L.A. Groundlings, Cherie Kerr is the founder, and since 1990, the Executive Producer and Artistic Director of the Orange County Crazies, a sketch and improvisational comedy troupe in Santa Ana, California. She also serves as the group's head writer.

Kerr has taught improvisational comedy to actors for the past thirty years, and teaches other classes as well, including a class on how to write sketch comedy and one on how to develop original characters. She has studied with some of the best improv and comedy teachers in the business, including Gary Austin, founder of the L.A. Groundlings, and a former member of the highly acclaimed group, The Committee; Michael Gellman, a Director and teacher for Second City, in Chicago; and Jeannie Berlin (an Academy Award nominee and Elaine May's daughter). In her formative years, she studied at the Pasadena Academy of Drama.

Kerr founded ExecuProv in 1983, and has provided a variety of classes on presentation and communication skills to hundreds of business professionals. Her clients include ARCO, Nissan Motors, Mitsubishi, Ingram Micro, Bank One, Delta Dental, Foothill Capital, PacifiCare, Universal Studios, Condor Freight Lines, Boise Cascade and Office Depot among others. She has also worked for a number of governmental agencies including the L.A. City Attorney's Office, the L.A. District Attorney's Office, and the County of Orange. She is a certified Provider for the Continuing Legal Education Program for the State Bar of California, and has served as that organization's official speaker-trainer for its Board of Governors.

A writer for more than 30 years, Kerr has owned an award-winning public relations firm and still works as an occasional consultant in that field. She has written, produced and directed an original full-scale musical comedy, is a member of ASCAP, and has been honored as an award-winning journalist and publicist. Kerr was named, along with Disney's Michael Eisner, as one of the "Top

Ten Most Sensational People in Orange County" by *Orange Coast* magazine. She is also a humor columnist for *The Orange County Register* newspaper.

In addition to lecturing and teaching ExecuProv, both in classroom situations and in private, one-on-one tutoring sessions, Kerr provides speechwriting services for many of her clients. Kerr also provides her creative services to large companies for corporate comedy industrials. She also serves as Artistic Director and head writer for "Law Revue," a yearly show that features lawyers and judges in satirical sketches and song parodies.

Kerr is frequently sought out as a keynote speaker relative to presentation and communications skills and humor in the workplace.

In addition to *"When I Say This ... ," "Do You Mean That?"* Kerr is the author of a book on public speaking using improv comedy techniques, *"I've Asked Miller To Say A Few Words"*; a sketch writing book used in companies, colleges and at theater schools, *"Build to Laugh: How To Construct Sketch Comedy With The Fast And Funny Formula"*; and *"Networking Skills That Get You The Job You Want."* Kerr is currently writing two additional books for her ExecuProv series, *"What's So Funny?"*, that teaches speakers how to get good story-telling and humor into speeches, and *How To Think Fast On Your Feet (Without Putting Them In Your Mouth)*, a manual to help business professionals handle pressure and tension during difficult communication situations.

In addition to her self-help books, Kerr is also authoring a novel about her father's life as a jazz string-bassist, *Charlie's Notes.*